How to
Find a Job on
LinkedIn,
Facebook,
Twitter, and
Google+

How to Find a Job on LinkedIn, Facebook, Twitter, and Google+

Second Edition

Brad Schepp and Debra Schepp

New York   Chicago   San Francisco   Lisbon
London   Madrid   Mexico City   Milan   New Delhi
San Juan   Seoul   Singapore   Sydney   Toronto

The McGraw-Hill Companies

2 3 4 5 6 7 8 9 0   QFR/QFR   1 8 7 6 5 4 3

ISBN: 978-0-07-179043-7
MHID: 0-07-179043-8

e-ISBN: 978-0-07-179044-4
e-MHID: 0-07-179044-6

Readers should know that online businesses have risks. Readers who participate in online business do so at their own risk. The author and publisher of this book cannot guarantee financial success and therefore disclaim any liability, loss, or risk sustained, either directly or indirectly, as a result of using the information given in this book.

Library of Congress Cataloging-in-Publication Data
Schepp, Brad
 How to find a job on LinkedIn, Facebook, Twitter, and Google + / by Brad Schepp and Debra Schepp. — 2nd ed.
      p. cm.
   Includes index.
   ISBN 978-0-07-179043-7 (alk. paper) — ISBN 0-07-179043-8 (alk. paper)
   1. Job hunting—Computer network resources. 2. Online social networks. 3. Facebook (Electronic resource) 4. MySpace (Firm) 5. Twitter. 6. LinkedIn (Electronic resource) 7. Business networks. 8. Internet. I. Schepp, Debra. II. Title.
   HF5382.7.S34 2012
   650.140285'6754—dc23

                                                                              2012000541

McGraw-Hill books are available at special quantity discounts to use as premiums and sales promotions, or for use in corporate training programs. To contact a representative, please e-mail us at bulksales@mcgraw-hill.com.

This book is printed on acid-free paper.

To all the job hunters still searching for work in the midst of historic unemployment. We hope our efforts support and encourage you. And we wish you well.
BS & DS

CONTENTS

PREFACE TO THE SECOND EDITION

We had heard that a year in Internet time is worth about seven years in the "real" world, but we never quite believed it—that is, until we updated this book. In a little over two years, social networking has undergone the kind of change that used to take *decades*. Not only have all the social networks covered in this book's first edition grown tremendously, social networking itself also has gone mainstream. Nearly everyone and their mothers have Facebook pages. Twitter has been credited with starting and helping to broadcast revolutions. LinkedIn now has virtually no competition in the professional social networking space.

As you'll see, as social networks have grown larger, fortunately, the tools they offer for sorting and searching them also have improved greatly. You'll read about LinkedIn's new InMaps feature, Twitter's Lists feature, Facebook's Lists and Smart Lists features, and newcomer Google + 's Circles feature. BranchOut, a Facebook application, turns your Facebook friends into a LinkedIn-like network. All these tools will help you to organize the networks you create so that you can use them efficiently and effectively. Plus social networking has gone mobile, allowing you to access your networks through mobile devices, including Android phones, BlackBerrys, iPhones, and more.

With all the changes over the past two years, the book you hold in your hands today is a much different book from the first edition. One thing both editions share is that they were both meant to be used almost like workbooks. We heard from many readers who used the book at their computers while they made changes to their profiles and built their networks based on what they were reading. You also could say that this book appeared on a few nightstands as well, given how often people told us they enjoyed all the many success stories we included. These stories are about real people who found jobs and real work through social networking. For this edition, we actually had to stop soliciting more stories! We could have created a book more than twice as big just with success stories, but we wanted to get the book into production and into your hands as soon as we could! Here are just a few examples to whet your appetite.

- New grad Johanna Franco landed her dream job with Hawaiian Airlines thanks to LinkedIn.

- Jim Chadman used LinkedIn's Groups to land a job allowing him to move his family back home to Pittsburgh.

- Consultants such as Joseph LaMountain can thank LinkedIn for hundreds of thousands of dollars in new business.

- S. E. Day used his LinkedIn network to identify and solidify a five-figure book contract and a permanent position as a corporate spokesperson.

- Through Twitter, Kathy Colaiacovo built a six-figure virtual assistant business in fewer than three years.

- Crystal Kendrick hires 20 to 30 people per year through her company's Facebook page.

- Katie Lorenz, a former Miss America contestant, was contacted by *Bloomberg* for an extensive article after locating her through her LinkedIn profile.

The best part of writing the first edition of this book was not the chance to present it at the National Press Club (although that was a thrill). The best part was the many, many letters and notes we received from people who told us that the book truly helped them to navigate through a dreadful job market and invigorate flagging job searches. We hope to hear the same from you once you've landed your own next great job. Share your stories with us, and we promise that we'll try to include them in this book's next edition!

Brad and Debra Schepp
bradanddeb.com

ACKNOWLEDGMENTS

It's always a challenge to thank every person who has helped us turn a manuscript into a book. Under any circumstance, that represents a pretty big crowd. Open that up to the 135 million people currently on LinkedIn, and Hercules would begin to get nervous. If we go on to consider the hundreds of millions of people on Facebook and Twitter, then add in a touch of Google +, we're willing to bet that Hercules would have gone back to bed. All we can do is our best and hope that anyone who doesn't see his or her name here will understand that at some point thank-yous have to stop and the book begin. We appreciate every e-mail you sent, every question you answered, and every bit of wisdom you provided to us. So here goes—our best shot.

First of all, we'd like to thank our agent, Bill Gladstone, of Waterside, Inc., for once again being a true advocate for our work. You've never let us down, Bill, and we appreciate that. Knox Huston at McGraw-Hill has rightfully earned a place among our favored editors. He's smart, savvy, kind, and agreeable. What else is there for writers to ask for? On the McGraw-Hill production team, we'd also like to thank Daina Penikas, Jim Madru, and Penny Linskey. We hope our manuscript wasn't a headache-producer!

So many people were kind enough to respond to our requests for information about how they used social networking sites: Sharon DeLay, Kristen Kouk, David Becker, Steven Burda, Virginia Backaitis, Elizabeth Garzarelli, Rayanne Langdon, Miriam Salpeter, Ruth-Ann Cooper, Jocelyn Wang, Dr. Scott Testa, Susan Schwartz, Leslie Carothers, Josh Chernin, Anne Pryor, Chuck Hester, Mike O'Neil, Pinny Cohen, Terrence Seamon, Stephen Weinstein, Gary Unger, Guy Battaglia, Mitch Neff, Fabroce Calando, S. E. Day, Jordan Harbinger, Amybeth Hale, Chris Perry, Kathy Colaiacovo, Joanne Petitto, Megan Montplaisir, Meggie Clemons, Brook Burris, Asia Bird, Alexander Parks, Trenton Willson, Ed McMasters, Joseph LaMountain, John Herndon, Sarah Baldwin, Michael J. Case, Tadd Rosenfeld, Donna Svei, Wallace "Walls" Jackson, Debby Afraimi, Greg Hutchins, Jacob Bettany,

Jim Chadman, and Johanna Franco. Without your input, we'd have missed important insights, and sharing your stories made working on this book a joy. We're sure that reading them will be the same treat for our readers, too.

We tapped public relations and press representatives often, and they were always responsive to our requests and supportive of our research. We'll start with a special thank-you to Krista Canfield, the public relations manager at LinkedIn. This book simply still would be in the making were it not for your competencies at your job. Your colleague, Erin O'Harra, also was a big help, and we thank her. Thanks to Peter Shankman (and his invaluable "Help A Reporter Out" website), to Andrew Lipsman (of Comscore), and to Jim Prosser (of Google), who was quick to help us with details of Google + . We wish you all success in your careers.

On a smaller scale, we'd like, as always, to thank our family, who listened to endless conversations about social networking. We can easily grant our kids and their significant others the discovery of this amazing phenomenon and thank them for first sharing it with us. We hope to have paid you back with a book you can use throughout your own careers, which have already begun to dazzle us, as your achievements always have. So Ethan, Stephanie, Andrew, and Laurel, thanks for listening and sharing too! To relatives and friends far and near, we're now open to accepting invitations to dinner and weekend getaways, so please invite us again, especially if you're willing to pay.

And last, a little thank-you to Max and Mollie. Throughout this project, not a single mouse ran across either of our desks, which was truly helpful. Plus, the notification system you two devised to let us know when food bowls were empty was simply brilliant.

INTRODUCTION

I t was noon in Manhattan, circa 1980, and we were in one of those delis with heaping sandwiches named for Milton Berle, Jack Benny, or some other comedian, lots of colorful people and waiters all talking at once, and no elbow room. If you've ever seen a Woody Allen movie, you know just what we mean. Across from us was Uncle Nat, a much revered but little known relative who had "made it big" in Manhattan. He was there to help us start our careers.

Frankly, Uncle Nat scared the heck out of us. He was everything we were not. He was rich, successful, polished, and part of the exciting world of New York advertising. To us, as brand-new college graduates, this was a world that looked fantastic and impossible to fathom at the same time, certainly no relation to any life we'd yet experienced. No wonder we were scared! Uncle Nat could be our meal ticket into that world. A shortcut! We couldn't disappoint him.

That lunch did lead to an "information interview" with someone very much like Uncle Nat, another "master of Manhattan." And that led to . . . nothing. You can understand. When the spotlight was on us, all we could say was, "Yes, we wanted our first job, and here is our résumé, and didn't we take all the right college courses? Isn't it clear how hard we worked and how smart we are?"

With the shadows of encounters such as these still lingering, no wonder "networking" still intimidates us to this day! And thank goodness our kids will never have to go through that. And neither will you, thanks to social networking sites such as LinkedIn.

Are you looking for a job or more work for your own business? If you're not now, chances are that you soon will be. Although the deep recession of 2008 to 2009 officially has passed, for many of us it still doesn't feel that way. Even if you've come through reasonably unscathed, the memories and feelings of those dreadful economic times may linger forever. You've probably heard since you first starting looking for a job that the best way to find work is by "networking." You need to connect with others in a position to help you. This is good advice, but it freezes many people in their tracks. (You may have made it to Manhattan, as we did, but no further.) And what if you're too young to have developed much of a network? What if you've lost track of your coworkers? What if you're shy, and picking up the phone intimidates you?

We understand. And for all these reasons, social networking sites finally make it possible for all of us to do what we should have been doing all along—connecting with others, staying connected, sharing resources, and networking.

LinkedIn, Facebook, Twitter, and Google + —they're all known as social networking sites. But LinkedIn is actually more about business networking than being social, and even the other sites have become host to what could be called "business." The point is that all these sites can be key tools that should be a part of every job search. And at least two of them should be part of your Internet routine whether you're actively searching for work or not.

Absolutely, your top network should be LinkedIn, which we'll go on the record here as calling the most important tool for business communications since e-mail. We devote Part 1 of this book to that site, and by the time you reach the end, you'll know how to create a standout profile, connect with others, gain expertise through answering questions, and find work.

In Part 2 we show you around Facebook, Twitter, and Google + and explain how they can help you to get a new job or more business. You'll find many examples of people who have done just that. We'll also include information for students and new graduates who, although they may be digital natives, are newcomers to the world of job hunting. We will step you through creating an online profile that highlights your strengths and experience most effectively. Then we'll help you to tailor it for each network you decide to join. Your LinkedIn profile should be different from your Google + profile, even though it will include some of the same information. You simply don't have to start from scratch each time.

As for LinkedIn, once you join, you'll see that it's important to use the site often. Social networking sites, much like all tools, have a learning curve before you've really mastered them. Before too long, you'll be using the site's resources not just to find work but also to accomplish some of the tasks you face on the job, day in and day out.

To give you a head start, here are just a few tips for using social networking sites:

- Update your status often.
- Keep your information fresh and current.
- Connect with others and offer help whenever you can.
- Comment on what you see.
- Use the medium: Post pictures, videos, music, whatever is appropriate to the site and your situation.
- Be respectful of others' time.

Before you give the clerk your cash or credit card for this book, you deserve to know a little about us and what makes us qualified to write such a book. We've written about technology, and specifically the Internet, for many years. It never stops amazing us, and that well of wonder we have hopefully shows in this book. At the same time, we've also written career books, so between our Internet and business-book background, we're confident that we're well qualified to explain how to use social networking sites for business purposes.

What can you expect from this book? Well, what does a plumber expect from a wrench, an accountant from a calculator, or a writer from a computer? You can expect to come away from this book with the knowledge of how to use arguably the most important tools job hunters now have at their disposal: social networking sites. You will never have to hunt for work in the same way again. We think Uncle Nat probably would be proud of us after all.

PART 1

Getting
LinkedIn

CHAPTER 1

Putting the *Work* in Social Networking

As we write this book, the world has passed an amazing milestone, almost without recognition: There are now more than 2 billion global Internet users. Social networking is just the latest Internet phenomenon to become part of our daily lives. At one point, the fact that your thoughts and information could be passed from person to person was the big step forward, but e-mail was easily adapted to, and most of us did so without much difficulty. Internet shopping was the next innovation to surmount. Once, only the brave ventured onto eBay and Amazon, and then only because they couldn't resist the temptation of good prices or rare collectibles. Most of us, at first, considered that a little too risky. Now a galaxy of safe and reliable Web shopping destinations has supplanted the original e-commerce models. Sure, you still may find a few holdouts who don't trust Internet shopping, but you're much more likely to talk to people who research, locate, and purchase all kinds of commodities on the Web. It's simply no big deal.

Social networking, however, is a little bit different. It began largely as a phenomenon of the young. In 2002, programmer Jonathan Abrams created a website where like-minded people could gather in virtual communities, exchange profiles, and greatly broaden their scope of friends. His site was called Friendster. A year later, MySpace sprang from Friendster, and within months, Facebook came along, too.

When Facebook was just starting out, it was strictly for college students. Those of us watching students pour hours into the site began to wonder what all the hype was about. If you were fortunate enough to share your life with members of this demographic group, you could see pretty quickly what kept them glued to the site. Here was a chance for newly minted high school graduates to go off to their separate college campuses but take along with them all their best friends from high school. Because we had been writing about online technology since the 1980s, this seemingly sudden blossoming of social networking came as absolutely no surprise to us. Almost from the very moment people began to dial out from their computers over their telephone lines and log onto "online services" such as CompuServe, Prodigy, and America Online, they did so with, more than any other purpose, the hope of connecting with people sharing their thoughts, goals, and philosophies.

Once people began to understand the power of the Internet, they also began to understand the value of networking with people across time zones and without regard to geography. Consequently, it didn't take Facebook very long to branch out and invite parents and other grownups to join its social network (even if the students redoubled their efforts to bar them at the door!). And now, Facebook has more than 800 million users worldwide! But, with the phenomenon of social networking growing at dizzying rates, it was only to be expected that the grownups, the professionals, the people with so much work to do ultimately would need their own place to network. Today, LinkedIn can serve as a combination Chamber of Commerce, where folks come together to enhance their professional connections, and office water cooler, where like-minded people swap advice and expertise. The difference is that you are no longer limited to networking just with the people who live within your sphere or belong to your own organizations. LinkedIn literally brings the whole professional world into your life and invites you to join.

WHAT EXACTLY IS LINKEDIN?

Simply put, LinkedIn is a professional's dream come true (Figure 1-1). It's also the Promised Land for job hunters. Short of calling it a magic job

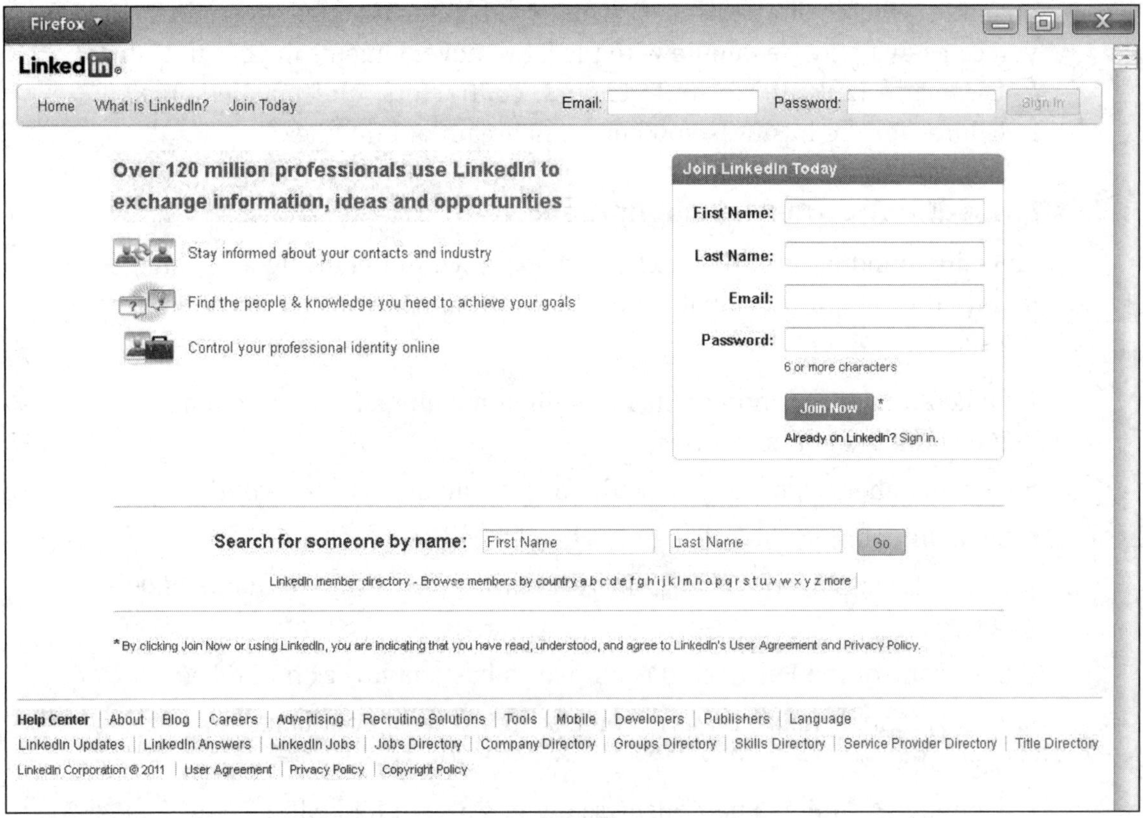

Figure 1-1: The main LinkedIn screen, which you'll see only until you set up an account.

machine, which, of course, is only hype, LinkedIn is a professional social network that allows you to connect with millions of potential colleagues who come together to share their career expertise, their experience, and their passion for their work. There is no magic job-hunting machine. LinkedIn won't simply throw out the perfect job and award it to you after you enter the right combination of data into the site. But LinkedIn will allow you to build a strong and vibrant network of professional connections that will permit you not only to job hunt more efficiently but also to enhance your job performance and career goals, no matter what phase of your career you happen to be working on.

Just out of school? LinkedIn can help you to find mentors, stay in touch with your favorite professors, and locate the hiring managers within your chosen career. Have you been in the workforce for a while? Well, LinkedIn will allow you to move throughout your career, never losing touch with colleagues you respect and admire, no matter where your paths may diverge and cross. Throughout your career, you can stay up to the minute with the latest developments in your industry. You can use LinkedIn to find vendors, contractors, and maybe someday new hires for the business you currently dream of building.

LinkedIn: An Internet Phenomenon

Since its founding in 2003, LinkedIn has grown dramatically and changed forever the way professionals interact. Consider some statistics culled from the site:

- LinkedIn now has more than 135 million members from more than 200 countries and territories.
- New members sign up to LinkedIn at the rate of two *per second*.
- LinkedIn members are 51 percent female and 49 percent male.
- The average LinkedIn user is 46 years old and earns more than $88,000 per year.
- Every one of the Fortune 500 companies has employees on LinkedIn.
- In 2010, more than 2 billion people searches were conducted on LinkedIn.
- Around 1.3 million small-business owners are on LinkedIn.
- There are 5.5 million high-tech managers using the site.
- More than 6.5 million students and 9 million recent college graduates use LinkedIn.
- In *Fortune Magazine's* most recent list of "100 Great Things about America," LinkedIn was ranked number 21.

LinkedIn has become a must-have tool for ambitious professionals, whether they're currently looking for a job or not. In just a few years, LinkedIn has grown into the largest and strongest business network in the world. Or, as LinkedIn tells potential advertisers and partners, it is "The world's largest audience of affluent, influential professionals."

Based in Mountain View, California, LinkedIn was spawned in 2002 in prototypical Silicon Valley fashion—from the garage of Reid Hoffman and cofounders Allen Blue, Jean-Luc Vaillant, Eric Ly, and Konstantin Guericke. The group formally launched LinkedIn in 2003, when they asked 300 of their most important business contacts to become part of the network they were building. Today, LinkedIn can safely boast that it has 135 million members across the globe, and the service is available in English, French, German, Indonesian, Italian, Japanese, Korean, Malay, Portuguese, Romanian, Russian, Spanish, Swedish and Turkish.

In terms of popularity and necessity, think of Facebook, but for serious professionals. LinkedIn members are more interested in productive networking than in learning about the music their friends now like or who their old high school flames are hooking up with. LinkedIn is the way to recruit top business partners, get that dream job, find venture capital, recruit that corporate superstar, or network with that college roommate from long ago whom you had given up ever finding again. Is your desk drawer cluttered with old business cards? Is your Rolodex gathering dust? Do you still spend way too much time hunting down old references or forging new contacts? LinkedIn is for you.

TIP

One of the driving forces behind the LinkedIn phenomenon is the concept of *pay it forward.* We heard this term and the idea behind it from countless active members of the LinkedIn community. In essence, it means that when you come to LinkedIn, be prepared to offer more than you ask for. You'll find countless ways to do this throughout the coming chapters, but it's important that you understand the philosophy before you even approach someone on the site.

The Inspiration Behind LinkedIn

In the March 2009 issue of *Saturday Night Magazine*, LinkedIn cofounder Allen Blue explained how the concept for LinkedIn came about:

> When you're an entrepreneur, you do almost everything with the people you know. The founders of LinkedIn knew this first-hand because we had all been doing it for years. With LinkedIn, we were looking to build a system that would let professionals not only stay in touch with friends, co-workers and college classmates, but also let them search their network for people that had expertise in certain areas. Every professional is more successful when they can get answers to tough work-related questions like "How do I begin a career in advertising?"

or "What vendor should I be looking at to help me solve 'X' problem?" from people they know and trust.

Why You Must Use LinkedIn

Your professional life exists on the Internet, whether you realize it or not. Just do a Google search for your name, and you're likely to find all types of references that you may or may not have known even existed. You can use LinkedIn as the dashboard that drives your professional Internet presence. Carefully crafted (and don't worry, we'll explain all this in Chapter 2), your LinkedIn profile will be among their first search results whenever someone prowls Google to find out more about you. Some people feel that before long, your LinkedIn profile even may replace a résumé or curriculum vitae (CV) as your professional work summary. Since you create that LinkedIn profile, and you can link it to more of your own good work, you gain control over what people are most likely to learn about you from searching the Web.

LinkedIn should be one of your regular online homes, where you spend time every day or at least every week. Here are just some of the things that you can accomplish through the site, all of which we'll explore in detail throughout this book:

- Market and promote your business
- Gain free access to top experts worldwide
- Do valuable, unique company research
- Create and maintain your online Rolodex
- Find professional peers you may have lost contact with
- Locate job postings tailored to your background

LinkedIn on the Go

Just in case we've yet to convince you that LinkedIn should be a vital part of your job search, you now can have access to the site and all it offers through your mobile devices. LinkedIn introduced free applications that allow you to access the site with your BlackBerry, iPhone, Android, or Palm Pre. Features vary slightly from one type of phone to another, but all of the apps allow you to stay connected to your LinkedIn community. For LinkedIn members who have other types of smart phones, you can get more information about connecting with LinkedIn remotely at m.linkedin.com.

Anne Pryor: Coaches Careers and Builds Wellness

Anne Pryor describes herself as a "master connector." Anne has spent much of her career in coaching and consulting with others who seek to find their best career paths and lead fulfilling lives. One of her first jobs was at a theme park called Berry Fair. "I spent 10 years creating memories for families," she told us. "I sold packages to companies for their employees." Anne's personality leads her to seek out people and find ways to help them. In her current role as career consultant and life coach, she's found LinkedIn to be the perfect place for a people person such as herself to thrive. Based in Minnesota, Anne has found abundant work. "We lost 30,000 jobs last month, just in Minnesota alone," she told us. "LinkedIn is a tool I'm teaching now at our company to help people connect." Anne was kind enough to share a story with us of one young woman who came seeking help.

"Jennifer" was looking for a job as a marketing director for a law firm when she came to Anne. "Her LinkedIn profile was about 75 percent complete," Anne told us. "First, we enhanced her profile. Her profile URL wasn't completed with her name . . . , so we fixed that to ensure that she would be picked up in Google searches. We plugged in where she graduated from, and we uploaded her classmates from the small college she'd attended in Minnesota. We saw that some of her classmates were marketing directors in the law firms with which she wanted to connect. She sent them invitations to connect through her network. They responded, and she followed up with a phone call. She accomplished this in four minutes!"

Anne Pryor looks at LinkedIn a little more broadly than many of the other career professionals you'll meet throughout this book. "My mission in life is to promote wellness—mental, spiritual, physical, and emotional—and to be well, people need to be connected. As someone with a background and interest in wellness and spirituality, I know we are all connected. LinkedIn offers a way that we can connect here on this earth. It's more than just business. People appreciate it when they see the value in connecting with

Anne Pryor helps her clients as a career consultant and coach for living an enriched life.

people they haven't seen in years," she continued. "Their eyes just light up! People go behind closed doors of the companies, and they close themselves off from people beyond those doors. I do my job by serving others and helping them succeed by reconnecting them with themselves and then connecting them with others so that they can easily and effortlessly manifest their desires. LinkedIn is the tool where we can connect and not be isolated," she said. "I'm grateful for this invention."

JOB HUNTING THROUGH LINKEDIN

Although by now it's clear that LinkedIn is more than just a job-hunting portal, that doesn't mean the arrival of this site hasn't changed a great deal about what job hunting is like in the twenty-first century. Still, some aspects of the task simply will never be easy. Job hunting ranks right up there with a root canal for so many of us. Maybe that's because you never know what you're going to have to contend with. You probably have your own share of horror stories. They're hard to avoid. Whether you're after your very first professional job or looking to break out into the next level of your career, job hunting is just plain difficult. Sure, sometimes interviews do go swimmingly. The planets align for you just so. You click perfectly with the manager interviewing you, you get an offer that suits you, and you're ready to start your new job. More common than those golden moments, though, are the times when you're likely to realize before the interview is over that the job's a poor fit. Or even more discouraging, you feel like you did a fabulous job only to have the interviewer disappear without a trace, not even a word. Then you know that you'll have to pick yourself up, brush off your battered ego, and face the same ordeal another day.

It's been said that job hunting requires that you endure a steady stream of nos before you can get to that one final yes. Your challenge is to turn on the flow of interviews that will let you swim past the nos and achieve that golden yes, meaning that you've landed a job that suits you. We admit that this has never been easy, even in the best of economies. During the great recession of 2008–2009, it was quite common for job seekers to send out hundreds of résumés and hear not a peep in response. But before you put this book down and go back to bed, let us remind you that you are much more empowered than job seekers have ever been before, even those who were job hunting as recently as a decade ago.

Thanks to social networking, the job of finding a new job has never been easier, with loads of opportunities and companies to choose from and mentors to turn to. (This is not to downplay the tremendous competition job seekers face, especially baby boomers and students.) Just think how wonderful it would have been in years past to have been able to talk to people who actually worked at the company you were interested in joining or to search for others who had the exact job you were dreaming of and then been able to follow their career histories to see how they got where they were. What about joining a group that permits you to approach the very people who are working at the career you're building? What if this group allowed you to see what these successful people are reading, discussing, sharing, and working on? Too bad we've all had to wait this long to have LinkedIn! No matter what the current state of the economy is, you're so fortunate that LinkedIn is here for you to use right now.

A QUICK GUIDED TOUR OF THE LINKEDIN SITE

Maybe you've already joined LinkedIn, and you're hoping to use this book to improve your social networking skills and land a new job. In that case, you already know at least a little about navigating the site. If you haven't joined yet, LinkedIn's home page doesn't offer much for you to explore. You can use the links there to learn more about the site and the benefits of becoming a member, but beyond those basics, you'll need to become a LinkedIn member. So, by all means, if you haven't joined LinkedIn yet, now's the time to do so. It's fast and free, and once you're signed up, the whole site opens for your exploration. Of course, you'll want to create your profile (see Chapter 2) and build your network (see Chapter 3), but that's getting a little ahead of ourselves. If you've already begun those two steps, you'll see in upcoming chapters lots of great advice for enhancing your LinkedIn image and building a powerful network. For this tour, we're going to show you the site through one of our own profiles. That way, you can get a feel for the whole site and begin to better understand the benefits of joining and using LinkedIn.

The LinkedIn homepage that you see once you've created a profile and connected with some people will resemble Figure 1-2. Prominently, front and center, you'll find LinkedIn Today. LinkedIn offers you top news stories based on the industry you follow and those most important to others in

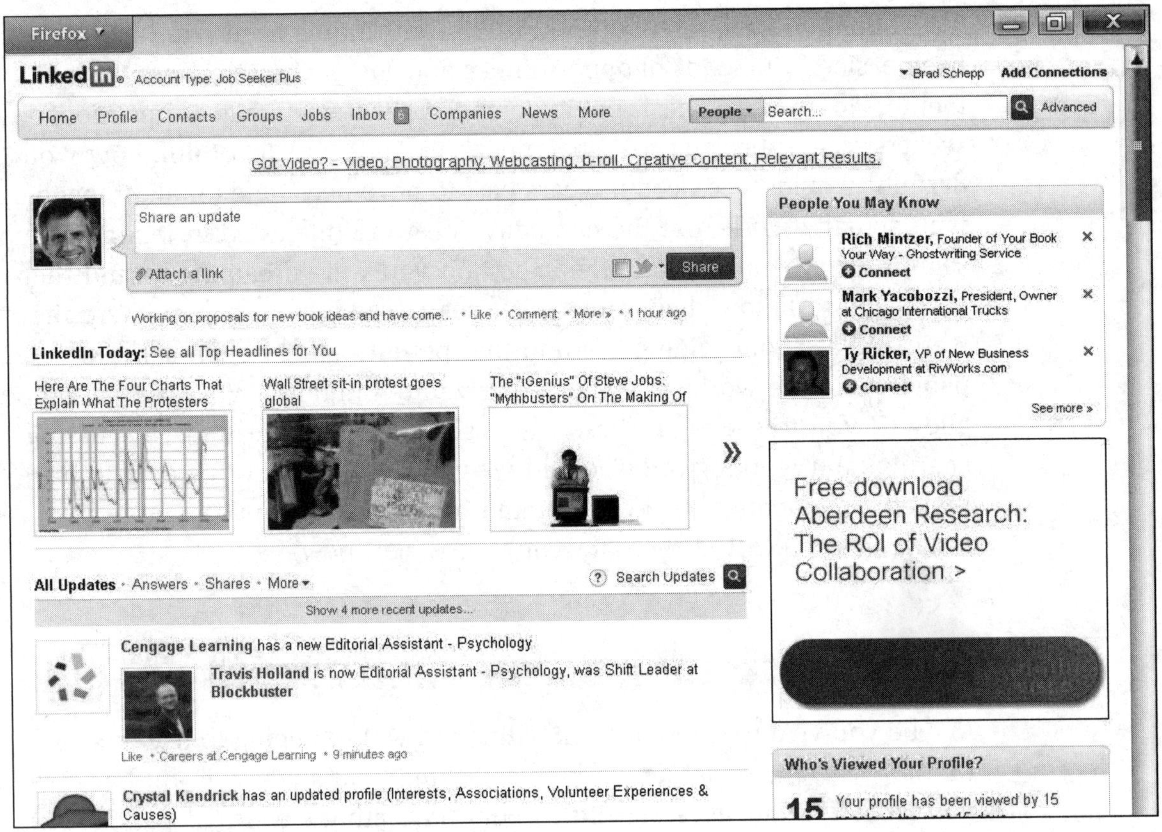

Figure 1-2: The personal homepage that appears once your profile is complete. This becomes your own LinkedIn homepage.

your network. If you're just starting out on LinkedIn and your network is sparse, you'll see three headlines of a more generic nature. As your profile and network expand, you'll see news stories targeted to your interests. The three types of stories you'll find are

- Stories your connections and coworkers are sharing
- Stories your industry peers are sharing
- Stories being followed by people beyond your industry

You can customize the publications you most want to follow, save your stories to be read later on your mobile device, or use the stories that appear as quick updates to your status on LinkedIn and other sites.

Through the navigation bar at the top of the page, you can get to all your customized content (all of which you'll learn more about in later chapters), including your groups, your profile, your contacts, your Inbox, and so on.

Also along this bar are hyperlinks from which you can quickly get to the main public areas of LinkedIn. These include "Groups," "Jobs," "Companies," "News," and "More." Under the "More" tab, you'll find links to "Answers" (a vital area of the site), the "Learning Center," and, well, more. Drop-down menus next to the hyperlinks will take you to specific content within these areas.

If you roll over your name at the top right corner of the page, you'll see the hyperlinks for "Settings" and "Sign Out." There are also links along the bottom of the page, the most important of which for your purposes now is the "Help Center" in the lower left corner.

Settings

You will want to click the "Settings" hyperlink as soon as you're up and running on the site. When you do, the screen in Figure 1-3 appears. From this, you can update your profile, change your profile picture, and set the many privacy settings that control what content relating to you others can view, as well as the content that's posted on your homepage for you and others to see when reviewing your profile. You can set your e-mail preferences, including the types of messages you'd like to receive and how frequently you receive them. You also can manage your Twitter settings, such as designating whether or not your Twitter account is part of your LinkedIn profile. You also can set your preferences for sharing your LinkedIn status updates with your Twitter followers.

Next, click on the "Account" link in the lower left-hand corner of the Settings page. Under the "Settings" heading on the screen that appears next, you'll find a link labeled "Customize the Updates You See on Your Homepage." Click on this link. This feature is especially important because it determines the content you view on your homepage. By default, LinkedIn will show you every kind of update from your network. You may want a less cluttered look, preferring, for example, not to know every time someone in your network has changed his profile photo, received a new recommendation, or joined a new group. However, if you're job hunting, you will want to be certain to receive new job postings and perhaps even notices of new discussions happening in your groups. Another way to control the

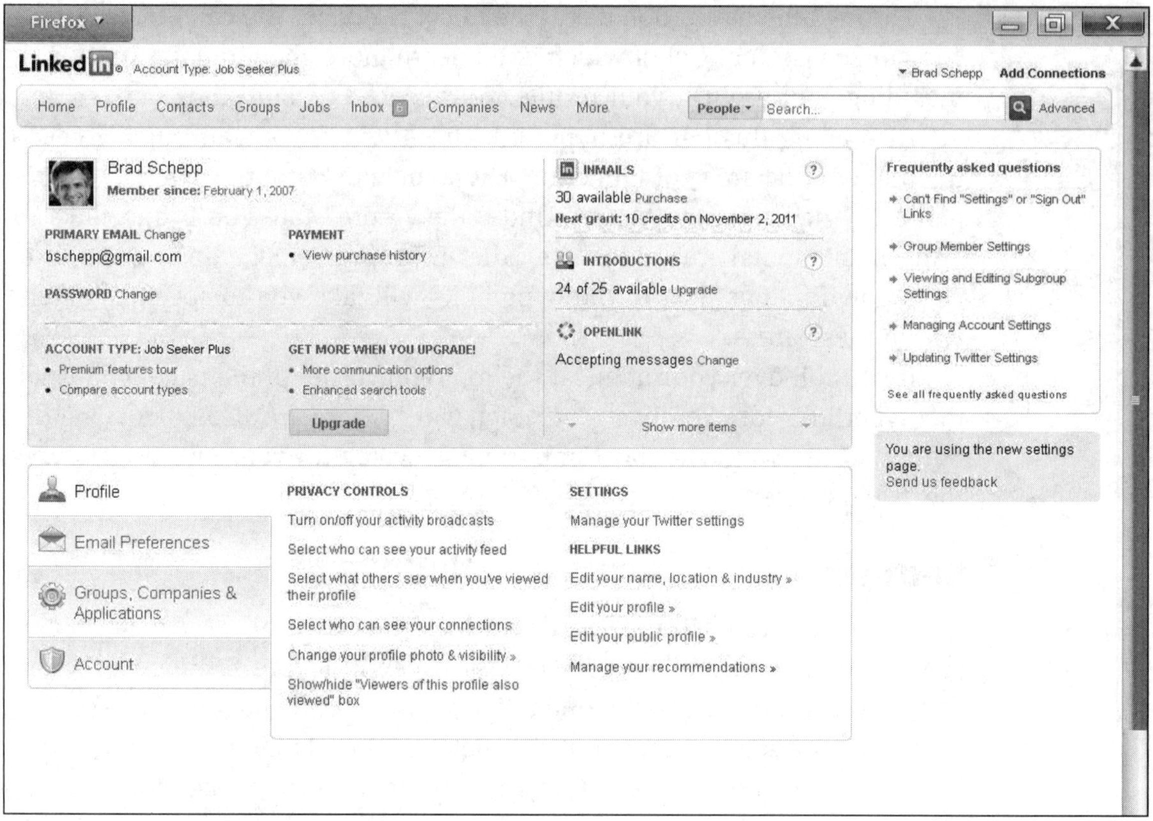

Figure 1-3: The Settings screen allows you to customize and control the information you receive and the views allowed to others interested in your profile.

amount of information you receive is by setting the number of updates shown to you.

Now your homepage will include your network updates, but other LinkedIn members who are just viewing your profile, of course, will not see all that information. It's your personal network, after all. Instead, they will see just the main facts about your background, including your summary, experience, education, and any links to sites such as your website and blog that you've added. Most of what you'll be reviewing when you go to your LinkedIn homepage is in the middle area that you can view by looking back at Figure 1-2. This includes the number of messages in your Inbox and, depending on your personal settings, other information that includes network updates, group updates, and information on the number of people from your employers and schools who have just joined LinkedIn. To the right of this area is additional information for you to review and possibly act on. This includes people you may know that LinkedIn has found for you, details about how many people have viewed your profile recently, events you may be interested in from the groups you belong to, and answers from your network, as well as job postings.

Finally, you also will want control over what people see when they find your LinkedIn profile through a search engine. This is called your *Public Profile*. From the Settings page, click on "Profile," and then under "Helpful Links," which appears in the middle part of the screen, click on "Edit Your Public Profile." From there, you can manage how you appear when people find you through a search engine, for example, whether your picture will be included, your summary, your current positions, your education, and so on.

Using Social Networking Sites Securely

Social networking makes Internet hacking easier and quicker, *USA Today* noted in a recent article. As with every other part of the Internet, there are people who use social networking sites to trick others into revealing sensitive information such as passwords, personal identification numbers (PINs), Social Security numbers, and the like. It seems to be a truism that wherever humans come together, some of them arrive with larceny as their goal. Don't let this happen to you! We want to encourage you to use social networking, but we also want to help you to learn to use these sites securely.

For suggestions about how users of social networking sites could protect their computers, as well as their online reputations, we spoke with cyber-security expert Joseph Steinberg. Mr. Steinberg has worked with high-profile personalities and Fortune 500 companies alike to ensure their safety from computer hacking.

His number one bit of advice: Do not use a password that's highly guessable, such as 12345, your name, or even your mother's name. Beyond that, log on frequently to check your privacy settings. "Remember it's not your Facebook, it's Facebook's," he cautioned. Facebook and LinkedIn are not static products. "So you can't just set these settings and then forget about them."

Every day Mr. Steinberg hears stories involving fake hyperlinks posted on social networking sites inviting people to click here and "learn how I just got an iPad for $50." He suggests that people use common sense and not click on links that seem out of place for the site they are using. The old adage applies: If it seems too good to be true, it probably is. "If iPads were being sold for $50, that kind of news would be on CNN or a deals website, and not on Facebook." If you click on that link, it may, in turn, be posted on your Facebook wall.

We all know that it's crucial to have virus protection and some way of securely backing up your data if you're using a laptop or desktop computer. But what about when you're using your smart phone? "If you're using a smart phone, you probably are using it more for texting, for e-mail, or for surfing the Internet than you are for making phone calls," Mr. Steinberg said. "So you have to treat it like a computer and install security software for it." The software should include the normal protection against viruses but also remote wipe technology that lets you erase your phone data remotely should your phone get lost or stolen.

Finally, he also had some advice about how to protect your online reputation. The fact is that there are now people entering the workforce who have always lived with social media, and they may not be aware of the repercussions of postings an employer might find objectionable. "Remember the hiring manager may not be in the same age group as the person applying for the job," he noted. People should remember that anything they say on a social media site probably will be around for longer than they are. So be sure to clean up anything that anyone might find objectionable on ethical or moral grounds, as well as offensive to a potential employer.

All the social networking sites are aware of the potential security risks that come with using their sites. We can tell you from personal experience that Facebook notified us when one of our profiles had been hijacked before we even realized that this had happened. A friend posted a note on our wall saying that something may be wrong. As we logged into e-mail, we already had a message from Facebook security that explained what happened and gave us clear steps to take to secure our profile. Help was just that swift and simple.

LinkedIn's Help and Learning Centers

The LinkedIn Help Center is where you'll want to go for answers to specific questions about how to accomplish things on the site. For example, there are links to articles on managing your account settings, importing contacts from your e-mail account, and changing, adding, or removing your e-mail address. The "Help Center" link is at the bottom of your homepage and many other LinkedIn pages, too.

Those new to LinkedIn will find a wealth of information about using the site through the separate Learning Center. Find the Learning Center by rolling over the "More" link that appears at the top of most LinkedIn pages. Another option is to enter learn.linkedin.com into your browser.

The Learning Center provides an excellent guide to everything on the site, with plenty of hyperlinks so that you can easily locate the areas you have questions about. Note that there is a section of the Learning Center just for job hunters at http://learn.linkedin.com/job-seekers/.

Also, at the bottom of most LinkedIn pages is a link for LinkedIn's blog, which will keep you up to the minute on all the new features the company rolls out.

You also may want to attend one or more LinkedIn webinars. You can get the details about these through the "Training Resources" link on the Learning Center's landing page.

LINKEDIN COMMUNICATIONS METHODS AND NETWORKING DETAILS

Every new technological advancement brings with it a new vocabulary and new ideas to understand and digest. Communicating on LinkedIn is the same. In order to be well versed, you simply have to understand the words you'll come across and have a feel for how everything on the site is structured. Don't despair. It's simple, intuitive, and relatively painless.

Your 1st, 2nd, and 3rd Degree Connections

Your connections on LinkedIn are made up of the people you invite to join your network and, by degrees, all the people in the networks of those linked directly to you. If you invite your coworker into your network, that coworker becomes your 1st degree connection. You also may share some other 1st degree connections with this individual because you both also may have invited other coworkers to join your networks.

Your 2nd degree connections include all the people in your coworker's network who are not also in your network. For example, if your coworker's boss from her last job is her 1st- degree connection, that boss would be your 2nd degree connection. In order to reach that boss directly, you would ask your coworker for an Introduction (or send an InMail for a fee). If your coworker agrees that the two of you would share commonalities, she'll most likely be happy to make the Introduction, at which point you'll be able to invite your coworker's former boss to join your network and therefore become a 1st degree connection for you, too.

Your 3rd degree connection may be the boss of your coworker's friend. Suppose that your coworker has linked with her friend at her old job who has your exact title. That's her 1st degree connection, of course. But she may not even know who her friend's boss currently is. Of course, if you have some reason to want to meet the equivalent of your supervisor at this other company, you still can work your way through your network and your coworker's network to get in touch.

You simply would ask your coworker to ask her friend about making the Introduction between you and his boss. You'd have to supply some reason why you think that boss would be interested in your work or background, and that may or may not have to do with a request for a job interview. Suppose that you're working on a presentation that you believe this manager at another company would be interested in. That could be a perfectly valid reason to want the Introduction. Provide your coworker with the details, and ask if she'd speak on your behalf. Once again, another option is to send an InMail for a fee.

In most cases, your 1st degree connection should be happy to help you reach out. In the end, after some communication, that 3rd degree connection easily could become a 1st degree member of your network, and you'll gain an ally and colleague at yet another company. If the day comes when you're ready to make a move, you'll have a 1st degree connection who also may be looking for someone just like you. Of course, by then, you'll know each other well enough to avoid a lot of the stress that comes from job hunting.

Your fellow Group members (more about Groups in Chapter 3) are also considered a part of your network. You may contact them directly or through the discussion feature that's a part of your Group.

Communications Methods

Throughout the chapters of this book, you'll learn a great deal about how you can identify and approach other LinkedIn members. To put you one step ahead, let's look at the different forms of reaching out to others and the structure of the network you'll begin to build.

Invitations. These can be sent to anyone you have an e-mail address for, whether or not they happen to be on LinkedIn. Once the parties you invite accept your Invitations, they become your 1st degree connections, and you can send messages directly to them through LinkedIn.

Messages. These are used to communicate directly with the people already in your network. One of the biggest advantages of using Messages is that once you've made a connection on LinkedIn, you never have to track that person's e-mail address again. You will always be able to reach the person directly through the site. You can send Messages from your Inbox or through your My Connections page.

Introductions. You just saw how you'd use Introductions to get in touch with people who are connected to your 1st degree connections but not directly to you. With the basic free membership on LinkedIn, you'll be able to request five Introductions per month. If you find that you need more, you'll know you're ready to upgrade to a paid LinkedIn subscription. You'll learn more about that in Chapter 6.

InMails. These are private messages that allow you to contact any LinkedIn user directly while protecting the recipient's privacy. If the person you send an InMail to is not in your network, you'll only be able to view her name and e-mail address, and then only if she accepts the InMail. With a free account, InMails are available only when purchased individually at the cost of $10 each. You will gain access to InMails with the premium LinkedIn accounts (discussed later in this book). LinkedIn guarantees a response when you send an InMail. If you don't get a response, LinkedIn will credit your account appropriately.

🔲 🔲 Mitch Neff: Was It a Case of Lemons or Lemonade?

"Getting laid off was the best thing that has happened to me this year," Mitch told us. "It advanced my opportunities well beyond where they would have been had I been secure in my previous job." Mitch went on to recount what had happened to him in the three weeks between his pink slip and our conversation. "This week alone I have had second interviews with a top 10 interactive agency and two major technology companies, and tomorrow with a local TV network affiliate. Next week, I will be flying out to meet one of those companies." Mitch also was in talks to syndicate a web show he does, and he'd signed a local client to keep the money coming in while he looked for his next professional home. "This is 100 percent from referrals and connections within my social networks," he noted.

Mitch fully admits that he's probably more "social savvy" than most, but he was quick to confirm that what he's done can be done by anyone in any field. He shared with us his concepts of "social capital" and "social tribes," two concepts that seem important as you set out putting your job hunt into the realm of social networking. We'll let Mitch explain them in his own words.

"Social capital is the notion that you build some type of equity by providing value. The more social capital you have in your networks, the more value you will receive when needed. I make sure to post interesting articles that I find on topics related to the subject. I engage with people who have questions I may be able to answer. I interview so-called influencers and post my questions to them either in my blog or on my web show. The flip side is that I now have an audience out there that enjoys the content I put out. When the folks I engage with most often found out that I had been laid off, they came out in force. Many messaged me privately to tell me they knew of some opportunities and companies that could use someone who 'lives and breathes this stuff.'"

"Social tribes are the groups that we run with. Some are purely digital. Some are in real life (IRL). Some are a mix. When your tribes recognize the value that you provide, they will literally go out of their way to help you when they feel they can. I try not to think about building social capital. I prefer to think that it is a by-product of helping others. It's a simple matter of a 'what can I do to help' attitude. It is as effortless as taking 20 minutes a day to scan your social feeds to ask and answer questions. This isn't rocket science; it is being human."

We started talking with Mitch on a Saturday. Within 2½ weeks, he sent us this final e-mail: "I just found out today that I landed an *awesome* job I found via someone I met on Twitter." We may not all currently share Mitch's social networking savvy, but since we are all human, let's proceed with the confidence he has that this is all it takes to make social networking work for us, too!

Best Jobs

Ten of the Best Jobs to Get Through Social Networking Sites

We think that you can get just about any kind of contract work or new job with the help of one or more social networking sites. Now, you wouldn't necessarily turn to Twitter to get your next job as an actuary. Then again, LinkedIn may not be as helpful to you if you are a musician looking for new gigs. By using a combination of these sites, though, we're convinced that you can land that next job faster. If that job happens to be one of the following, your task is even simpler. We present these in no particular order.

1. *Social media strategist.* Of course, you can demonstrate how adept you are at using social media sites, whether it's creating company-specific pages or providing clever status updates. Many companies now realize how essential it is that they have at least one person on board who can use sites such as Facebook and Twitter to provide customer service, seed the market with news about the companies, dispel rumors, and much more.

2. *Public relations (PR) manager.* Whatever you want to call it—communications manager or PR director—as a professional communicator, you really should be able to make your online profile sing. Just about any company has someone in a PR role and may be looking for someone just like you. Even if a company isn't currently in the market for someone with your skills, you can keep your name in front of the right people by careful and frequent networking through the sites we discuss in this book.

3. *Musician.* Many musicians promote their gigs and get new ones through sites such as Facebook. They create Pages, which their fans can "like," meaning that news of this appears on their Facebook walls. The status of MySpace is uncertain as we write this, but if it's still viable, it is definitely another source for musicians to check out.

4. *Blogger.* Everyone's attention span is shrinking to that of a fly, and sites such as Twitter don't help. But we all make time to read the words of someone who can help us to do our jobs better or maybe just better

understand the world we inhabit. Whether your goal is to be an independent blogger or to blog for a website or corporation, social networking sites can help you to promote your work to millions of people.

5. *Copywriter.* With so many sites offering you the chance to let everyone know your current status or to microblog about what's got your gears going, writers of all types have powerful new showcases for their talents. Copywriters are just one type, but a good representative example.

6. *Consultant.* If you're in business for yourself, you should be spending a good part of each workday marketing yourself and your skills. An excellent way to do this is through LinkedIn's Answers section, where you can demonstrate your expertise in a worldwide forum and unobtrusively include your background information just in case you've inspired someone to hire you.

7. *Information technology (IT) worker.* Many programmers, software engineers, and their managers use social networking sites; they've always been early adopters of new forms of electronic communications. These sites should be one of the first places you turn to when you're looking for that next IT job, but you probably already knew that!

8. *Virtual assistant/worker.* Many companies now hire people to do administrative tasks from afar rather than go to the expense of having them onsite. They may do receptionist work, scheduling, billing, writing, social media site updating, and many other tasks. Companies save on office space costs and benefits, and workers can work from the comfort of their home offices.

9. *Web designer.* Businesses of all sizes need web designers to help them get their sites up and running and then webmasters to keep them going. You can demonstrate your skills in this area in many ways while using social networking sites. Such skills include the design of your Google + or Facebook page, the multimedia portfolio you include as part of your LinkedIn profile, or the questions you answer on those ubiquitous discussion boards.

10. *Marketing manager.* Prove that you can sell yourself, and you may have an easier time convincing someone that you can move products for them as well. Social networking sites make it much easier for you

to sell yourself to a worldwide audience through your words and accomplishments and reach people who care.

Now, if you haven't found your own profession on this list of the top 10, don't despair. The opportunities are nearly boundless, and this is just a small sampling to show you what's possible. In researching this book, we found people from all walks of life connecting, expanding, and building their careers through social networking.

I GOT A JOB ON LINKEDIN

Throughout the first part of this book you'll meet many people who have found jobs or additional contract/freelance work thanks to LinkedIn. To get things rolling, we present a few examples here. We could have presented many, many more. LinkedIn is just that powerful.

Pinny Cohen: Consumer Behavior Consultant

In his interesting line of work, Pinny Cohen works with many different types of businesses, from manufacturing companies to distributors to retailers, by helping them understand consumers better from a psychology/statistics perspective and to develop plans to increase conversion rates on a site, increase sales in a store, or increase positive feelings toward a company. For example, Pinny has worked with car dealership groups to refine their sites and offline marketing, rug manufacturers to improve their trade-show displays and boost distribution of their products, and restaurants to enhance their patrons' dining experience.

Here, in his own words, he describes the many ways he uses LinkedIn to drum up business. You'll learn more about these methods in subsequent chapters.

I found clients in the following ways:

By type of company. When I had a service to offer a particular type of person, industry, or geographic location, I used the advanced search to target the decision makers.

Pinny Cohen's consulting business enjoys a new profitability thanks to his efforts on LinkedIn.

By niche. I joined groups in the targeted area and discussed topics that were "buzzworthy" in that group.

By targeted company. If I had a lead for a particular company or was blocked by a secretary, I could follow the chain of command by looking at all employees from a particular company and get to the right person right away.

Introduction. I built up an army of contacts, all of whom are very kind and will send an Introduction to any of the 7.5 million people I end up getting connected to by two degrees away.

Answers. I would answer questions in my niche and display expertise, often getting a follow-up message that could be converted into business.

Second contact. I often would add a contact to LinkedIn after my initial discussion with him or her—within 24 hours to keep my name fresh in the person's head (making use of some of my own expertise on marketing/psych). Then I would follow up with more information a day or week later. In a way, the second stepping stone was LinkedIn.

Profile optimization. I would add keywords into my profile to get ranked well in Google and get the right searchers looking at my profile and getting in touch with me.

Display icons. I place the LinkedIn icon on my blog and other places to make it easy to connect. Someone reading my content is much more likely to already trust me, and LinkedIn is an easy way for them to "officially" get in touch.

Show expertise. I bring my blog into LinkedIn as an application so that any visitor to my LinkedIn profile can instantly see some of my work and that I'm active on the site. If users don't see that, they won't risk spending time getting in touch with you.

Explain. I explain what I can offer (value-wise) to someone reading my profile so that they are thinking about how they can be helped, instead of just saying, "Oh, that's an interesting person," and then leaving.

Johanna Franco: Account Executive

Recent college graduates have been struggling to get a toehold into the labor market. Many are settling for jobs that are way below their abilities just to gain some experience and make ends meet. Johanna Franco is a recent college graduate who landed her dream job thanks to LinkedIn.

Johanna wanted to work for Hawaiian Airlines. She knew that blindly sending them a résumé through e-mail probably would not be adequate. She set her goal to talk to someone in the corporate office. "I called the number on their website to get in touch with someone in human resources, but they were only reachable via e-mail," she told us. "I wanted to talk to someone over the phone so that I could be advised as to what position would work best for me."

When her plan to reach someone directly failed, Johanna turned to LinkedIn. "I searched 'Hawaiian Airlines' and saw that a friend of a friend worked there in the corporate office!" she recalls. Johanna then set about working her network. She requested an Introduction, and this new contact passed her résumé on. "One of his coworkers contacted me in regard to an opportunity she saw appropriate for my skill set," Johanna recalls. "I spoke to her and then applied on their website. I continued to interview with her entire team and her department head. The company flew me to Hawaii for a final round interview, and I was offered the job."

Johanna Franco used LinkedIn and a little luck to find her dream job.

Now Johanna works with the Hawaiian Airline's customer loyalty program. When we asked her to offer advice for a newcomer to LinkedIn, her response surprised us.

"I'm a light user, and I typed in 'Hawaiian Airlines' on a whim. I was quite shocked when I had a connection to their corporate office—and that was just what I was looking for. I would encourage all light users to try and learn how to use LinkedIn even if they don't feel very familiar with it. The site can have a huge impact on your job search."

Is Johanna's story a matter of pure serendipity? Well, serendipity may well have played its part, but there's no denying that so did LinkedIn!

Kristen Kouk: Public Relations Executive

Kristen Kouk was eager to share her LinkedIn success story.

"I found my current position [partner of a PR agency] through LinkedIn's Update e-mails. I realized one of my former classmates at the University of Texas had recently started her very own company, and I immediately messaged her through LinkedIn to get more information. I sent her my résumé so that she could verify my experience, but she already knew my accomplishments in the PR industry from my LinkedIn profile. She knew I was the perfect fit for her growing agency."

When Kristen Kouk reconnected with an old college friend, she also found a great new job.

LOOKING AHEAD

Throughout this first section of this book you'll learn a great deal about the ins and outs of using LinkedIn. Each chapter will end with a quick look ahead at what the next chapter will bring, but in this first chapter, let's plot your course throughout your LinkedIn exploration and beyond.

The first order of business now is to make your own place on LinkedIn by creating a complete and dynamic profile. Chapter 2 will give you plenty of help. It may take some time to get your profile just right, but every moment you spend on perfecting it will be rewarded. Also, your profile is never exactly finished. As you move throughout your job and career, you'll keep an eye on how you can enhance your profile to reflect your own advancement and goals at the time.

Beyond Chapter 2, you'll learn about building a strong and vibrant network in Chapter 3. Chapter 4 will give you invaluable advice about actually hunting for a job on the site. Chapter 5 will clarify for you the powerful tool that is the Answers section. Having access to a world of experts who are willing and eager to share what they know will make everything about your work life easier. Chapter 6 will look at the many ways you can use LinkedIn to enhance your job performance. Chapter 7 will address some of the special tools and services LinkedIn and Facebook have developed to help students and new grads. Whether you currently have the job of your dreams or are still in search of the perfect spot for you, once you've got a job you care about, LinkedIn will help you to do it all so much more effectively.

Finally, we'll send you out to explore some other social networks that are also great places for locating jobs and business opportunities, as well as for business networking. These include Facebook, Twitter, and the newest service—Google +. You'll want to take a careful look at how these other sites can help you. You may be surprised to find how effective they can be when added to your mix of business tools and social networks.

CHAPTER 2

Create Your Best Profile

ow many times have you sat through a presentation for work about a subject you knew so well that you actually could have made the presentation yourself? How dreadful is it to have to be polite while someone explains in tedious step-by-step detail something so simple that you easily could have done it yourself? It's a universal human struggle and one you won't be subjected to in this chapter. We know that the mechanics of creating a LinkedIn profile are simple. LinkedIn has worked hard to make them so. If you follow the recommendations on the form you'll use to create a profile, you'll easily be stepped through every aspect of creating a complete and useful profile on the site. Not only that, LinkedIn has added a tool called *Improve Your Profile*. This remains live on your profile page, and you can access it at any time for suggestions on how to make your profile stronger and more dynamic.

Instead, we're going to focus on the philosophies and theories behind a great profile. We're going to talk about the place your LinkedIn profile will take in your total online presence and existence. When we do give you some nuts-and-bolts advice about making your profile sparkle, we'll ensure that those tidbits have the value-added features you'll need to make your profile work better. For instance, we won't just tell you to include links; instead, we'll tell you how to maximize the links you include. We're simply not going to torture you by repeatedly detailing things that you are clearly able to accomplish on your own. Because you've come to LinkedIn with millions of people already occupying the space, we have a lot of great advice about what makes a terrific profile terrific and also what makes your profile reflect negatively on you. We'll guide you—but only where you need guidance.

THEORIES AND PHILOSOPHIES

You will find almost as many different opinions about what makes a great LinkedIn profile as you will find profiles. Every time someone completes the profile form, another profile comes to life. Some experts will tell you to make sure that you include only the most relevant and detailed professional-looking profile. Others will tell you to be sure to let your personality sparkle so that people reading your profile will leave feeling like they know a little more about you as a real human. We're here to say that we agree with both those statements.

You don't want to include a lot of trivial personal information on your LinkedIn profile. For example, this isn't the place to declare the minutiae of your life. You can go to other networking sites if you want to update your friends with the latest stomach bug your family is fighting, but don't put that kind of stuff on LinkedIn. As one savvy LinkedIn user told us, "Keep religion out of it, duh!" The things that may be most dear to your heart are not necessarily the things you should include on LinkedIn.

On the other hand, LinkedIn would not be terribly useful if everyone stuck so rigidly to the same information in their profiles. We'd all look too much alike. Your LinkedIn profile isn't just a résumé. It's a portrait of who you are as a professional, and this means who you are as a person. There's nothing wrong with letting your personality show through. Just do it in a way that supports your professional life. You can manage this easily, for example, by linking your blog or website to your LinkedIn profile. This is a way to share more information with people who are already interested in your background enough to want more insight into who you are. They have proven that by their conscious decision to click through to learn more.

Now, the basic information you provide when you first create your LinkedIn account is enough to get a "profile" for you up on the site, but it's far from complete at that point. Once you click on the "Profile" hyperlink,

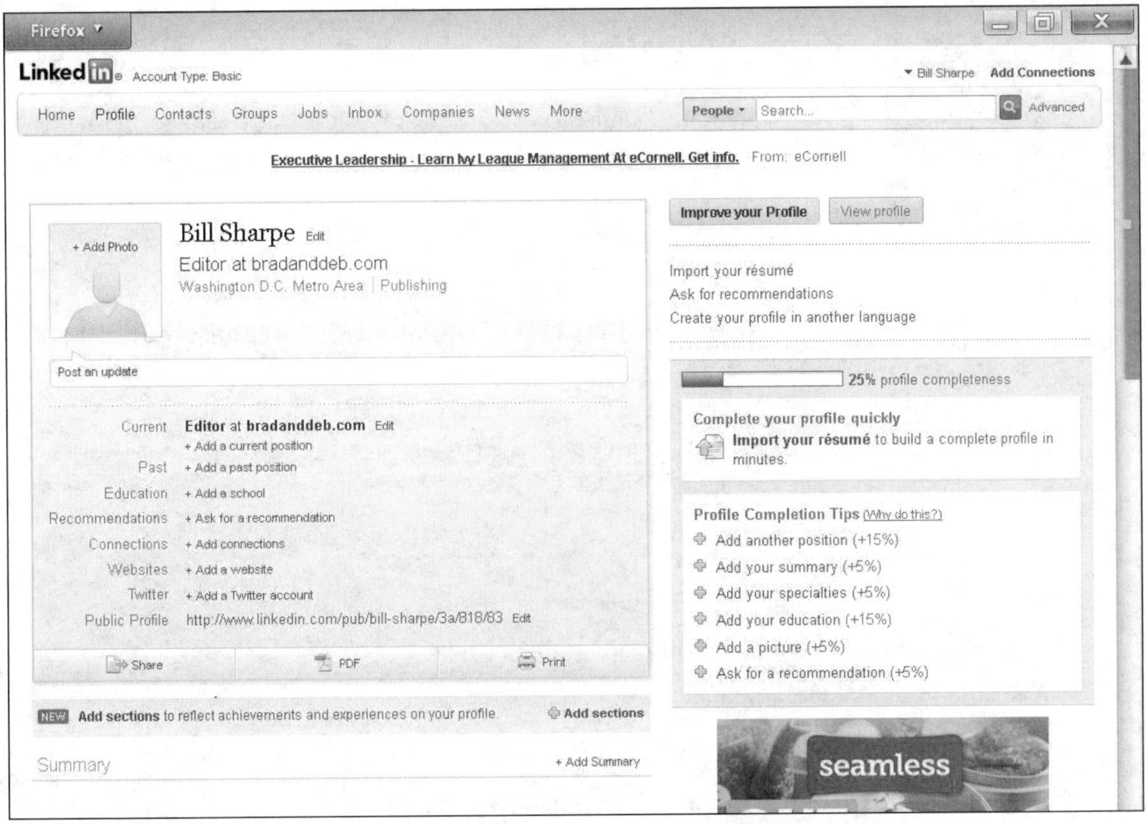

Figure 2-1: Use this screen to fill in all the details needed for a complete LinkedIn profile.

you can fill in all the details about your work background, education, and much more (Figure 2-1).

A Perfect LinkedIn Profile

There's probably no better way to dive in than to include an example of an extraordinary LinkedIn profile, and for us, that means taking a tour of Krista Canfield's profile (Figure 2-2). Krista is senior manager of corporate communications at LinkedIn. Who would be more likely to have a stellar profile? Her Summary tells you that Krista works in public relations but retains the heart of a reporter. This early experience as a reporter helps her Summary read like a compelling story. She knows how to use a lead sentence and make her audience want to keep on reading. Read on through

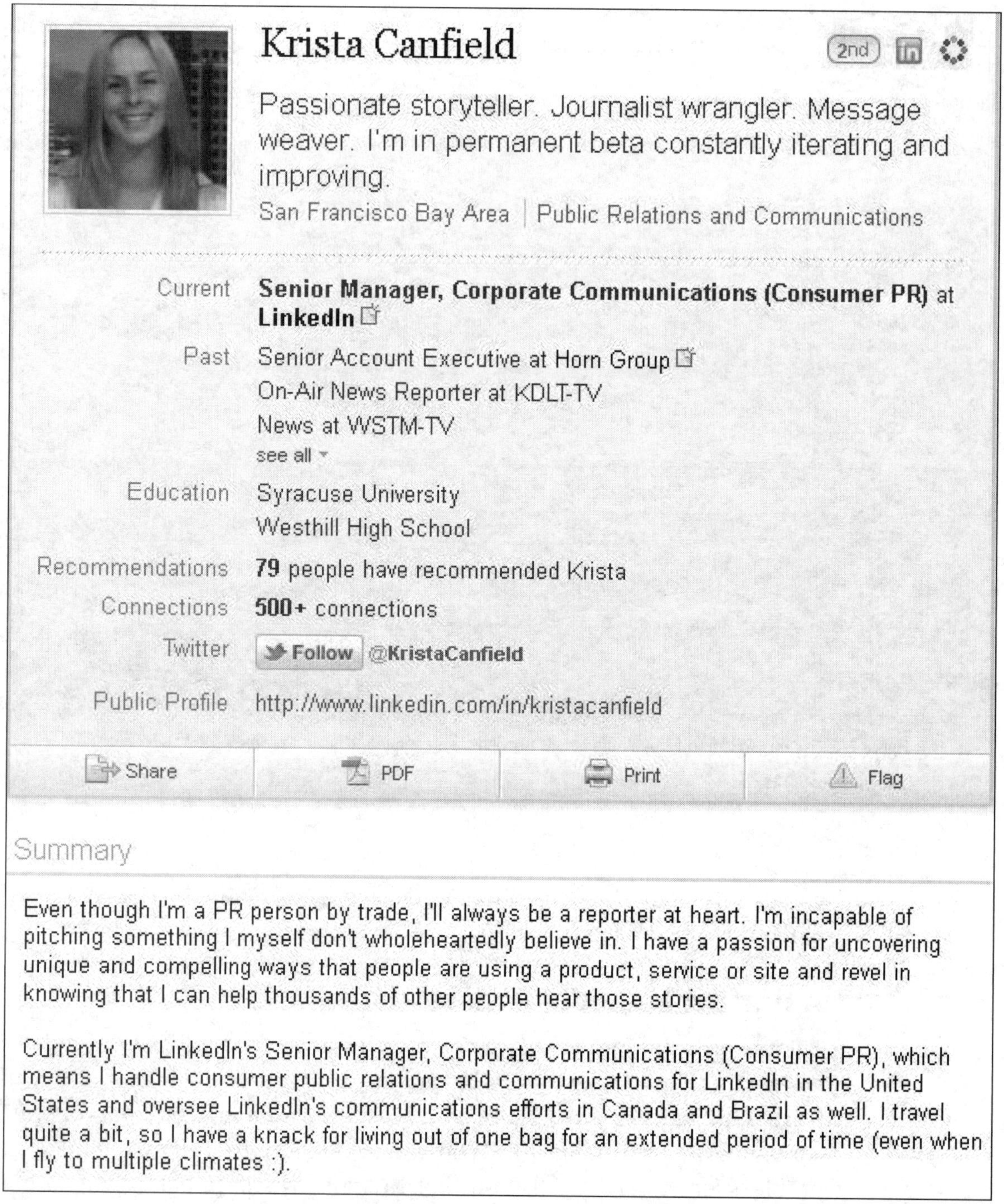

Krista Canfield

(2nd) in ⚙

Passionate storyteller. Journalist wrangler. Message weaver. I'm in permanent beta constantly iterating and improving.

San Francisco Bay Area | Public Relations and Communications

Current	**Senior Manager, Corporate Communications (Consumer PR)** at **LinkedIn**
Past	Senior Account Executive at Horn Group
	On-Air News Reporter at KDLT-TV
	News at WSTM-TV
	see all ▾
Education	Syracuse University
	Westhill High School
Recommendations	**79** people have recommended Krista
Connections	**500+** connections
Twitter	➤ Follow **@KristaCanfield**
Public Profile	http://www.linkedin.com/in/kristacanfield

Share	PDF	Print	Flag

Summary

Even though I'm a PR person by trade, I'll always be a reporter at heart. I'm incapable of pitching something I myself don't wholeheartedly believe in. I have a passion for uncovering unique and compelling ways that people are using a product, service or site and revel in knowing that I can help thousands of other people hear those stories.

Currently I'm LinkedIn's Senior Manager, Corporate Communications (Consumer PR), which means I handle consumer public relations and communications for LinkedIn in the United States and oversee LinkedIn's communications efforts in Canada and Brazil as well. I travel quite a bit, so I have a knack for living out of one bag for an extended period of time (even when I fly to multiple climates :).

Figure 2-2: Krista Canfield shares both her professional expertise and her out-of-office interests on her LinkedIn profile.

her Specialties (by viewing her profile on the site), and you can easily believe that when she says that she stays cool under pressure and that she is someone you can rely on, she means it, and it's true.

Krista has rearranged the sections of her profile so that her Reading List by Amazon comes directly after the first two sections of her profile, where most people jump right into their experience. This simple-to-add application is a tool we'll cover more fully in a few pages, but by placing her reading list here and up front, Krista allows you to look over her shoulder and see what she considers to be interesting. When we checked, she had 152 people following her reading list, getting updates each time she adds a new title. This proves that we're not the only ones who consider Krista to be a thought leader.

When you look at her Experience, you'll see that Krista not only claims to be who she is, but she also backs up her statements with cold, hard facts. For example, she tells you that from the time she joined LinkedIn until the day we checked, the company expanded from 18 million members and 200 employees to over 100 million members and more than 1,000 employees. This single fact alone proves her next statement, which is simply, "I thrive in fast-paced, hypergrowth environments."

By the time you've reached the end of her profile, you'll know that for 14 years Krista was a competitive amateur figure skater, competing in many regional competitions and ice shows. You'll also see that she supports a great many charitable causes from children's issues to animal rights and welfare and women's health. You come to the end of Krista's profile knowing that she is a high-achieving professional, and a person with a broad range of tastes and interests. You feel as though you've learned a lot about her in both these spheres of life.

CONTENT AND APPEARANCE

Of course, what's right for Krista may very well be all wrong for you. LinkedIn offers you lots of options for making your profile individual. Although, visually, LinkedIn profiles all resemble each other, what you choose to include in yours and how you present your content will blend to form a profile that's unique to you. Creating the profile that best speaks of you and your work is all that matters. How well you tell your story will be strictly up to you, and that will be shaped largely by your own career goals.

The first thing you need to consider is what exactly you want to achieve through your profile on the site. Once you answer some of those basic but core questions, you'll be able to craft the profile that best moves you toward those goals.

For example, if you are a freelancer or consultant, you may want to create a profile that showcases your specialties. If you are a writer or artist, the feel of your profile is likely to be quite different from that of an engineer or banker and more like Krista's. If you're currently job hunting, you'll choose to highlight certain elements that wouldn't be as important if you were settled in your position and coming to LinkedIn for expertise requests. Those elements might include greater detail about your accomplishments at other companies, complete with lots of figures (for example, "Boosted global sales 200 percent during my tenure"). But no matter what you want your final profile to say about you, all profiles have to share common elements.

Go Google Yourself

You always should know what others are learning about you on the web. We don't know how LinkedIn accomplished this, but your LinkedIn profile is likely to be among the top hits on a search results page when you Google yourself. This is why your profile has to speak well of you; then you can use it as a dashboard to drive your entire web presence. Linked to your website or blog, the profile becomes a gateway to everything you want professional contacts to know about you on the web. Once someone is checking out your LinkedIn profile page, he merely has to click a quick hyperlink to move over to your website. Conversely, when you put a hyperlink to your LinkedIn profile on your website, anyone who happens to find your website through a search engine will have your entire professional background available through a single click.

A site called Vizibility (vizibility.com) allows you to gain even greater control of the links people are likely to come across first when they Google your name. You just go to the site and fill in your name and perhaps where you've worked. The Vizibility wizard then asks you to provide keywords that you feel are especially relevant to the image you'd like to project, as well as to list some words that are not relevant. Soon you'll reach a place where you can designate the top five search results that you'd like people to see when researching you on Google. The site then helps you to create a "Google Me" link to these results, which you can list on your LinkedIn profile as one of your websites. With 1 billion people worldwide using Google, you can bet a lot of people will click or tap on that "Google Me" link.

Michael J. Case: Managing Director

Today, Michael Case is the managing director of Wahl & Case K.K., which he says is the fastest growing recruitment firm in Japan. Before he branched out into his own business in 2010, Michael was the head of executive search and staffing at Apple for the Japan region. "I hired most of the current executive team at Apple Japan," he told us. Before his stint with Apple, Michael was the head of recruitment for Morgan Stanley. So, clearly, he has a long history of evaluating job candidates and a global perspective on what makes a good impression on a potential hiring manager. To top it all off, Michael has been actively using LinkedIn to identify and attract strong candidates since 2004. "We use LinkedIn heavily on a daily basis, and we see great profiles and terribly neglected profiles," he said. Fortunately, he shared his expert philosophy with us to help you to put your best face forward.

Michael J. Case knows a good profile when he sees one.

"First, always keep your audience in mind and remember this is a professional document that represents you publicly," he advised. "Therefore, one must be very, very careful in crafting this profile and take even more care than one would with a résumé because this is likely to have even wider reach and impact," Michael said. He also emphasized the importance of making sure that your profile is complete. "The more information that is there," he reasoned, "the more a potential employer or recruiter will have to work with. It's worth the effort."

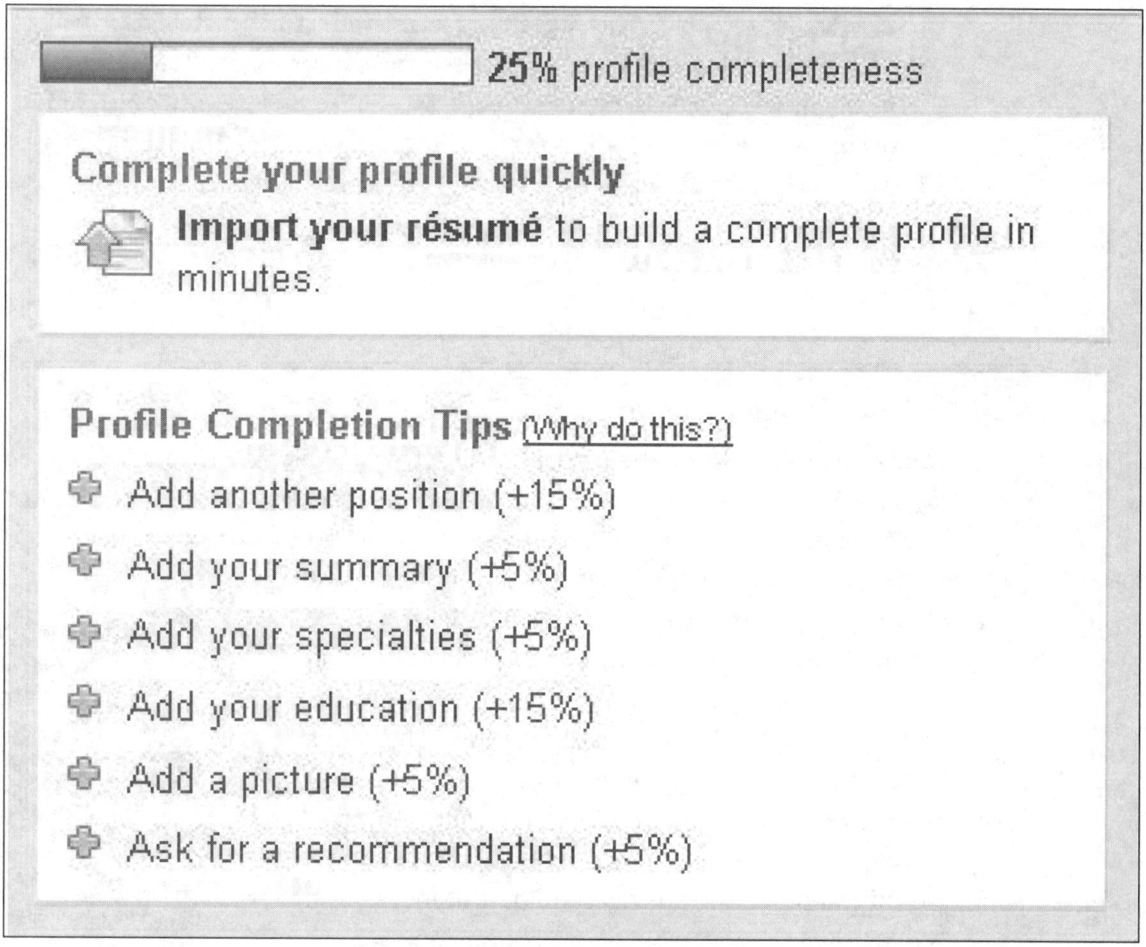

25% profile completeness

Complete your profile quickly

 Import your résumé to build a complete profile in minutes.

Profile Completion Tips (Why do this?)

✛ Add another position (+15%)

✛ Add your summary (+5%)

✛ Add your specialties (+5%)

✛ Add your education (+15%)

✛ Add a picture (+5%)

✛ Ask for a recommendation (+5%)

Figure 2-3: LinkedIn keeps track of how complete your profile is and lets you see very clearly the remaining steps you can take as you work your way toward 100 percent completeness.

■ You Need 100 Percent

On LinkedIn, a complete profile means that it's 100 percent finished. How do you know that you've reached this milestone? LinkedIn notes your progress right on your profile (Figure 2-3). A brand-new profile is likely to be only about 25 percent complete. "Make sure their profiles are 100 percent complete," advised career consultant Anne Pryor. "Nothing much happens on LinkedIn until your profile is at 100 percent," more than a few successful users told us. Fortunately, LinkedIn will step you through the process as you work your way toward that 100 percent profile. We'll look at the nuts and bolts of maximizing the elements of your profile a little later in this chapter, but for now, know that, among all the other things that you have to include, you'll need a photo and three recommendations. Let's look at these two elements first.

Your LinkedIn Photo

Throughout this book, you'll meet many different LinkedIn users who have chosen their photos for their own specific reasons. Most of us select a photo because we find it flattering. That's good, of course. But remember that the photo you put on your LinkedIn profile will be the only way to get your face before the people you specifically want to attract. It doesn't matter if you're a glamour-puss in this case. It matters that your photo be bright, well lit, and positive. "However you look at work is how you should look in your picture," advised Chuck Hester, a LinkedIn LION. (LION stands for LinkedIn Open Networker, and as we'll describe in Chapter 3, a LION is someone who links with as many people as possible.) You don't have to wear a suit, for example, although cutoffs on the beach aren't a good idea either. Figure 2-4 makes an interesting first impression. Look a little closer, and you'll see that Theresa Hummel-Krallinger lists "Laughologist" as one of her job titles. This may be just the right impression to attract her particular type of client!

Recommendations

You can complete all the elements of your profile, but until you've received three recommendations, you're not going to hit the 100 percent mark. Even more important, LinkedIn says that people with recommendations are three times more likely to receive inquiries through LinkedIn people searches. Recommendations on LinkedIn don't differ too much from recommendations you'd get anyplace else. It's actually kind of a funny game we humans play. You know you can't make a good professional impression without recommendations, yet you also know you wouldn't solicit recommendations from someone unless you were sure that they would be strong and positive. Still, as flawed as the human system of recommending may be, it's vital to your profile. "A lot of people use the recommendation feature," noted David Becker, a branding professional. "I think that's viable if it's

Theresa Hummel-Krallinger

Trainer, Coach, Laughologist

Greater Philadelphia Area | Professional Training & Coaching

Current	**Director, Organizational Development & Training, North America** at **Almac Group** ☐ **Faculty Member** at **Temple University** ☐ **President** at **High Five Performance, Inc.**
Past	Director, Organizational Development & Training at Almac Clinical Technologies ☐ OD & Training Consultant at ICTI President, Board member at Greater Philadelphia ASTD ☐ see all ▾
Education	Chestnut Hill College Lansdale Catholic Villanova University
Recommendations	**36** people have recommended Theresa

Figure 2-4: Theresa Hummel-Krallinger has found the perfect image for her LinkedIn profile photo. After all, she's a corporate trainer and a "laughologist"!

done well. It can backfire if you just have one recommendation. It makes people wonder, 'What about all the others?'"

Unlike in real life, on LinkedIn, everyone can view both the recommendations you receive and the ones you leave for others. Bryan Webb, a technical marketing professional, uses recommendations frequently when evaluating someone on LinkedIn. "I look for the recommendations they have given and received," he told us. Keep in mind that not only do your own recommendations speak to your work, but those you leave for others probably reveal even more about your character and values. People are clearly judged by how they present themselves in a public forum, so look at every recommendation you write as an opportunity to show who you are while you shine the spotlight on a colleague or friend.

The immediacy with which others can evaluate you through your recommendations is another thing that separates LinkedIn from older ways of doing business. It used to be that checking references was reserved for the last phase of the hiring process. You wouldn't check references unless you were close to making an offer to a candidate. Now you can use LinkedIn to see what others have said about a prospective employee or business partner before you've even met. "It gives me a better insight into the person," noted Bryan when we asked about recommendations. "With LinkedIn, you don't have to wait to review references from someone." Those recommendations are there and always waiting for the world to see who you are in the eyes of others.

It's best to have at least one recommendation from each of your most recent jobs. If you've had several short stints with companies recently but a much longer tenure with a company before that, then be sure to include at least one recommendation from that previous employer.

Ideally, your recommendations are from managers, preferably the people who managed you directly (or, for contractors and consultants, from actual clients who hired you). It's also good to include recommendations from coworkers at your same level, especially if they worked with you in the same group. Finally, recommendations from people who you've managed also can be telling if they attest to your skills as a manager. Just make sure that they're long on specifics and short on saccharin!

Requesting Recommendations

There are several things to keep in mind when you request recommendations from your colleagues, friends, and business partners. "LinkedIn is excellent for demonstrating your expertise," said David Becker. Of course, there are many places on the site for doing so, including the Answers area we'll cover in Chapter 5, but your recommendations also should feature your specific attributes and contributions.

To ask someone to write a recommendation for your LinkedIn profile, use the form shown in Figure 2-5. This appears when you click on the "Ask for a recommendation" hyperlink shown in Figure 2-1. Note that the form is filled in with a boilerplate note, which you should customize. When you customize that note, include some specific details you'd like to have featured from the part of your career you shared with this person. Give a few specific talking points as suggestions when you send your request. This

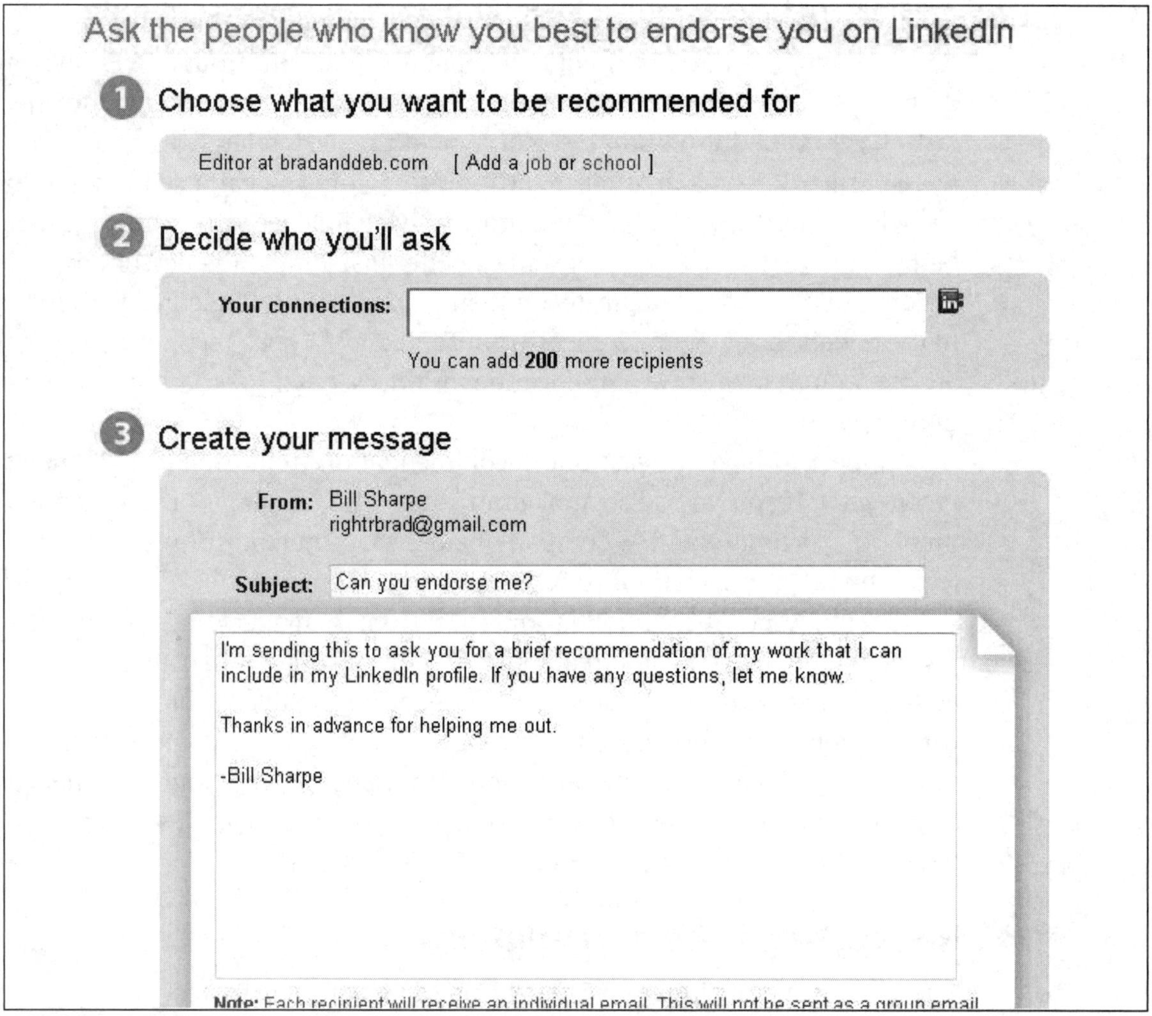

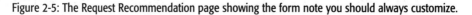

Ask the people who know you best to endorse you on LinkedIn

1 Choose what you want to be recommended for

Editor at bradanddeb.com   [Add a job or school]

2 Decide who you'll ask

Your connections: [   ]

You can add **200** more recipients

3 Create your message

From: Bill Sharpe
rightrbrad@gmail.com

Subject: Can you endorse me?

I'm sending this to ask you for a brief recommendation of my work that I can include in my LinkedIn profile. If you have any questions, let me know.

Thanks in advance for helping me out.

-Bill Sharpe

Note: Each recipient will receive an individual email. This will not be sent as a group email

Figure 2-5: The Request Recommendation page showing the form note you should always customize.

not only makes it easier for the person who has agreed to recommend you, but it also makes the recommendation more closely tailored to the results you want. Again, what you'd like to spotlight will vary depending on what you're hoping to achieve with your LinkedIn presence. If you're job hunting, you'll want to look across the breadth of your career and request recommendations from people who can spotlight the most important attributes for the type of job you're seeking. Former managers can attest to what you accomplished for them and suggest to your next manager what you are capable of. If you're looking for business partners, on the other hand, you probably want some recommendations that highlight your ability to meet deadlines, manage budgets, and supervise projects, for example.

"Request as many recommendations as is appropriate from your previous employers, colleagues, professors, and clients," recommends Chris Perry, brand and marketing generator for Reckitt Benckiser. "They don't have to be long, like traditional recommendations. They just need to be genuine and supportive of your personal brand and the value you hope to continue providing future employers and clients."

Finally, when you come across former colleagues who you respected or enjoyed working with, why not write unsolicited recommendations for them? If you send those without expecting to receive any in return, you are living the creed of LinkedIn by doing more for others than you ask for yourself. Your former colleagues will have the chance to review your recommendations before accepting them into their profiles, so they will know immediately what you've done for them. You'll certainly make someone's day, and it's quite possible that you'll also get a few good recommendations to fill out your profile, too.

NUTS AND BOLTS

Let's turn our attention now to the details of putting together a great profile. You already know that you need a photo and some recommendations, but what are the other things to consider as you build your profile? We've gathered some great advice and tips from experts all over LinkedIn to help you create a great profile of your own. "The first thing to realize is that your LinkedIn profile isn't a résumé," said Mike O'Neil, CEO of Integrated Alliances and a LinkedIn trainer. "That's a fast way of getting something up there, but it's not a profile." Your LinkedIn profile lives and breathes in a way that your résumé simply cannot. Since your profile is the home base for everything else you do on LinkedIn, the more active you are on the site, the more activity will show on your profile. Everything you do on LinkedIn from writing and requesting recommendations, to asking and answering questions, to joining groups will show up on your overall profile.

Starting at the Top

Although you're not getting a step-by-step tour of the form you'll use to complete your LinkedIn profile, certain parts of the profile are so important that we should look at them together. Starting at the top of the page shown in Figure 2-6, you'll see a photo, a headline, and a status update. You've already spent some time planning for the photo, so let's take a look at the other two elements. They actually are more than they seem.

Your headline should consist of the most telling and persuasive things you most want people to know about you. Think of it as the pitch you would use if the hiring manager for your dream job stepped onto the elevator with you in a parking garage. You may have only 15 to 20 seconds to say

Debra Sorkowitz Schepp

Writer, editor, co-founder at bradanddeb.com
Washington D.C. Metro Area | Publishing

Debra Sorkowitz Schepp Talking to lots of interesting job hunters as we work on revising our LinkedIn book

Like • Comment • Share • See all activity • 37 seconds ago

Current	**Library Associate II** at **Frederick County Public Libraries**
	Co-founder at **bradanddeb.com**
Past	Production Editor at Rowman & Littlefield Publishing Group
	Associate Editor at Datapro (now Gartner)
Education	Rutgers, The State University of New Jersey-New Brunswick
Recommendations	**3** people have recommended Debra
Connections	**79** connections
Websites	bradanddeb.com
Twitter	bradanddeb

Figure 2-6: The top of a LinkedIn profile. The headline and status area are two quick ways to gain interest and attention from others viewing your profile.

something that would grab this executive's attention. What would it be? "I'm looking for communication styles," says Chuck Hester. "The writing style should be concise and precise." This advice is especially useful when considering your headline. Get right to the point, leaving no room for speculation about what you offer through your best skills and experience.

Now, if you are currently employed, and especially if you're content where you are and your LinkedIn profile is meant to showcase your employer as well as you, it's perfectly acceptable just to include your full job title within your headline. But we're assuming that you're looking for advice about what to include if you're between positions or at least want to keep all options open.

Here are some actual examples from LinkedIn of status headlines that should achieve results:

- Experienced marketing analyst with GE + Navy leadership experience
- Pricing professional specializing in management, market segmentation, price optimization, and process improvement
- Radio Host, Author, Public Speaker
- Entreprenuer, Executive, Startup Advisor
- Wildly Creative Namer, "Eat My Words"

A Complete and Attractive LinkedIn Profile

Monique Cuvelier, CEO at her own web design firm, Talance.com, has quite an enticing profile on LinkedIn (Figure 2-7). She has honed it to show her best experience and has loaded it with keywords that will attract new clients and potential business partners. You may notice that her profile includes a link to an article she's written. Were you to click that link, you'd be taken to her company's blog. From there, it's just another simple click to get to the website itself and glimpse first-hand what Monique can do in creating a strong and vibrant place on the web.

Notice also Monique's Specialties. Within this area she details a dozen specific terms relevant to web design. This list includes everything from the software she's worked with to the details of her job, such as editing, training, and management. Her company's blog is also linked to her profile through the WordPress application on LinkedIn, and she adds to it frequently to keep her content fresh and relevant. "My goals with my LinkedIn

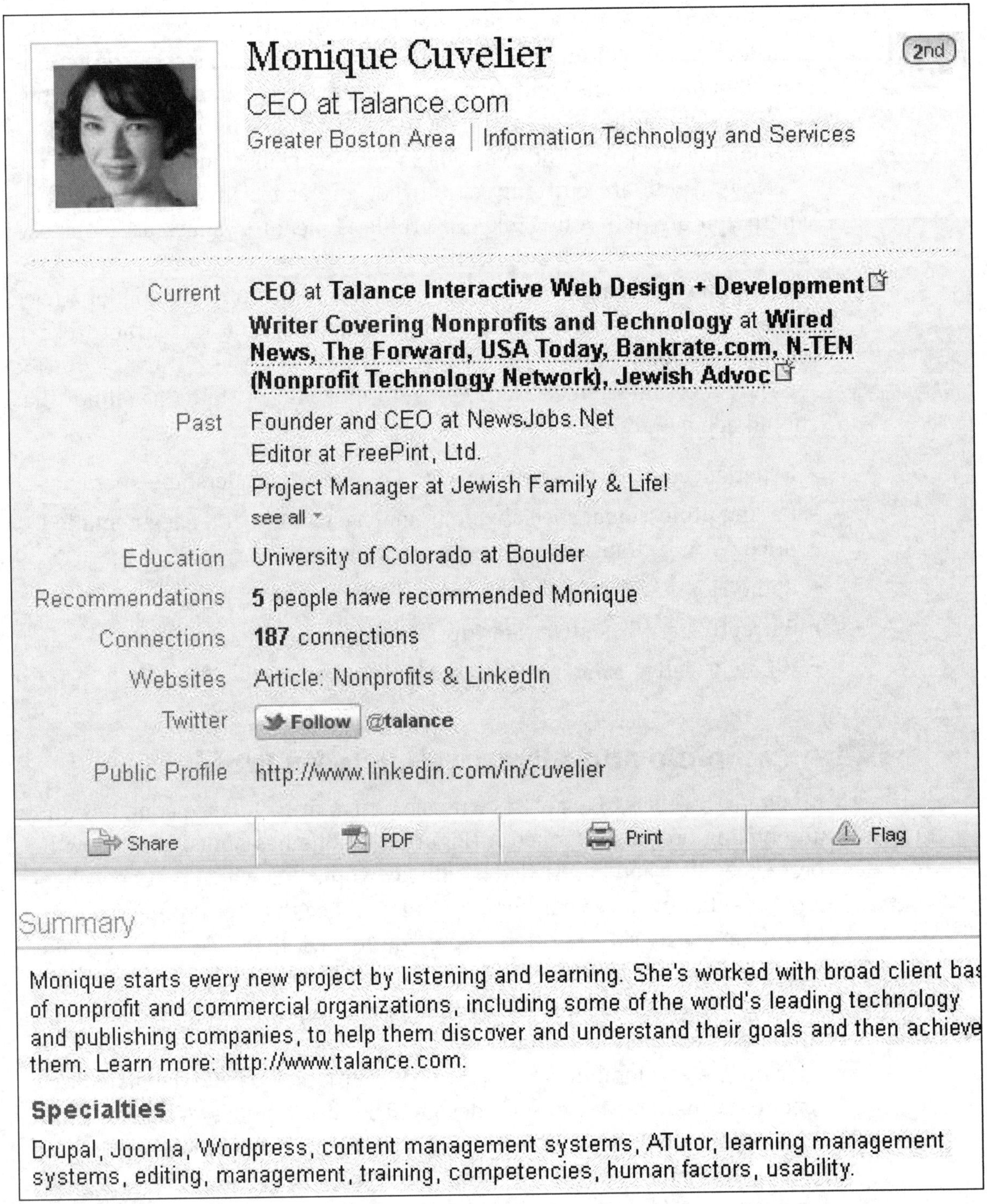

Monique Cuvelier (2nd)

CEO at Talance.com

Greater Boston Area | Information Technology and Services

Current	**CEO** at **Talance Interactive Web Design + Development** ⬀ **Writer Covering Nonprofits and Technology** at **Wired News, The Forward, USA Today, Bankrate.com, N-TEN (Nonprofit Technology Network), Jewish Advoc** ⬀
Past	Founder and CEO at NewsJobs.Net Editor at FreePint, Ltd. Project Manager at Jewish Family & Life! see all ▾
Education	University of Colorado at Boulder
Recommendations	**5** people have recommended Monique
Connections	**187** connections
Websites	Article: Nonprofits & LinkedIn
Twitter	**Follow** @talance
Public Profile	http://www.linkedin.com/in/cuvelier

Share	PDF	Print	Flag

Summary

Monique starts every new project by listening and learning. She's worked with broad client bas of nonprofit and commercial organizations, including some of the world's leading technology and publishing companies, to help them discover and understand their goals and then achieve them. Learn more: http://www.talance.com.

Specialties

Drupal, Joomla, Wordpress, content management systems, ATutor, learning management systems, editing, management, training, competencies, human factors, usability.

Figure 2-7: Monique Cuvelier often receives compliments on her complete and attractive LinkedIn profile.

profile are to try to establish my own expertise and create another entry into my company's website and services," she said. "According to my website traffic, it does drive people our way, and it's garnered some compliments, so that's another plus!"

"I think profile writing is a little like writing a résumé," Monique said. "There are sure-fire mistakes you can make, but a really good one is harder to define. Weird or blurry pictures are a minus," she added. "Poor punctuation is a turnoff, and skimpy information seems useless," she further noted. "Those would be the top picks for what makes a bad profile."

Just below the headline is your status bar. Here's where you can have a little fun and keep your profile lively and dynamic. This status bar isn't unlike those on other networking sites such as Facebook and Twitter. It's meant to be updated often, say, several times a week, and be the most current part of your profile. Just don't update your status with extraneous entries. It's not the place to talk about the weekend hiking trip you just took unless you're looking for work as a hiking tour guide. Instead, use the space to promote your latest business-oriented blog entry, article published, product launched, award won, or anything else that's going on right now in your professional life. The more lively and dynamic you make this, the better it speaks to your productivity and engagement with your career. Your LinkedIn network will be alerted when you have updated your status. Your network also will have the chance to "like" your status, as well as respond with a comment. These responses can result in the start of useful dialogs.

So once again update your status frequently. It shows that you're working and contributing to the LinkedIn community by sharing your news. And be sure to include a hyperlink, if relevant, because it makes your status update that much more useful and provocative.

Some examples of provocative status updates from LinkedIn include

- Cher Lon Malik RT @BadBoyBrad: Vote for me to be the face of @ aboutdotme on a Times Square billboard, http://t.co/dAxLGpQ.

- Jacob Bettany Video: Classic cars rev up their investment credentials, http://t.co/s582gHhP.

- Jay Grandin is trying to blend inflammatory language into a highchair ad.

- Alexandra Watson is naming corporate conference rooms after cereal brands. Meet me in Cap'n Crunch at 3 p.m.

Every Word's a Keyword

As you're contemplating how best to describe yourself, your work, and your goals and aspirations, keep in mind that every word of your profile is a potential keyword. Now this is not to say that a good profile is simply a string of eye-popping keywords because no one wants to read that, and ultimately, it doesn't give anyone a feel for who you are, just what you've done. But consider that keywords help people to find your profile, and you should make sure that you use a lot of them, especially ones that are specific to your own industry. "Southwest Airlines started using 'cheap flights' in their profile because that's how people searched for flights," said Krista Canfield, LinkedIn's public relations manager. "That upped their search engine optimization (SEO) because that's the search term used most commonly. Fill your profile with keywords that will come up in Google searches."

Brand and marketing consultant Chris Perry agrees. "Leverage your Headline, Summary, and Specialties," he said. "Plug your personal brand, supporting pitch, and strengths directly into your profile. Make sure viewers of your profile know exactly what you offer. All of these are places where targeted industry/function/expertise-specific keywords are ideal for optimizing your profile in "People search" results." Okay, fair enough, but how do you know which words to choose? Turn right back to LinkedIn. No matter what your job or level of experience, you're going to find others on LinkedIn who are very much like you. Search for the job title you currently hold or dream of holding. Then search the profiles that come up for keywords that you may not have thought of on your own. "Go to the People search and look for titles you're interested in, like Project Architects," advised Anne Pryor. "See their profiles and the words they use. Then see what groups they're in." Now you have not only the keywords that can add zip to your own profile but also some new destinations to consider as you begin joining groups.

Avoid These Buzzwords

Just as clichés convey little real meaning, there are words that appear in LinkedIn profiles again and again. You may think that stating that you're a seasoned professional, for example, will help you to stand out from the crowd, but instead, it's more likely to cause you to blend right in—this is not what you want. LinkedIn has provided users with a quick and handy list of overused terms and phrases. Here are the top 10 phrases U.S. professionals tend to fall back on:

1. Extensive experience

2. Innovative

3. Motivated

4. Results-oriented

5. Dynamic

6. Proven track record

7. Team player

8. Fast-paced

9. Problem solver

10. Entrepreneurial

Now that you know these phrases tend to be clunkers, you can avoid them. Better yet, as you build your profile, let your actions replace the words. If you are results-oriented, state your results. Team players can cite examples of how their team-building efforts solved a problem for an employer or brought a project to fruition. Show your talents rather than providing empty words.

Your Summary

Your Summary is the space for you to elaborate on your professional life. If people reviewing your profile have gotten this far, they've already learned your name and seen your photo, headline, and perhaps status. You don't want to lose them here! You have plenty of room in this space to describe what you do, what you've done, and what spins your propeller. Just be sure to let some of your personality show. The people who read your profile want to come away feeling as though they know something more about you when they're done, so reward them with the tidbits that help to describe you. You're giving them not only facts but also a flavor for what you may be like as a person. Fill it with keywords, sure. Even include some bullet points if that's a good way to detail what you've done. But don't make it simply a dry listing of jobs, tasks, and history.

Your Specialties

Here's the place to really pack in the keywords. Fill this area with every detail you can think of that would entice your next employer to take a closer look. "You should consider where you want to work and tailor your profile accordingly," said Jacqueline Wolven, graphic designer and marketing professional. The Specialties area of her profile includes nearly 15 separate and searchable keywords describing her services and experience. Just keep in mind that in the wise advice of Chuck Hester, "Everything you put in your profile has to be traceable." Make sure that you can back your claims with hard facts before you make them.

Inside Tips for a Great Profile from LinkedIn

Of course, LinkedIn's public relations manager Krista Canfield clearly has an advantage over most of the rest of us when it comes to creating a great profile. She was kind enough to share some insider information that will make your profile even better. Here are two of her most important pieces of advice:

1. When you fill in the box for your website, click on "Other." This lets you put your actual website's name there instead of the URL. Then use one of the other two links for your company's website so that people can gain more information about the nature of your work. Finally, save the last position in the field for your latest article, award, achievement, or whatever else happens to reside online. This will help you with SEO on your name.

2. Customize your LinkedIn URL. When you first sign on to LinkedIn, you'll receive a generic URL supplied by the site. It's very easy to overlook this simple but practical piece of advice to improve your own branding. Change your LinkedIn URL to be exactly the same as your name is known professionally. For example, if you're a married woman who has taken your husband's name, you might want to put your maiden name in your profile name. That way, people who studied or worked with you prior to your marriage still will be able to find you. However, when it comes to your URL, change it to be the same as the name you are known by professionally. It makes it easier for people to remember you and your profile location if you include that name. No one will search that field for your maiden name. The same will hold true for anyone whose given name is different from his common name; for example, substitute Bill for William or Chuck for Charles if that is how you're known.

To customize your URL, select "Edit Profile" from the "Profile" hyperlink at the top of the page. In the box above your summary, look for "Public Profile." Click on "Edit." From there you can reach the page where you can customize your URL.

Your Experience

As you go about completing your profile, you'll want to detail your experience at your current job and each of your previous employers. This is not the place for dry iterations of the tasks and action items you completed at each stop along your employment journey. You want to make this section sparkle. "You want to make your profile shine," says Bryan Webb. "Add and expand on your experience and what you've done at each position. If I'm reviewing a profile and don't find it compelling, I will not take it any further. Make your experience compelling and exciting," he advised.

Don't just list what you've done; add details about how you did it. Your well of experience should be broad, but here's the place to make sure that it's deep as well. What other departments did you work with to achieve success with that big project? How did you manage people? What were the proudest moments while you were at any particular job? Give people something to distinguish you from all the others who may share your job titles and your employment history. Make the person reading about your experience want to know more so that she'll be enticed to contact you. If this sounds like a lot of work, it is. But it's also your best shot at making yourself desirable in the eyes of that next employer.

TIP

Once you've completed your LinkedIn profile, include the customized URL within your e-mail signature as part of all the e-mail you send. In this way, every time new contacts hear from you, you'll be increasing the chances that they'll click through to your LinkedIn profile. You've built it carefully; now let it start paying you back for all that time and attention!

Add Additional Sections to Your Profile

To further enhance and personalize your LinkedIn profile, you can choose to add sections that don't appear automatically in the standard profile form. These sections will vary depending on your industry and professional background, but they include

- Certifications
- Courses
- Languages
- Organizations
- Projects
- Patents
- Publications
- Skills

These additions to your profile not only allow you to add new details to your story, but they also represent new areas of keyword-rich text that will make your profile more likely to appear in search results. "This is another great way to feature your strengths and capabilities (for example, web development, marketing consulting, professional speaking, etc.) on your profile while also optimizing your profile in another search filter," Chris Perry recommends.

By adding a tab for Organizations, you now can feature your volunteer activities on your LinkedIn profile. Very often the work we do for nonprofit organizations will add other elements to our work experience that paid employment may be lacking. For example, if you serve on a charity's board of directors, you are likely to be making decisions that include budgeting, public relations, and event planning. You can further round out your experience to include team building, presentation skills, and writing. Many of us do volunteer work, but we don't ever think of those efforts as adding to our skill sets. They do! Now you can include them on your profile for even greater keyword exposure.

To further personalize your profile, you also can rearrange the sections of your profile to determine in which order they will appear. If you're relatively new to the workforce but you went to a stellar university and graduate school, you may want to move your Education entries up to just above your Experience section. Rearranging the sections of your profile is a matter of simply dragging them and dropping them. Once you've got the sections in the order you think is right, test that by clicking "View profile." Now you can decide whether you've got everything exactly where you want it before others view your changes.

LinkedIn Applications

LinkedIn's Applications are fabulous tools for making your profile and your life on LinkedIn more vibrant and engaged. To reach the Applications area, mouse over to the "More" link at the top of your profile page. The pull-down menu that appears displays popular applications and a link from which you can view others. Rather than step you through each application, some of which may have changed by the time you read this, we'll look at the purpose of the applications and just what you may be able to do with them.

One favorite application that couldn't be simpler to add to your profile is Reading List by Amazon. Here's where you can create your own personal bookshelf that will reside on your profile. Include reviews of books you're currently reading. Spread the word about titles you've found intriguing but haven't yet gotten to read. Creating this list gives you just one more way of connecting with your fellow LinkedIn visitors on a personal and human note. Of course, feature books that support your work life, but don't hesitate to include that latest page-turner, too. This is a simple, easy, but quite direct way to let your personality and taste shine through your profile.

Bloggers have two options on LinkedIn. You can create your blog through WordPress, a hugely popular member of the blogging universe.

Once you create your WordPress blog, you can easily link it to your profile. That way, every time you add a blog entry, your profile will reflect the new addition. Bloglink allows you to connect your existing blog with your LinkedIn profile. Through Bloglink, your network will be notified every time you update a blog entry. Likewise, you'll be notified when members of your network have updated their blogs, too. This will go a long way toward building your own personal brand, both on LinkedIn and on the web in general.

Still another useful and dynamic application is SlideShare Presentations. With this feature, you can upload an existing presentation to your profile to showcase the work you've done. Anyone visiting your profile can click through the slides to gain more detail about your work life. Figure 2-8 provides an example of a presentation career transition coach and organizational developer Terrence Seamon included on his profile to spotlight some of his accomplishments.

You also will find LinkedIn's Creative Portfolio Display application useful if your work falls within the realm of visual creations. Once you install this application, you can upload your portfolio in the free Behance Network, an online network for creative professionals. Now you can offer viewers of your profile an unlimited number of examples of the work you've created for clients, employers, or as a student.

Among the other applications currently offered on LinkedIn are document-sharing functions, a poll-creation feature, and an application that enables you to see legal updates relevant to your business. You'll also find a real estate application for tracking listings and completed deals and even a travel application. Use this last one the next time you're planning a business trip to see if you'll be able to meet some of the members of your LinkedIn network face to face.

▣ ▣ Add Your Tweets to Your Profile

If you're on Twitter (as you should be if you're job hunting), you can join your LinkedIn and Twitter accounts so that you can share status updates and tweets between the two sites. To add your Twitter ID to your LinkedIn profile, switch to "Edit my profile." In the box below your Summary box, scroll down to the "Twitter" field. Then click on the "Add a Twitter account" link. You'll then need to authorize LinkedIn to "use" your Twitter account. (Don't worry, this is just so that you can add your tweets to your profile or tweet your updated LinkedIn status.)

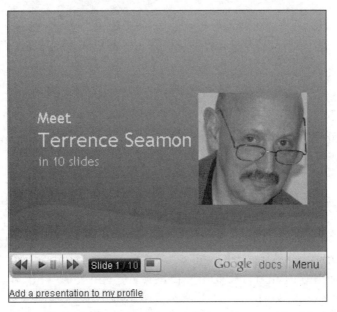

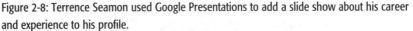

Figure 2-8: Terrence Seamon used Google Presentations to add a slide show about his career and experience to his profile.

Keep in mind that LinkedIn and Twitter each have their own uses and neti-quette, and what you post on one site, you may not want posted on the other. Both LinkedIn and Twitter give you the opportunity to decide in each case whether a given status update or tweet is posted to the other site. On LinkedIn, for example, you'll need to check the little box next to the Twitter symbol and then click "Share" to have that update tweeted. For more information, click the LinkedIn "Help Center" link at the bottom of most pages.

Profile Dos and Don'ts

Elizabeth Garzarelli is a recruiter who spends hours every day on LinkedIn. She was kind enough to share not only her own insights into what grabs her about a profile but also a detailed list of some basic dos and don'ts to consider as you go about building your profile. "I first look at someone's current job title," she said. "Then I read through their past job titles. Next, I look at the responsibilities they had at each job, and in some cases, I look at their education degrees and/or their geographic location, if that's applicable." We grant you that this is just a matter of one person's taste and opinion, but it's an opinion built on having reviewed many thousands of LinkedIn profiles.

- *Do put in as much information as possible.* Be sure to include not just your job titles but also your responsibilities at each job. Put down your educational degrees, and include any foreign languages that you speak.
- *Do state that you are open to "career opportunities" under Contact settings.* If you're concerned that this will signal to your boss that you're looking for a job, at least put that you're open to expertise requests because then I will feel comfortable asking you who you know who might be right for the position I'm trying to fill. (Then you can raise your own hand if you'd like.)
- *Do put in keywords that relate to your areas of expertise under Specialties.* I have a friend who listed her title as "Multimedia Producer" and discussed CDs and DVDs, but by adding the words *audio* and *video* as keywords, she'll likely have more people contact her.
- *Do add your picture.* It makes people feel more connected to you, and people like to do business with people they feel they know.
- *Do join appropriate professional and alumni groups.* It makes you more accessible to recruiters.
- *Don't put in "cutesy" titles such as "Marketing Goddess of the World," "Head Geek," or "Chief Bottle Washer."* This will not attract my attention; it will cause me to skip over you.
- *Don't be vague with your job title.* "Experienced Finance and Marketing Executive" is too generic. Much better is "VP Marketing at XYZ Company," and then put *finance* as a keyword under your Specialties.
- *Don't change your job title to "Consultant" if you're recently unemployed unless you're actively looking for consulting assignments.* Just leave your most recent job title there. The dates of your employment will tell me if you're still there or not.

- *Don't brag about how many connections you have.* If you have more than 20, I'm suitably impressed. Boasting "2,700 + connections!" makes me think that you'll link with just anyone.

I GOT A JOB ON LINKEDIN

 Cher Lon Malik: Office Manager

Not only did Cher Lon Malik find her current job through LinkedIn, but she's also found at least 75 other people senior-level executive jobs. It all began about six years ago when Cher Lon, then in advertising sales for AOL/Time Warner, read articles in both *Forbes* and the *Wall Street Journal* encouraging all professionals of every variety to find a place on LinkedIn. The advice was convincing, stating that even if you weren't job hunting, LinkedIn could help to uncover sales leads and all manner of market research.

So Cher Lon got busy and created a profile, although she was very happy at the time in her position with AOL. She wears many hats, including military wife, philanthropist, and charity board member, and this new form of networking seemed quite promising. "I'm consistently seeking new opportunities to expand my network," she said. Cher Lon is also dedicated to both helping veterans transition to civilian jobs and assisting others who are seeking expanded business opportunities. Soon recruiters were calling her daily. Although she had no plans to leave AOL/Time Warner at the time, a persistent recruiter contacted her three times about the same position. He convinced her

Cher Lon Malik wasn't even looking for a job when her current job found her on LinkedIn.

that with her skill set, based on her LinkedIn profile, she needed to work for Informatica, and Informatica needed her skills. "I finally listened," she said, "and I'm glad I did." The job was for an office manager at Informatica, and it called for her to contact some of the same types of people she was already reaching out to at AOL/Time Warner. She still loves her job five years later. "I have been blessed to be part of this phenomenal company and its leadership," she said.

Cher Lon attributes her good luck to the quality of her profile. "I believe the recruiter found me because of the keywords in my profile," she said. "At Informatica, I have to reach out to CIOs," she said, and "I've found that LinkedIn gives you a reputation. I've been 90 percent effective in contacting senior-level professionals I've located through LinkedIn." Cher Lon feels that this has a lot to do with the quality of the people using the site. "If you're on LinkedIn, you must be a good person," she said. "It gives you an automatic reputation." Cher Lon also noted that the LinkedIn community is very protective, working hard to keep the quality of the site high. "They will correct people who misspell a lot of words," she said.

Cher Lon is very enthusiastic about the changes and improvements she's seen since joining LinkedIn. "LinkedIn has made such great user-friendly touches to its platform. It is simply goof-proof," she noted. "It is a database that is priceless, that remains the most accurate even against those who charge for information. It has been and still remains the best source of networking and discovering data."

Cher Lon belongs to 40 to 45 LinkedIn Groups and has found scores of job postings on the Groups discussion boards. She's a firm believer in LinkedIn's pay-it-forward philosophy and, as an old hand on LinkedIn, has reposted the jobs she's found in other discussion groups. As a result, she's helped many people find new jobs all because of her skill at using the site and her willingness to help others.

Sarah Baldwin: Vice President, Marketing

Sarah Baldwin used her LinkedIn profile to prove to her prospective employer that she was who she claimed to be. "I used it to introduce my professional background after I cold called the owners of a company with which I wanted to partner." She admits this approach is a little backwards, using her profile to prove her gravitas rather than working her network to help others find her.

Sarah came across a compelling product that she was eager to help market, Goodnighties Recovery Sleepwear. After she called the owners of the company, she invited them to view her full LinkedIn profile. "I have been fortunate to work with some high-level people, such as the former CEO of Monsanto," she explained.

Sarah Baldwin used her LinkedIn profile to validate her professional credentials.

"I felt that that alone legitimized my background." Today, Sarah has the exclusive worldwide marketing and sales rights to the product line, and the sleepwear is sold "everywhere." "I love this site," Sarah exclaimed! "I tell people it's like match.com for businesspeople!"

LOOKING AHEAD

As we began this chapter, we told you that the steps you'll take to complete your profile are carefully detailed and supported on LinkedIn. All the rest is as much an art as it is a science. It would be wonderful to claim that we had all the answers about what you should and shouldn't put into your LinkedIn profile. Honestly, we only had some of those answers. The beauty of LinkedIn is that each profile, created by an individual, is bound to reflect that individual. You most likely know better than most people what puts your work history, philosophies, and expertise in the best light. Keep working on it, and you'll have a profile that will make you proud. With that profile complete, you are ready to begin enjoying everything else on LinkedIn. In the next few chapters you'll learn about many of the amazing features the site offers and the wonderful things you can learn and accomplish there. Your next step is to take that 100 percent, ever-changing, ever-vibrant profile and start building your network. Chapter 3 will help you with all the necessary details and strategies you'll need to create your own corner of LinkedIn populated with some very interesting people.

CHAPTER 3

Build and Work Your LinkedIn Network

othing much can happen on LinkedIn until you've created your profile. But your profile won't take you very far without a robust network to draw on. So now that you've created your own profile on LinkedIn and it's 100 percent complete or nearly so, let's turn to building the network that's going to make everything else take off. Your network on LinkedIn is at once very much like the network you've been working to build ever since you asked your high school teacher for that first recommendation and unlike anything else you've ever experienced.

There are two schools of thought about what makes a great and effective network on LinkedIn:

1. Link with as many people as possible, without regard for whether or not you actually know the person. The larger the network, the better.

2. Link only with people you actually know; be selective when building your network.

We'll look at the differences between these philosophies but let you decide which approach is right for you.

In many ways, your network is the hub of everything else that happens on LinkedIn, and it can even serve as the hub of your professional life. You know that networking is important to your professional success. But what happens when you have the power potentially to network with more than 135 million people? The possibilities before you expand quickly and in sometimes unexpected ways.

In the classic 1991 Albert Brooks movie *Defending Your Life*, yuppie Daniel Miller, played by none other than Brooks, dies and finds himself in Judgment City, where he is asked to defend his actions during his brief lifetime. Now, Miller never quite conquered his insecurities to become the assertive, self-confident type of person who gets to move beyond life on earth. But we can forgive him once his defense attorney reveals that Miller uses only about 3 percent of his brain! Please, don't feel too superior yet, because according to Rip Torn, who plays the attorney, no one on earth uses more than 5 percent of their brains. There are simply better parts of the universe for better-wired individuals, such as Torn himself, who happens to use 48 percent of his brain.

Now, there are no data to suggest whether we use 3 or 48 percent of our networks, but we *do* know that when it comes to networking, most people are a lot more like Albert Brooks than Rip Torn. Most of us reach only a tiny percentage of the people who potentially could help us find a new job or solve a pressing business problem when we're stumped. It works the other way, too. We're just as likely to be overlooked by the people we know who could truly benefit from our knowledge and experience. We're limited by our Rolodexes, our disorganization, our past, our personalities, the stack of business cards we all seem to keep, and even time. Computers have helped us to organize some, but the Internet actually can make things even more of a mess. Searching for key business contacts on the web is hit or miss. Besides, how are you going to go about finding experts when you're not even sure who they may be or where to start looking? Then there's the challenge of vetting them.

LinkedIn improves our networking IQ immeasurably and has the potential to make us all networking geniuses if we use it to its full potential. In fact, this is what LinkedIn is all about—connecting with other people who can help you to accomplish more as a professional. The ability to network is what compelled many of LinkedIn's 135 million members to be a part of the site in the first place. It's why everyone on the site has created profiles and searched for connections and why many have gone on to join groups, answer questions from strangers, and much more.

YOUR VERY OWN LINKEDIN NETWORK

LinkedIn will become whatever it is that you work toward making it. Seeing LinkedIn as a tool, you'd be hard pressed to find a more effective way of tracking down colleagues, mentors, apprentices, and friends. "At first I thought, 'Oh no, another site like MySpace or Facebook,'" admitted LION Steven Burda. "But on LinkedIn, I met my professors, businesspeople, those who I have heard at speaking events! I went home and created my own profile." Of course, Steven has pinpointed the essence of LinkedIn. Build a network, and a world of professional experience opens before you. Everyone knows that when you're looking for a new job, it's especially important to network: Speak to colleagues who may know of appropriate openings, neighbors, family, anyone who can help you to land that new job. Yet many of us have looked at the prospect of this task and thought, even among all the people I know, I still don't know anyone in a position to help me land this or that particular job.

Dig Your Well Before You're Thirsty

Your LinkedIn network can be a valuable asset to your business life whether you're currently working or not. But both Seven Burda and Chuck Hester told us about the importance of having an active and vibrant network in place *before* you need to look for a job. Once you've found yourself in need of a new job, however, you can really crank your LinkedIn networking into overdrive. So don't despair if you happen to be reading this after your thirst has set in. You'll use many of the same techniques to build your job-hunting network as you'd use to cement a network while already employed.

Determine Your Goals Before You Dig

It's difficult to create something without an understanding of what it is you wish to have once you're finished. This is not to say that you should be so rigid as to eliminate the delightful serendipity that can come from being on LinkedIn. But just as you thought carefully about what you wanted your profile to say about you before you put the finishing touches on it, you'll need to decide what role your LinkedIn network will play in your life before you actually can create the most effective network for you. Building a solid, well-rounded network not only will help you to find and land that next job, but it also will be there to provide expertise, referrals, and support once you're sitting behind your new desk.

LinkedIn: A Recruiter's New Best Friend

In all her years of matching job candidates with job openings, Virginia Backaitis has seen a little bit of everything. Without question, though, LinkedIn has helped her to do her job even better. Not only does she use the site to find, vet, and connect with potential candidates and employers, but she also uses the Answers section to research questions and issues to support her journalism work. Virginia writes frequently for the *New York Post*. She described to us what makes LinkedIn such a great place for recruiters, hiring managers, and job seekers.

> If I post a job listing on Monster.com, for example, by the time I get to my office, I may have 500 responses. That's too many to be helpful. But if I get a response from my friend, then at least I'll do a phone interview out of loyalty to that friend. Hiring is risky, so I almost always go with someone who has a recommendation. On LinkedIn, I think, "What companies would hire people to do this job?" Then I go look for people who might know someone who would be right. I generally unearth a candidate, maybe someone who isn't even looking for a job.

> If you're looking for advancement but your boss isn't dying, you may need a new place to move up.

> I actually have recruited people to fill jobs through LinkedIn, for example, an equity research person at one of our financial companies. I simply put in the names of those companies to see who I might know working in similar positions. Then I ask some questions. "Who's good at this?" "If you were going to leave your company, who would you want to take with you?" LinkedIn lets me know that these people are already good, because someone I know knows them. My real job is qualifying them through due diligence, but we already know that the person can do the job. We're left with a personality, geography, and compensation fit.

Even with all her experience and expertise, Virginia doesn't support the concept of "open networking," or connecting with everyone who asks you to be a part of their network, whether you know them or not. "Know who you are linked to," she advised. "Some people want to have the biggest network possible. Make sure that you're linking to people who really like and support you."

LINKEDIN OPEN NETWORKERS (LIONS)

A LinkedIn LION (sometimes called *superconnectors* or just *open networkers*) literally will link to just about anyone who requests a connection. Some of the LIONs who were so generous with their time and ideas while we researched this book have tens of thousands of connections. Of course, each of those connections has a network, so the more connections LIONs make, the greater number of people they can gain access to. "I have about 16,500 contacts," said LION Todd Herschberg when we first spoke. "Of the 30 million people on LinkedIn [at that time], I could reach out to any one of about 18 million people to find a job." Now, for some, that is an absolute windfall of humanity, but for others, the question may remain: What exactly am I suppose to do with 18 million people once I've found them?

The official word from LinkedIn goes against the LION philosophy. You'll find advice all over the site to connect only with the people who you know and trust. What's more, LinkedIn has a cap of 30,000 on the number of connections you may have. LinkedIn notifies members who are at or will exceed that cap if they attempt to invite or add additional contacts that will push them over the limit.

For the most part, we found that the LIONs were already super networking connectors in their real lives before they discovered LinkedIn. Some of the LIONs we met actually were building their own networks in hopes of someday becoming recruiters themselves. Others used a combination of LinkedIn and in-person networking to connect with as many people as they possibly could. "You don't know what's lurking around the corner," said Gary Unger, LION and LinkedIn trainer. "The downside is that someone may try to sell you something, but I can always delete that person."

A Den Full of LIONs

Let's take a look at some LIONs so that we can better understand what motivates them and see if those same motivations appeal to you. Then we'll consider why becoming a LION may not be such a great idea. By the time we get to the details of actually building your network, you'll have ample information to decide for yourself which side of this coin looks most appealing.

Chuck Hester: "I use LinkedIn as a database. I contact 1,000 people routinely. The others are occasional when we have some common business. When I travel, I reach out through LinkedIn to network within the city I'm visiting, and I do LinkedIn dinners or breakfasts that meet face to face. At a minimum, 10 show up, but I've had as many as 35. When I first came to LinkedIn, I tried to connect with the connectors. There's a top 100 list. I went to the top 50 and invited them into my network. Mostly all of them accepted. For each one I connect with, I find five connections in their network. Once I reached 500 connections, I stopped inviting. Now people invite me."

Todd Herschberg: "I may be the forty-sixth most linked-in member on LinkedIn. I know I'm in the top 50. I have about 16,500 connections. I've met, in person, about half of those. I'm a very outgoing type of guy. I'm always happy to connect because you never know where the next opportunity or job offer will come from. I've also founded the largest networking group in Orange County, California. There are now more than 3,000 members."

Steven Burda: "Is having so many connections a good thing? There are two sides to every story. Some say it's quantity versus quality. I am from the MySpace generation. I was one of the first to use social networking. It's not what you know, but who you know. I keep track of people in three ways: I have a good memory (I remember names), I put two and two together, and I make a note in my folder. There is no way I know every single person in my network, but I try to add five to ten people each week."

BUILD LIKE YOU BREATHE

Well, maybe not quite that often. But adding to your network in a more organic and simple way is the other alternative. If you've decided that you're no LION, you'll find that your network still can grow to impressive proportions. Since you gain the connections of all your connections, your network expands at a dizzying rate. For example, if you have 274 connections, LinkedIn may report that your total network gives you access to more than 8 million professionals. Although that number sounds a little preposterous, you'll find that depending on your connections' networks, you really do have an enormous pool of potential colleagues and associates.

Building your network by starting with the people who you know and trust and then moving out in a more gradual way is the path many LinkedIn members recommend. It's also the strategy LinkedIn as a company supports. "LinkedIn was founded to work on the relationships you already have," explained Krista Canfield. "If you connect with people who don't really know you, they can't vouch for you. LinkedIn should be like your Rolodex, and you wouldn't just pass that along to strangers. This site isn't meant to just find people." Instead, LinkedIn was meant to be a gathering place for sharing professional goals and career development. "Look at LinkedIn as if it were a business lunch," said Krista. "You wouldn't just blanket the whole network. You wouldn't announce your needs to a room full of people. Don't forget your manners." If you think of LinkedIn this way, it's a little embarrassing to consider that you'd just blast your requests to everyone at once.

Embarrassment aside, another possible disadvantage of becoming a LION is the amount of time and effort it will take to keep track of that enormous network. Think about it: If you have tens of thousands of connections, every time someone in that network changes his or her status (which, as you remember, is important to do frequently), makes a connection, or answers or asks a question, you may get an update. Do you really want to know that much about all these people on a weekly or even daily basis? Maybe so, but it does require a good amount of work to tend this network once you've built it. "As you grow professionally," noted Krista, "you know it isn't necessarily how many people you know but who the people you know are."

These Aren't LIONs, but They're also Not Pussycats

Many people on LinkedIn have large, vibrant, thriving networks without opening them up to anyone and everyone. Through our research, we met people with many dozens of connections, and they call on their networks to support their careers and solve pressing work issues. If by now you've come to think that you're not of the personality or nature to become a LION yourself, don't despair. You actually may be better off.

Bryan Webb: "I came to LinkedIn about three years ago after attending a networking meeting at the University of Waterloo. A facilitator recommended that if you were looking for a way to improve your networking, you should use it. If I am going to connect with someone, I need to have some dialog with them, some e-mail exchanges, for example. Tell me where we met, what common ground we have. It's not just about the numbers; it's the quality. I don't have time to be a LION. I consider myself connected, and I have just shy of 1,300 connections."

Stephen Weinstein: "I have about 400 connections, but I'm not an open networker. I add a connection with a reason in mind. Usually, I've had a real-world connection with them."

Jacqueline Wolven: "You should have as your connections people you really clicked with at places where you worked, but not everyone, says this marketing specialist. I dislike the LION concept. That distorts your connections. They are not true connections. I don't have a relationship with those people. I don't know their connections. They are so busy connecting! I took out anyone who was a LION in my connections."

WILL THE LIONS AND THE NON-LIONS EVER AGREE?

Will the Democrats and Republicans ever end the partisan gridlock in Washington? Will the Hatfields and McCoys make peace? Will the Trix rabbit ever get his breakfast? All these are questions left to posterity. Your challenge is to decide which type of network you personally feel will serve your professional needs best of all. And that decision is not necessarily set in stone. Your LinkedIn network is a living, breathing entity. It's bound to change and grow along with your own professional needs and circumstances. Who's to say that you won't start out dead set against becoming a LION, only to discover that you've come to believe in the doctrine of "the more the merrier"? On the other hand, you may just find that your own little corner of LinkedIn provides you with ample connections and networking opportunities, and then you'll leave well enough alone. Either way, you've got lots of great ways to build out that network and then use it to advance your business and career goals.

BUILDING YOUR LINKEDIN NETWORK

Soon after you began to complete your profile, you were prompted to add connections to LinkedIn by entering your e-mail addresses and passwords. This is absolutely the fastest way to get your network started. Presumably, some of the people you already have in your address book are people you'd like to include in your network. Figure 3-1 shows you just how simple it is to upload your e-mail address books to LinkedIn to build out your network.

If you're brand new to LinkedIn, you may be intimidated about giving out your e-mail address *and* password, but there's no need to be concerned. This is a secure network, and LinkedIn doesn't store the information you provide. Once you supply that information, you'll be able to pick and choose among the people in your address books to invite into your network. For one thing, as you're browsing through your address book, you'll be able to see who among your contacts is already on LinkedIn. Those will be the people who LinkedIn presents to you first. LinkedIn recommends that you start with those people. Since they're both on the site and on your radar screen, they're good candidates. Once you've gotten those already familiar with LinkedIn to join you, LinkedIn will show you another list culled from your e-mail contacts—those who are not yet on LinkedIn. But whether you decide to invite everyone, as the LIONs advocate, or be more discriminating and invite only those contacts who really know you is your choice. Note that if you use this method to add connections, you will not be given the option of customizing your invitations, something we definitely recommend. So you pay something for the convenience and ease of adding connections simply by importing your e-mail address books.

Using LinkedIn's Outlook Connector

If you use Microsoft Outlook, you may want to download the LinkedIn Outlook Connector. Through this tool, you can access your LinkedIn network from within Outlook, check out the people your connections are connecting

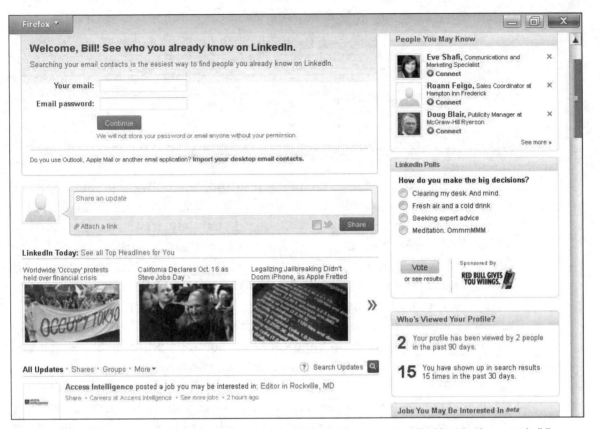

Figure 3-1: LinkedIn provides a simple, secure, and reliable way to use your e-mail address books to start building your network.

to, find out when your connections have updated their profiles, send invitations to connect from within Outlook, and retrieve e-mail addresses, photos, and other profile information from a folder marked "LinkedIn." Click "Tools" at the bottom of your homepage to learn more about Outlook Connector. We discussed managing your account through the Settings area in Chapter 1, but it's important to discuss settings here in the context of building a network. To reach that area, click the "Settings" link on the top right of your homepage (it appears when you roll over your name). Check out the items under the heading "Email Preferences." Click on "Select the types of messages you're willing to receive." From the page that appears next, you can control the manner in which LinkedIn members can contact you, let other members know the kinds of opportunities you are open to, and provide advice to others interested in contacting you. This is important information because it lets others know how open you are to forming new connections and the kinds of things you would like to be contacted about, such as consulting offers and job opportunities. You may want to update this information as your circumstances change.

Adding Connections

Once you have your network underway by uploading your e-mail address books, LinkedIn will help you to add connections that you may not have already considered. Click on the "Add Connections" link that appears under the "Contacts" hyperlink on your homepage. You'll then see four tabs presenting new possibilities for connections on the site. You can import your e-mail contacts, which you've already done. Or, if you use Outlook, Apple Mail, or another similar e-mail application, LinkedIn gives you the option of importing your desktop e-mail contacts file from that application. The file you upload must be in .csv, .txt, or .vcf format.

Click on the "Colleagues" tab, and LinkedIn will show you a listing of all the companies you entered when you created your profile. Now you can browse the LinkedIn database to see who else from those companies is already on the site, making it very easy for you to find former coworkers to connect with. The next step would be to consider sending direct invitations to those people.

Fabrice Calando: Digital Strategist

"Even if I'm not actively looking for anything, I get job leads once a month on average through LinkedIn," Fabrice told us. Of course, that's not how his LinkedIn story began. Although Fabrice has been on the site for years, he activated his network only fairly recently. He saw that Facebook had some promising opportunities for job hunting and resource sharing, and he came to recognize that LinkedIn would be even more robust an online destination for his objectives. "My main objective has always been to be exposed to interesting job opportunities; my secondary objective is to find interesting prospects for the companies I work at," he said. Here, in his own words, are the steps Fabrice took to ramp up his LinkedIn presence. These are easily transferable to anyone on the site, no matter what your industry may be.

Fabrice Calando Digital Strategist TMP Worldwide

The first thing I did was rework my profile a little. I wanted to get it 100 percent complete, and I wanted to make sure every position had a strong description of what I had accomplished. I also beefed up the Summary section to include industry keywords and added a few applications such as Tweets, Amazon, and WordPress. After a few months of increased activity on LinkedIn, I still wasn't satisfied with my profile—I felt it was not doing a good enough job "selling" me. I've actually always had a hard time selling myself; updating my CVs was always a struggle, and my LinkedIn profile was suffering the same fate. To remedy this, I actually worked with a professional copywriter. He helped me structure what I wanted to say. The main lesson was "answer the question: What can I do for you?" so when someone finds my profile, they immediately know if I'm the person they need.

The second thing I did was find relevant Groups to participate in—industry groups first and groups in my area second. The most interesting group turned out to be a regional one—Linked Québec. The group had for its mission to regroup professionals in the Province of Quebec and was by far the most active and professional (i.e., no spam comments). I later found out the founder of the group was dedicated to making this the largest group of the type and spent a large amount of his time promoting the Group within LinkedIn and moderating discussions. I was actively participating in the Group by starting discussions and participating in others. When the Group got large enough, there was a call for moderators to help keep the group clean. I jumped on the opportunity—not only would it get my name more out there, but I would really get a chance to learn what works and what does not on LinkedIn.

Fabrice's third step was to focus on his network:

Connections on LinkedIn are important—both the quality and the quantity. I started actively inviting people to join my network. I only invited people that I personally knew or had worked with, were in my industry and potential employers, but I accepted most invitations. Quality of contacts makes sense, but so does quantity. I find that as people search for people on LinkedIn, the site tends to rank people in order of relevance and degrees of separation, so the more connections you have, the more you increase the chance that you'll be connected to the searcher on a 1st, 2nd, or 3rd degree.

I'm currently a Digital Strategist at TMP Worldwide, a recruitment advertising agency. They're the ones that reached out to me for this opportunity, and one of the first comments I received from them was "you really have a great LinkedIn profile. We could immediately tell you were the person for us." No joke.

All in all, I find a strong profile is the most important. You want people who find your profile to know exactly what you are, what you can do, and if you're the right fit for them. Participation in Groups and adding contacts helps to bring people to your profile."

So just in case you thought we were overemphasizing your need to polish your profile and consider it a living entity that you cultivate like a carefully tended garden, now you know that's not just our opinion! What an enviable position to occupy. Fabrice is happily employed and still fielding job opportunities on a monthly basis. If he can do it, so can you.

Ten Ways to Bother and Annoy the LinkedIn Community

1. Use form e-mails without personalizing them.

2. Post blatant sales pitches disguised as Answers or within e-mails you send to other LinkedIn users.

3. Post nonanswers in the Answers area just to get your name and a hyperlink to your profile posted.

4. Ask questions that have been asked many times before.

5. Invite people to join your network without explaining how you know them.

6. Ask for help repeatedly without providing help yourself.

7. Don't proofread your profile and other public comments.

8. Disregard legitimate requests for introductions or connection requests.

9. Treat LinkedIn as though it were Facebook or Twitter by posting trivial status updates, etc.

10. Shortchange the site by posting a bare-bones profile, not using the Company and Answers sections, or not building your network.

Colleagues

Once you've browsed your lists of Colleagues on LinkedIn, you can easily keep up to date with new arrivals to the site. LinkedIn tracks how recently you've checked for new Colleagues and offers you the option of viewing all Colleagues or only the new contacts who have joined LinkedIn since you last searched.

Classmates

If you were to click this tab, you'd see the schools you've included in your profile. Click on a particular school to view profiles for classmates whose attendance overlapped your own. You can also select the option to view only the people who graduated either while you actually were at the school or from up to four years out from your attendance dates.

People You May Know

When you click on "People You May Know," LinkedIn will use information from your profile, such as the schools you attended and the companies for which you worked, to show you some additional people with whom you may want to connect. The screen you see next will show you not only the individual's name and title but also the number of connections you have in common. Clearly, those with whom you have more than a few connections in common should prove a good starting point for expanding your network.

Tag Your Connections

As you start to gather your connections, you likely will be looking for ways to manage the list, making it easier to turn to specific parts of your network for specific reasons. LinkedIn allows you to create tags by which you can group your connections together based on commonalities they share. LinkedIn begins this process for you by grouping your connections based on the information you've provided. For example, your officemate already will be a Colleague connection. But, by clicking on the "Contact" tab and bringing up your whole list of connections, you can customize your tags, adding, deleting, or changing them as you see fit. Now you can group your connections based on commonalities you determine to be relevant. You can have as many as 200 unique tags at one time.

Creating Great Invitations

In your eagerness to expand your network, you may be tempted to send off dozens of generic LinkedIn invitations to the people in your address book. This is considered to be universally bad form. Think about it. Do you respond better to junk mail, even well-targeted junk mail, or to personalized letters? When we asked LinkedIn's Krista Canfield how receptive people are to invitations to connect, she said, "Very receptive, if you've done your homework. The more tailored and specific you can make your request, the better. Ask yourself, 'If this showed up in my e-mail, would I respond?'"

"I reject the boilerplate invitations that LinkedIn provides," said Bryan Webb. "When I send out an invitation, I personalize it." At the very least, never approach someone on LinkedIn until you've read her profile. You may find that she is currently not open to more invitations, and knowing that before you approach her can prevent you from accidentally alienating someone who could be a very good contact at some point in the future.

Profile Stats

The "Who's viewed your profile" box on the right side of your homepage provides an abbreviated list of LinkedIn members who have looked at your profile recently. Looking at this information is one way to assess how effectively your profile is attracting the types of members you are striving to attract. This information is scant, however, and the only way to see a more complete accounting is to sign up for one of LinkedIn's premium accounts (these are described in some detail in Chapters 4 and 7).

But we wanted to briefly mention the new Jobseeker Premium account here to give you an idea of the sort of additional information it provides. One of the advantages of the Jobseeker account is that you are given access to more detailed Profile Stats. You can see all the people who have viewed your profile recently, including their names, companies, geographic locations, and industries. (This detailed information is only available if the member has not changed his or her Privacy Controls. Otherwise, you may get the dreaded "Anonymous LinkedIn user" or simply a job title at a specific company such as "Director at Time Warner." Even so, you can learn more about those people by clicking on their hyperlink, which will show you profiles of LinkedIn members who match that description. You just may be able to figure out who actually viewed your profile from that information.)

We find that we look at those statistics pretty often. Aside from details on who has viewed their profiles, Jobseeker account holders also can see such statistics as the top search keywords people used to pull up their profile. In addition, they can view a chart showing views by industry. For example, most of the people who check our profiles tend to be from the publishing, writing and editing, or marketing and advertising industries. Finally, they can view a world map that shows where their views are coming from. So, if you're looking to reach people internationally, and 90 percent of your views are from the United States, you may want to take a close look at your profile to see how you can address that issue.

Using Advanced Search

Before you know it, you'll be ready to search around for new people to include in your network using LinkedIn's Advanced Search feature. Use this feature to narrow your search for people you share commonalities with.

From the box right under your name on your homepage you can do an "Advanced Search" of LinkedIn's mammoth database to research people, jobs, companies, and more. When you click on the "Advanced" hyperlink, you'll see the form shown in Figure 3-2. Using this form, (with People left as the default search on your homepage), you can select search parameters to include specific industries, groups, languages, companies, and titles, to name just a few. You also can sort your search results by relevance, relationship, or keyword. You'll want to experiment with this search feature to find the best way to locate your own good contacts, but we'll step you through an example to help you get started.

Let's say that we're looking for new connections among acquisition editors at book publishers. We'll plug in "acquisitions editor" in the "Title" box and select "Current" from the drop-down menu below it. We'll also select Publishing as the industry and, lacking foreign-language skills, limit our results to profiles in English. In addition, we'll select Senior as the seniority level. Finally, we'll select the basic view for our results and sort by relevance. After we click on the "Search" box, we're shown 32 different contacts that meet our search criteria (Figure 3-3). This is a perfectly manageable number, sorted by how they are currently connected to us. We also see generic listings for people who match our search requests but are

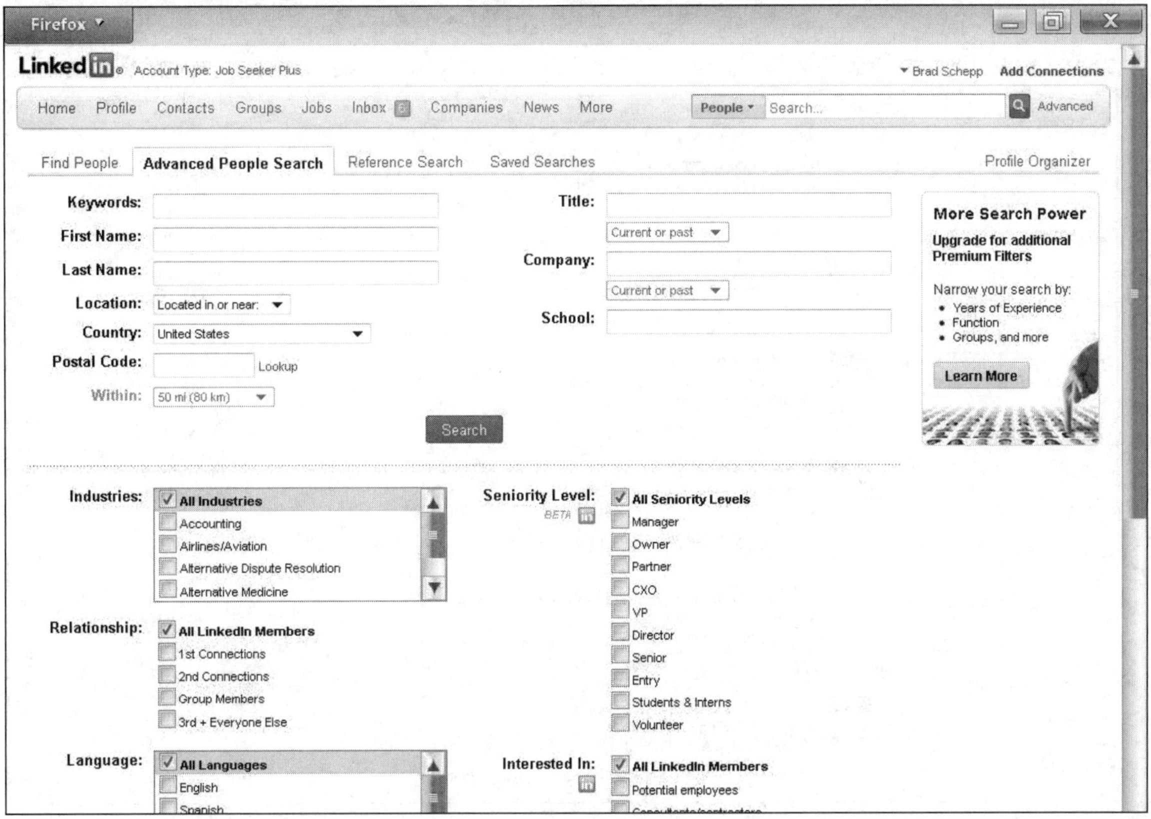

Figure 3-2: An Advanced People Search helps you to locate people relevant to the search parameters you set yourself.

outside our network. We then can read through our results to see with whom we may want to connect.

TIP

Use the Advanced Search feature to search for the job title right above yours in your company hierarchy. Then you can to see how others climbed that next rung.

Faceted Search

LinkedIn offers you the opportunity to refine your search for former colleagues, classmates, and associates through faceted searching. Every time

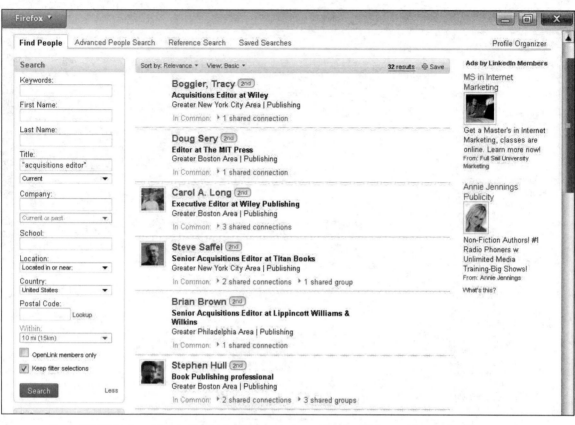

Figure 3-3: We've found hundreds of potential new contacts through an Advanced People Search.

you search for a person by name, you'll see a series of clickable boxes on the left of your search results page. These boxes allow you to hone in on the actual person you are searching for.

Suppose you'd like to reconnect with a college classmate who has a fairly common name. When you search by name alone, you may get too many results to work with effectively. As you scroll down the left fields of search-refining options, simply click open the "School" box, and check the box for the name of your college. Now your search results are automatically refined to include only those LinkedIn members with that name who attended your school.

With the standard LinkedIn membership, you can refine your searches based on Current Company, Relationship, Location, Industry, Past Company, School, and Profile Language. A premium membership will allow you to search by the additional terms Groups, Years of Experience, Function, Seniority Level, Interested In, Company Size, Fortune 1000, and Recently Joined.

Join LinkedIn Groups

One of LinkedIn's most powerful tools is its Groups feature, and with more than 1 million groups on the site, you're sure to find a few that will interest you. Once you join a few groups, you'll likely find many potential new connections among their members.

From the top of your LinkedIn homepage, you can access the Groups Directory by rolling over the "Groups" hyperlink. Click on the "Groups Directory" link, and you'll see the screen shown in Figure 3-4. Once you're there, you're ready to start searching for relevant groups. Of course, one of the easiest to find is your college or graduate school alumni group. Also consider joining alumni groups for companies where you've worked, as well as trade groups. If you happen not to find a group that seems right for you, you always can start your own group. "You can create your own group," said Krista Canfield, "as long as it's business-oriented. It has to be business-based. We want to be a site that your boss will want you to be spending time on."

Many groups require that you ask to join, but that shouldn't intimidate you. LinkedIn groups are quite well known for being friendly and informative places, so there's no need to hesitate to ask to join. Many other groups allow you to join just by clicking the "Join Group" button. "Joining a group allows you to connect with people without actually connecting directly to them," explained Krista. "You can reach out to anyone in a group, whether you know them directly or not." Once you've joined a group, that group's icon appears on your profile page. Having these icons makes your commitment to your LinkedIn network clear and speaks well of you as an active and engaged member of the LinkedIn community.

TIP

Be sure to follow the 80/20 rule after you've joined a group. In other words, contribute four times as much information as you ask for. This is part of being a good LinkedIn citizen. Examples of giving to your group would be posting relevant articles, answering questions on the discussion boards, and generally sharing your knowledge base with others.

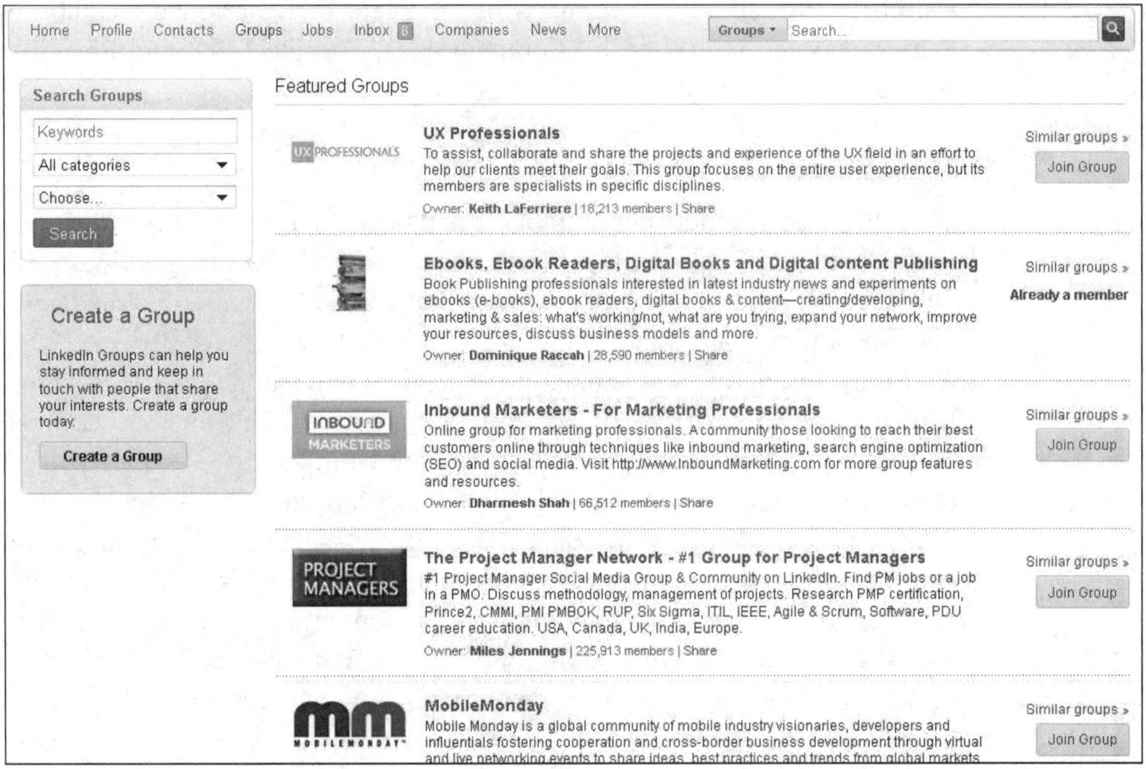

Figure 3-4: The Groups Directory makes it simple to find interesting groups to join on LinkedIn.

Click on a group name, and you'll immediately learn which group members are already in your network. It's a clear sign that you've found a good group for yourself if more than a few members are already in your network, especially if they are first-degree connections. You also will see a brief description of the group and an "About This Group" box showing when it was created and who owns it (the creator), as well as who manages it, if applicable. You also will see information about similar groups.

Once you've become a member of a group, you'll have access to everything that group has to offer, and we're not just talking about the other members. Most groups include a discussion board, news article archives, and membership lists. Some also feature a jobs section. Finally, you even can "follow" group members who you feel post especially interesting content. If you choose your groups wisely, you'll log on each week to find a wealth of information provided to you by others within your profession. Of course, you'll also be busy providing your own insights and knowledge to help the other group members. "I put my modified résumé up on my groups now that I'm job hunting," said Terrence Seamon, corporate trainer and organizational developer. That's a bonus to other members of Terry's group because they may just be looking for someone with his particular background, making their candidate search just a little bit easier.

 Mike O'Neil: LION, LinkedIn Trainer, and Group Advocate

"This is one of LinkedIn's best tricks," Mike told us enthusiastically. "When you join a LinkedIn group, and you can join up to 50 of them—it's like a club." Mike went on to explain how you go about finding a group that's right for you. First, he recommends that you search by a keyword relevant to your own background. The groups in the results page are sorted by how large a membership they have.

Then you can approach the leaders of the groups. "The leaders can always be approached," advised Mike. "You're doing exactly what the group founder wants you to do." Ask that leader to please consider you for inclusion in the group. "You don't solicit help," noted Mike. "You get the connection first; then you go back to thank them and offer your whole network as a resource to the group." The key to the groups is that once you are a member, you are free to search out and approach any other member of the group. You no longer have to work your way through your network connections to find someone willing to make an introduction for you. It completely eliminates the issue of whether you are one degree, two degrees, or three degrees removed from anyone else in the group. You all belong on equal footing.

LION Mike O'Neil is a big proponent of joining LinkedIn groups.

Posting Information Effectively

Asia Bird offers great advice for effectively posting information to LinkedIn groups.

Asia Bird is Social Sales Manager at Sociable Sales and a sales operations team leader at Rising International. She is very active on LinkedIn and writes frequently about using the site effectively for Sociablesales.com. She is a great supporter of LinkedIn groups, participating in many each week. She graciously offered to share her advice about posting to groups with us. You can find more insights from this LinkedIn success story at sociablesales.com.

Five Questions to Ask Before Posting Content in LinkedIn Groups

Now that you have joined a bunch of groups, you can start actively engaging the group community and providing value by posting new content and commenting on other people's content. Before you set up your first entry to post new content, take a moment and ask yourself the following questions:

Will the members of this group find my content valuable? Value always should be first on your mind when leveraging LinkedIn. What are you contributing, and how does it add value? Is it relevant, interesting, and/or new?

Is this post self-serving or group-serving? Generally, if you find yourself promoting your own content on LinkedIn, it's viewed as pushing information rather than providing value. There's a big difference. I rant about why you shouldn't promote your own content on LinkedIn all the time. If you're promoting your own stuff, you may want to find something else.

Discussion, Promotion, or Job?

It matters where you post stuff. You don't want to be labeled a spammer or have your content deleted. Make sure that you are posting properly: Links to articles, blog posts, events, news, and so on belong on the Promotion Board. Questions and conversations posed to the group community belong on the Discussion Board. Job posts . . . you guessed it! Job posts and announcements go on the Jobs Board.

When Did I Last Post to This Group?

How often should you post new stuff? If you are posting new content to the group more than once a day, you might be overdoing it. People can only handle so much information at one time, and you're not the only one posting content! If you are trying to stand out in the group and really get noticed, I'd recommend posting new content two to three times a week per group.

Did I Format My Entry Correctly?

Who likes broken links, cutoff sentences, and random bits of code in their information? Nobody. Once you hit the "Share" button, you can't go back and edit, so make sure to set it up correctly right from the start!

Asking yourself these questions before sharing content with your group community will improve your ability to provide quality content that group members can find, use, and appreciate.

WORKING YOUR NETWORK

It won't be too long before you'll find your network robust enough to begin making it work for you. There are as many different ways to work a LinkedIn network as there are individuals to make these networks work. No matter what you hope to accomplish on the site, you'll find great ways to bring your network to life and make it a vital part of your professional toolbox. Throughout this book, you'll find chapters devoted to some of the most dynamic areas of LinkedIn with plenty of good advice about how to best use those areas. Here, we'll give you a brief but satisfying taste of just a few.

"First, update your status on your profile," said Krista Canfield, when we asked what a job hunter can do to accelerate the job-hunting process. "Answer the question, 'What are you working on?' That lets your network know that you need help."

TIP

If you're in the midst of a job search and you have a lot of connections, it helps to be able to sort them by industry. Click on the "Connections" link on your profile page and then "Advanced Options." From there, you can filter your connections by location or industry.

"I can use LinkedIn for educational purposes," says David Becker of PhillipeBecker. "Let's say one of our clients is a wine company, and they're thinking of doing away with corks because it's better environmentally to use screw tops. I can go to the group and ask, 'What do you think about this?' I'll get responses that I would have had to pay for before LinkedIn."

LinkedIn InMaps

Now what good is it to amass a large network on LinkedIn if using it is too unwieldy? Frankly, we find it amazing that LIONs, with connections possibly numbering in the thousands, actually are able to use their networks efficiently. Even those with connections "only" in the hundreds may not have a clear enough grasp of who comprises their network. Fortunately, since we wrote the last edition of this book, LinkedIn has introduced one tool in particular that gives you a new way to look at your network: InMaps.

Through InMaps, you can get a visual fix on the makeup of your network. You can see how your connections are related to one another and how those connections group together into clusters.

Figure 3-5 illustrates what one InMap looks like. One thing you can't see is that the different groups are color coded. As LinkedIn explained on its blog, the colors can be used to represent different affiliations or groups, such as previous employers, people you went to college with, or industries you may work in.

People who are especially well connected in their fields will stand out—their names appear proportionately larger. Those people are especially influential and may be people you will want to stay in touch with. You also can share your InMaps with other people through LinkedIn, Twitter, or Facebook. When you share your InMap, your contact names will not be shown. We're not sure why you would want to share such a network, but we did want to mention that the capability is available. To access your InMap, go to www.linkedinlabs.com. Click the "InMaps" icon, and then log in with LinkedIn.

Finally, we also should mention that you can only use the InMap feature if you have at least 50 connections and your profile is at least 75 percent complete.

Jim Chadman: Materials Management Supervisor

Jim Chadman started a LinkedIn group called *Professionals Desiring Relocation to Pittsburgh.* He's the group's first success story:

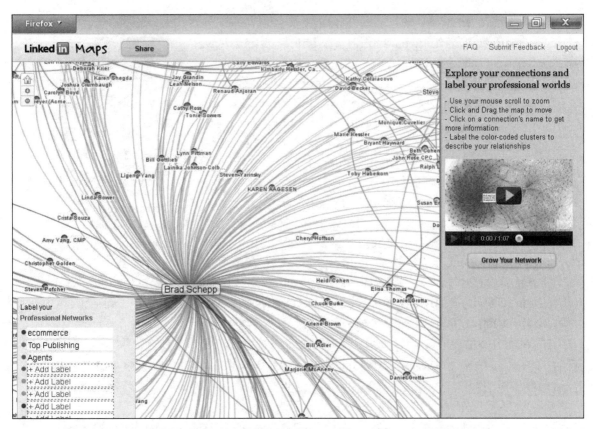

Figure 3-5: Here's one example of a LinkedIn InMap. Of course, it's much more useful if you can see the entire screen, in color.

Jim was living in Maryland and working in his field (warehousing and distribution), but he wanted to move back to the area he considered home. "I wanted to start a family and have my kids raised the way I was, with family close by," he told us.

Jim looked for a job in his field for eight months. He did everything he figured you're supposed to do these days, responding to ads on national job boards such as Monster and Hot Jobs as well as boards specific to his industry. After sending out 100 or more résumés and queries, he hadn't landed one interview (unfortunately, an all-too-familiar story these days). "I was going to give up," he said, although he still believed in himself. "I'm a professional," he told us.

Then, while he was on vacation, he received an e-mail inviting him to attend a webinar about how to use LinkedIn. It turns out the webinar was more or less a pitch for the webinar leader's $400 package of services—offering tailored advice on creating the perfect profile, connecting with others in his field, and so on. But Jim did learn some strategies that he found useful. He learned that companies don't want to hire people who respond to ads on job boards and the like; they still want that personal connection. They prefer to hire people they "know." The webinar leader advised people to build their networks by connecting with "superconnectors" in their fields. (*Superconnectors* he

Jim Chadman created a LinkedIn group to find the job he wanted.

defined as those with 500 or more connections.) Of course, on LinkedIn, you can't approach just anyone unless you already have some sort of connection with them. But, as you now know, once you join a group, you can approach any other member of that group.

So Jim started joining groups that were relevant to his industry or had some sort of tie to Pittsburgh. Jim used the following e-mail to gain the attention of LinkedIn members in Pittsburgh:

> I'm looking to expand my network in the greater Pittsburgh area as my wife and I are looking to relocate back home. Adding your network would greatly bolster that attempt, any help would be greatly appreciated.

> Thank you kindly,

> James Chadman

After four or five weeks of networking in this way, sending his message to superconnectors belonging to the groups he'd joined, including Connecting Pittsburgh Job Seekers with Employers and Recruiters, another LinkedIn member contacted him. This person worked for Pittsburgh's largest employer, UMPC, a multi-billion-dollar health enterprise. He asked Jim to come in for an interview, and when they met, Jim said that they found "commonalities." It was one of the best interviews he had ever had. It turned out that like Jim; the interviewer had moved out of the Pittsburgh area for a time and also really wanted to move back. Evidently, this is fairly common among people growing up in Pittsburgh—so common there's even a name for it: the *rubber-band effect*. People get experience elsewhere and then move back to Pittsburgh.

The interviewer also was familiar with the group Jim belonged to on LinkedIn and said that "he liked the group and its purpose." He didn't have a specific position at the time, but soon he brought Jim in for a second interview, and Jim got the job—supervisor of materials management at UPMC Mercy Hospital.

When we spoke, Jim said that his new employer is now interested in another member of his group, so there may be another success story to report on for the next edition of this book.

Using RSS Feeds on LinkedIn

One of the long-heralded pluses of the Internet is that once you identify information you want to receive regularly, you can set up a *feed* so that updates are delivered to you; you don't have go to the web to retrieve them. This type of technology has had many iterations over the years, from *push* technology to customized daily newspapers that, once set up, are delivered to your computer rather than to your doorstep. The latest version of the technology that delivers regularly updated information to you is called *Really Simple Syndication* (RSS).

There are many different RSS readers (called *aggregators*) that do the behind-the-scenes work for you. If you're unfamiliar with the technology, you should check out an overview such as Wikipedia's (http://en.wikipedia .org/wiki/Rss). We suggest choosing a simple web-based aggregator such as Google Reader if you're not an old hand at using RSS. Most web browsers, such as Mozilla Firefox, also incorporate readers.

On LinkedIn, you create two types of RSS feeds: public and personal. A public feed brings you information that's available to all LinkedIn members, such as updates on the latest LinkedIn features. An example of a personal feed is one that brings you the latest news from your LinkedIn network. Here's how to create an RSS feed for your Network Updates:

1. From your LinkedIn homepage, roll over to the "More" hyperlink right below "LinkedIn Today," and bring down the drop-down menu.

2. Click on "RSS."

3. Click on "Enable," which appears on the next page.

4. Click on the RSS reader of your choice, or click on the "RSS" icon.

5. Follow any further directions given for your particular reader.

You also can set up an RSS feed to receive new Answers to question categories you follow. You'll find a complete discussion of Answers in Chapter 5.

LinkedIn suggests that you check to see how your particular reader displays information because some actually will push your feed URLs to the web. From there, the information can be picked up by search engines. The company advises you not to use an RSS feeder to subscribe to personal information (such as your Network Updates) until you determine that your reader keeps such information private.

Reviewing Your Network Statistics

To see who is in your network, as well as the number of people you can contact through your network, go to the navigation bar at the top of your LinkedIn homepage. Under the "Contacts" hyperlink, you'll see a "Network Statistics" link. By clicking that, you'll get the screen shown in Figure 3-6, which will show you how many people are in your direct network, then those who are two degrees from you (friends of friends), and finally, those who are three degrees from you (people you have to reach through a friend and then a friend of theirs).

Removing Connections

After you have spent all that time and effort cultivating a connection, it seems counterintuitive that you'd want to remove a connection at some point. But it will happen. Relationships sour, a colleague becomes a competitor, and partners decide to go their separate ways. In such cases, you may no longer want that person to have access to your contacts, and under the circumstances, you may decide that the best thing to do is remove that person as a connection.

Since LinkedIn is all about adding connections and not removing them, it's not surprising that how you go about removing someone from your contact list isn't readily apparent. Here's how you do it:

• Click the "Contacts" hyperlink at the top of your homepage.

• Click the "Remove Connections" hyperlink in the right corner of the screen.

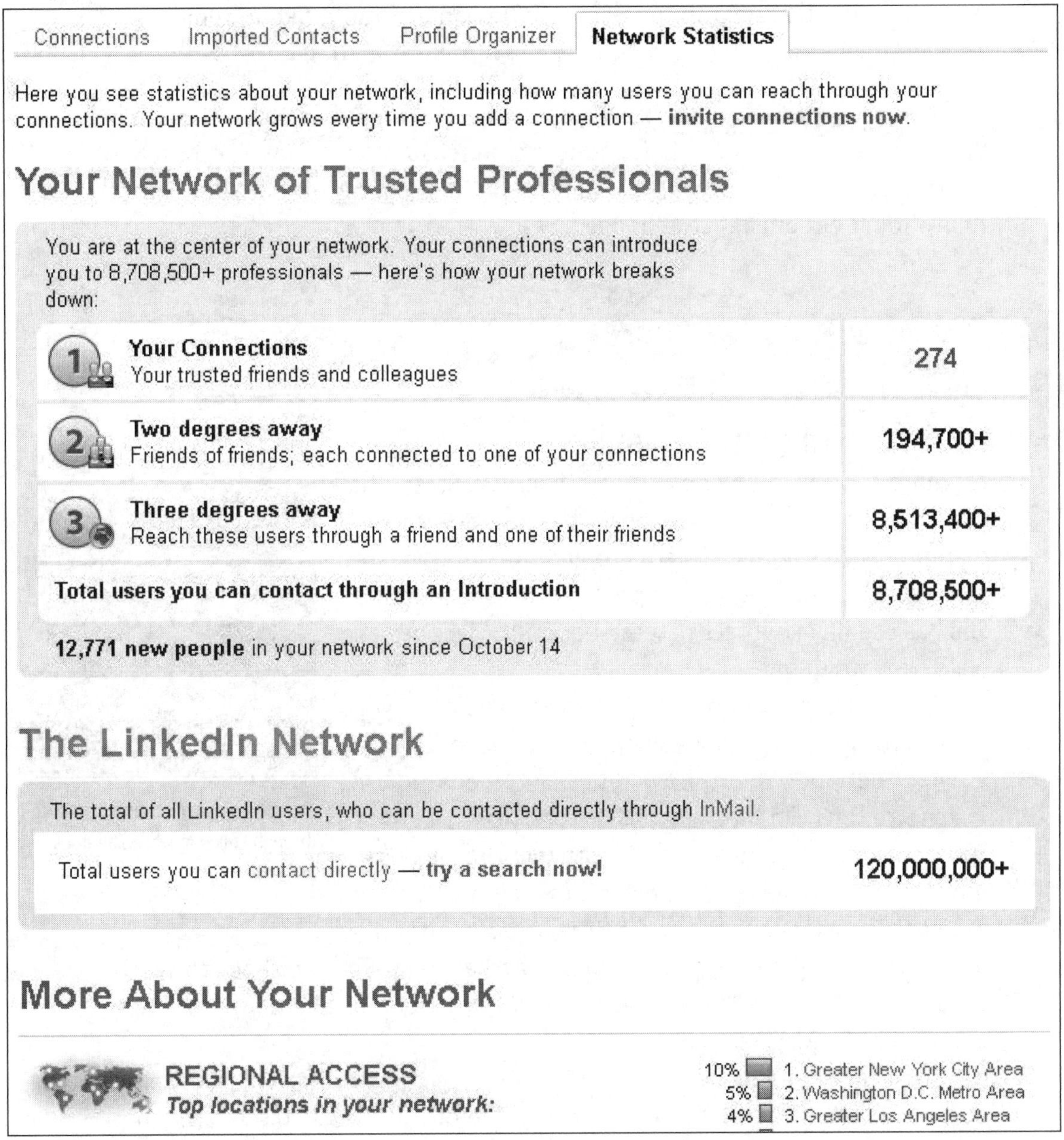

Connections	Imported Contacts	Profile Organizer	**Network Statistics**

Here you see statistics about your network, including how many users you can reach through your connections. Your network grows every time you add a connection — **invite connections now**.

Your Network of Trusted Professionals

You are at the center of your network. Your connections can introduce you to 8,708,500+ professionals — here's how your network breaks down:

1	**Your Connections** Your trusted friends and colleagues	274
2	**Two degrees away** Friends of friends; each connected to one of your connections	194,700+
3	**Three degrees away** Reach these users through a friend and one of their friends	8,513,400+
	Total users you can contact through an Introduction	8,708,500+

12,771 new people in your network since October 14

The LinkedIn Network

The total of all LinkedIn users, who can be contacted directly through InMail.

Total users you can contact directly — **try a search now!**	120,000,000+

More About Your Network

REGIONAL ACCESS
Top locations in your network:

10% 1. Greater New York City Area
5% 2. Washington D.C. Metro Area
4% 3. Greater Los Angeles Area

Figure 3-6: The screen that allows you to track your network statistics on LinkedIn.

- Click on the box next to the name of the contact you'd like to remove.
- Click the "Remove Connections" button.

Rest assured that LinkedIn wisely does not notify your connection that you have removed him or her, so there's no reason to fear any sort of retaliatory action. You also will be able to reinvite a connection at some other time should circumstances change.

I GOT A JOB ON LINKEDIN

Asia Bird: LinkedIn Consultant

Asia Bird has her own consultancy (Sociable Sales) that specializes in helping professionals, business owners, and entrepreneurs leverage LinkedIn to grow their businesses, increase their visibility, and open new revenue streams. She has used LinkedIn to increase her customer base and build her own business.

Asia Bird helps other users prosper through LinkedIn while she does the same.

Once she set about building out her LinkedIn network, her business grew quickly. "Since I started leveraging my LinkedIn network, the opportunities have been pouring in," she told us. "In two months, I went from just under 500 connections to nearly 3,000 connections," she said. Among the new work to come Asia's way are multiple business partnership opportunities, a radio interview request, speaking engagement requests, and a client who hired her to teach the art of using LinkedIn effectively. "I get at least one or two new consulting opportunities a day," she said.

We were intrigued by the steps she took to grow her robust network, and Asia was happy to share her experience. "One of the things I did to grow my network was to join groups and start participating in group discussions and posting interesting articles," she explained. "I also put my LinkedIn URL in the e-mail signature of all my outbound e-mails." This helped her in her efforts to get more people to come to her LinkedIn profile rather than directing them to find her on Twitter or Facebook.

"I saw the biggest spike in connection requests when I started asking and answering questions in the Answers section," she said. "Questions and answers turned into conversations, and when I mentioned what I do, people seemed really interested. This has resulted in consulting work and additional connections."

Asia offered some sage advice for people just starting out in job hunting on the site. "It's not necessary for job seekers to have networks in the thousands," she said. "It's much more important for them to be active in the networks they do have. However, the more active they are, the more their networks will grow. I am my own LinkedIn success story!"

Joseph LaMountain: President of SparkLight Communications

Joseph LaMountain is the president of SparkLight Communications and a member of the teaching staff at Georgetown University in Washington, DC. Joe's company specializes in helping organizations achieve their advocacy, marketing, and communications goals. He credits LinkedIn with increasing his firm's earnings dramatically. "I've secured at least $100,000 of consulting business in that time," he said. He's referring to the previous six months, during which he's been actively working his LinkedIn network.

Joseph LaMountain has ramped up his consulting business thanks to a vibrant LinkedIn network.

"Basically, I use LinkedIn as a Rolodex so that I can easily stay in touch with my business colleagues," he explained. "But what it also allows me to do is to see to whom they are connected. If I see that a friend/colleague is connected to someone with whom I may have a business interest, I ask them to introduce me. This results in a conversation that often leads to business opportunities."

"We asked Joseph if he could give us some specifics, and he was happy to share. "An example is the work I will be starting with the National Patient Advocate Foundation later this month," he said. "Troy Zimmerman, vice president of the National Kidney Foundation, is an old colleague. I hadn't spoken with him in a few years, but we are connected through LinkedIn. I reviewed his connection list and asked if he would introduce me to a few people. We exchanged a few e-mails, and he eventually introduced me to someone he knows at the National Patient Advocate Foundation. As it turns out, the foundation happened to be looking for someone to help enhance its grassroots advocacy program. That is one of the services I provide, and after a few meetings and discussions, the foundation decided to hire me."

"What's most amazing about LinkedIn is the sheer number of people you can connect with through your existing relationships. I have about 700 connections on LinkedIn, but those people are connected to another 5 million people! By selectively mining those data, you can hone in on the people with whom you have the greatest likelihood of finding work."

LOOKING AHEAD

Well, now you have a profile that is complete, or nearly so, and you have the beginnings of a vibrant and growing network of colleagues, classmates, and newly mined connections. You're ready to start pounding the LinkedIn pavement in search of your next great job opportunity. Throughout the next few chapters you'll gain lots of insights into how people are using LinkedIn to enhance their careers, move up the ranks, and solve everyday business problems. Chapter 4 will provide you with lots of great ideas for using the site to find the next stop along your career path. Let's get to work!

CHAPTER 4

Use LinkedIn to Job Hunt

ith your profile at 100 percent and your network expanding with each passing week, you will be ready to start exploring LinkedIn for new job and business opportunities any time you want to. Of course, when you have a keyword-rich profile, a strong network, and an active presence on LinkedIn, people with the power to hire may just be looking for you at the same time.

Yet "LinkedIn is a tool, not a magic machine that gets people jobs," says Steven Burda. Steven is absolutely right. As with so many other things in life, you won't find a magic solution on the site any more than you can trade a cow for magic beans. But you will find magic in the strong and vibrant network you've built, and recruiters, hiring managers, and human relations directors are all over LinkedIn looking for qualified leads. Your challenge will be to identify the ones who have jobs that are right for you, and to show them what you have to offer. Freelancers and consultants also will find that LinkedIn is a gold mine. If you already have a job, that's all the better because the best time to job hunt is while you are still working.

Because you built your network carefully, it's full of people who know you and your work, can vouch for your credentials, and have strong connections of their own to span the breadth of the Internet for opportunities. Your job now is to decide what type of job you truly want, determine which companies hire people for that type of job, and then start prowling your network for people who can introduce you to the decision makers at those companies. Because you also are committed to helping those in your network in the same way, you'll be operating from a position of strength as you go through your search. This chapter will take you step by step through many of the specifics of a job search on LinkedIn, but each individual who comes to the site brings an individual perspective. Your experience is likely to be as individual as and as different from those described here as your own tastes and style.

Of course, because you now occupy a spot on LinkedIn and the LinkedIn network is dedicated to helping professionals thrive, you'll find opportunities right on the site. The LinkedIn site is teaming with job postings, and finding those postings is easier than ever. Some even may find you, for example, by way of the "Jobs You May Be Interested In" box on your homepage. Finally, companies can post jobs on their own websites and allow candidates to apply using their LinkedIn profiles at the click of a mouse. Job hunting is still not easy, but using these tools can make applying for jobs simpler than ever before.

Just a very quick reminder as we begin: Before approaching others on LinkedIn, read their profiles carefully to ensure that they're encouraging messages and InMails at the moment. You don't want to approach people in a position to help you and turn them off in the process. If they have specifically stated that they are not open to contacts and you contact them, you'll do just that. It shows that you aren't looking at the network as a whole and instead are just looking out for yourself. That's contrary to the philosophy and scope of the site, and it can be difficult to recover from such a faux pas. So, with a little etiquette reminder and a lot of enthusiasm, let's travel step by step through what happens once you decide to start your LinkedIn job search.

YOUR PROFILE

Yes, we haven't forgotten that you spent hours on your profile after reading Chapter 2, but once you launch a job search, your profile is the first thing up for review. As your identity on LinkedIn (and increasingly your professional identity on the web at large), your profile lives and breathes much the same way you do. You are bound to refine your job-search goals as you explore opportunities. That will surely lead you to discover tweaks that should be made to your profile, so let's take a look. "I think employers don't want to see just credentials," explained David Becker of PhillipeBecker. "They want to see proof of those credentials. Demonstrate your expertise." Now is the time to make your profile as specific and quantifiable as possible. If you increased profits at your last company by 40 percent, say so. If you supervised a staff of 20 people, get specific about what your group actually did and how your leadership led to its success. The more detailed you make your profile, the more a prospective employer will know about you before ever scheduling an interview.

You'll find plenty to think about in terms of the keywords you use in your profile, too. As your job search moves along, you'll view profiles of potential competitors, read the profiles of people who work at companies that interest you, and gain insights into what those companies are searching for. Every industry has its own vocabulary, so the more you explore, the more you are sure to discover new and strong keywords that others in the industry are using. Keep a constant eye open for keywords you may have missed that could enhance your chances of showing up in important search results. Then be sure to edit your profile to include them.

Your Status Line

An up-to-date status message can be vital to your job-hunting efforts. "If you are out of work, put 'Open to Opportunities,'" recommended Krista Canfield of LinkedIn. "It's better than 'Unemployed.'" Such positive phrasing can mean many things besides "Unemployed," but even if everyone on LinkedIn comes to view the phrases as interchangeable, keeping a positive spin is always important to a job search. Plus, it's the truth.

As tempting as it might be to pad your status with descriptors such as "Freelancer" and "Consultant," use these words only if they represent the truth. "Don't say consulting or freelancing unless it's true," advised Krista. "It will come up in an interview, and that's very awkward." Of course, if you're claiming to be a consultant, a prospective employer will want to know the details about that. Most of us aren't good enough liars to fabricate a whole group of experiences we've never had, and interviewers are pretty savvy at recognizing such fabrications even for those of us who are.

USING RECOMMENDATIONS

As you were building your LinkedIn profile, you searched your growing network for good sources of recommendations to include. Simply speaking, it is not possible to reach a 100 percent complete profile without a few recommendations. Besides the fact that recommendations will help you to reach that 100 percent complete milestone, they also increase your visibility and appeal as a candidate. LinkedIn members with recommendations, according to the company, are three times as likely to receive inquiries through LinkedIn searches.

You're probably quite familiar with the process of asking for recommendations. As a matter of fact, going back into your high school years, you knew you'd have to have a few great recommendations before your college applications were complete. And ever since, you've been told to leave any job on good terms to enhance the likelihood that your former boss would be willing to write you a great recommendation. LinkedIn simply brings this whole process into the digital age, and that can be at once both a bonus and a challenge. "I think a lot of people use the Recommendation feature," notes David Becker. "I think that's viable if it's done well."

The bonus part comes with the realization that conceivably you can have dozens of different people willing to write a recommendation for you. With each recommendation you request, you can offer a recommendation in return. That way, you never have to feel as though you are imposing on someone. You are merely offering a free exchange of goods. Additionally, whenever you write or receive a recommendation, a notification goes out to the entire network of both parties involved. If you're swapping recommendations with a colleague who has hundreds of connections, your good work is going to be flashed before hundreds of people. Who knows which person in this list just may be looking to hire someone like you?

Be careful with tit-for-tat arrangements—you write a recommendation for me, and I'll write one for you—because these can work against you if the new

The challenge in using recommendations is to get good, solid, and specific recommendations from colleagues who actually know you well and to get more than one of them.

So your task begins with soliciting recommendations, but it also goes beyond that. You need to make sure that your recommendations are specific enough so that they actually offer real value to someone who comes to LinkedIn to screen your background. Once your colleague agrees to write a recommendation for you, help that person out. "Scrap the generic request for recommendations, and point out what you need to have included," Krista Canfield told us. "Give them an idea of what you're looking for. The more specific you are, the better. Plus, it makes it simpler for the person filling out the form." As long as your associate has agreed to recommend you, it's time to make sure that the recommendation gives you exactly what you need.

Now, in order to know what you'll need, you can search through your groups and networks to see the types of tidbits your potential competitors include. Your recommendations are displayed prominently on your profile, and so are all the recommendations you yourself have written for people in your network. They are one of the best ways to make your profile a standout. If you've built your network carefully, you may find that in addition to the recommendations you solicit, every now and again a former or current colleague may just add one spontaneously. Either way, you have the opportunity to review all recommendations before they appear on your profile. You actually post them; your colleagues just deliver them. When you've received a recommendation, you'll get a message. It's up to you whether or not you wish to add a particular recommendation to your profile.

WORKING YOUR NETWORK

With your profile polished, including recommendations, you're ready to start working your network in search of that new job. The most exciting thing about this search is that there's simply no way to know for sure which contact is going to turn the key to your next great opportunity. "It's relationships that get you jobs," said Jacqueline Wolven, owner at Moxie Marketing and Public Relations. "Something I did 15 years ago is helping my client today," she continued. "That's the neat thing about LinkedIn; it allows you to keep connected. I used LinkedIn to connect my client with someone I'd worked with 15 years ago!" Now, all parties are happy and thriving.

As you saw in Chapter 3, the first rule of connecting on LinkedIn is clear. Don't use the standard, canned LinkedIn e-mail forms. Before you approach anyone for help, make sure that you know enough about them to write with a voice that says you know each other. Don't hesitate to remind your contact how you met, where you may have worked together, and what your common affiliation is. "It's not all about connecting with all the people you can," Krista Canfield said. "It's about finding the people who have the 'right' connections." Of course, once you're job hunting, your goal is to find the person who may have an opening to the job you seek. If that person is in your network, you're golden. However, if you have to crawl around your network a bit to find the right connection, don't despair. This is what LinkedIn was meant to do.

But exactly how do you go about crawling around your network? Ed McMasters shared his LinkedIn success story with us as a great example of what the network can do. When we spoke, he was enjoying his new job as marketing and communications manager for Flottman Company, a pharmaceutical printing company in northern Kentucky. Ed's story begins while he was still with the regional tourism network CincinnatiUSA.com. Here, in his own words, is the story that led to his new job.

The position was posted by the owner of the company on his LinkedIn profile. From there it went viral to one of his friends at Kroger and then to a mutual friend at the Cincinnati Airport and from there to a good friend of mine at the Cincinnati Visitors Bureau. She forwarded it to me, and the chain was complete once I inquired about the position. The key to LinkedIn was opening the awareness—I believe that the folks at Flottman did not post the job on a job-search site or place it through a recruiter.

Ed was fortunate in that his network included a variety of people who were well connected both online and in the real world, but don't let that discourage you if you are not yet equally networked. LinkedIn was designed to help you broaden your reach, and the actions you take on the site every day will help you to do just that.

"Get active," advises Chris Perry. "Start being active and contributing value from day 1. Share interesting news with your network via status updates, post links to intriguing articles, and join in discussions in your LinkedIn groups. Offer insightful answers to questions on LinkedIn's Answers forum, add your blog feed, or share your recommended reading list. This will increase your visibility on LinkedIn and will help you to share and enhance your personal brand in front of your network."

Krista Canfield shared some LinkedIn advice: "Don't just network when you need something. A 'gimme, gimme' mentality is a surefire way to lose professional contacts and get deleted from peoples' networks. Take the time to help others in your network, not because you're expecting something in return, but because you truly want them to succeed. Opportunities often arise when you reconnect with people and take time to listen to what they are thinking about and working on."

"What I like best about LinkedIn is that it takes away the 'cold call,'" said Joe LaMountain, president of SparkLight Communications. "When a friend introduces you to a friend, it's no longer a cold call, but simply friends introducing one another." So, as you build your network, be sure to make yourself one of the "friends" who adds value to your network and keeps an eye out for others. It isn't just the decent thing to do; it's also the most likely way to reap rewards.

Bryan Webb Gets a Job

Bryan Webb saw a posting on the Canadian website www.workopolis.com for a sales manager with a company he knew he'd like to work for. The posting called for him to send his application to the human resources director, but he decided to try a different route. Here's his story in his own words:

I decided to use LinkedIn to see if it could help me reach the hiring manager. I went to the Advanced Search page, typed in the company name, and found three names of company employees in my expanded network. This list included the chief operating officer (COO), who was a third-degree connection. I wanted to get an edge, so I sent a request for an introduction to this person to one of my contacts (a great guy). In my request, I said, "I would like to get an introduction to your contact. Would you mind forwarding this introduction?" He recommended that I should be given an opportunity to meet.

Bryan Webb, sales manager at AZZ/ Blenkhorn and Sawle, Ltd., got his current job through LinkedIn.

When I contacted the COO via the LinkedIn introduction, I told him I'd applied to his company and would like more information about the work they do. Within three days, I'd gotten a response through this request. I also got an offer from the human relations department to come for an interview. When I arrived, I found the interview was with the COO, who I'd so recently contacted through LinkedIn.

Normally, first interviews are 45 minutes, but after 90 minutes, he asked me when I could start. After two hours, I asked for a formal offer letter to be sent. It turns out that the COO said he'd gotten a request to be introduced to me from a contact of his on LinkedIn, someone he respected very much. The quality of that introduction is what got me the chance to meet the hiring manager. My experience on LinkedIn led directly to my getting the job. I continue to use LinkedIn in my new company to gain access to potential customers and employees.

You're Searching for Others, but Others Are also Searching for You

Soon you'll be learning about how recruiters use LinkedIn to find great candidates for their clients. Remember that just as you are harnessing LinkedIn's power to search for your next great opportunity, you also should assume that from now on, anyone you interview with will have already learned a great deal about you through your LinkedIn profile and activity on the site. This is the reality of social networking, and this reality has caught many a student in its snare. That photo on a social networking site that shows an 18-year-old athlete with a beer can in his hand attending a party in a state where the legal drinking age is 21 certainly can derail the young man's scholarship hopes. Of course, your profile is completely professional after all your efforts based on Chapter 2, but it's still so important for you to comport yourself with total professionalism while on LinkedIn.

David Becker explained how he uses LinkedIn when qualifying potential candidates. "We see who they are connected with," he explained. "For the most part, it gives more depth to a candidate. It's an interesting place to see how people interact." David continued to explain that LinkedIn is the perfect place to demonstrate your expertise. "Employers can see that," he said. "If you're an insurance broker, for example, be involved in an insurance group, and position yourself as an expert."

Mark Montgomery, a consultant providing college admission and planning advice, agrees. He noted that while he hasn't found a job per se on LinkedIn, he has gotten consulting work from people who first found him through the site. Krista Canfield spoke to us of a wedding photographer who got many jobs from within her network of friends and colleagues simply because she mentioned his work. Steven Burda agrees. "The more descriptive you make your profile, the more people in your field will reach out to you," he said.

RESEARCHING COMPANIES

While you're working on getting noticed and connecting with the decision makers, you also can be researching companies that might be perfect candidates for your next job. You'll use LinkedIn to research companies you're interested in through the Companies tab. Behind this tab (Figure 4-1), you'll find information on more than 2 million companies.

The best thing about LinkedIn's company information is that it all comes straight from LinkedIn members and their profiles. Nothing comes directly from the corporate headquarters by way of the public relations department, the latest annual report, or the investor relations department, for example. To create this area of the site, LinkedIn started with companies that have the greatest number of employees. Then LinkedIn staff spoke with representatives at the companies to determine the information that would be most useful to both LinkedIn users and the companies themselves.

You can search the Companies area by industry and other criteria, including location and company size. You even can add a company—your

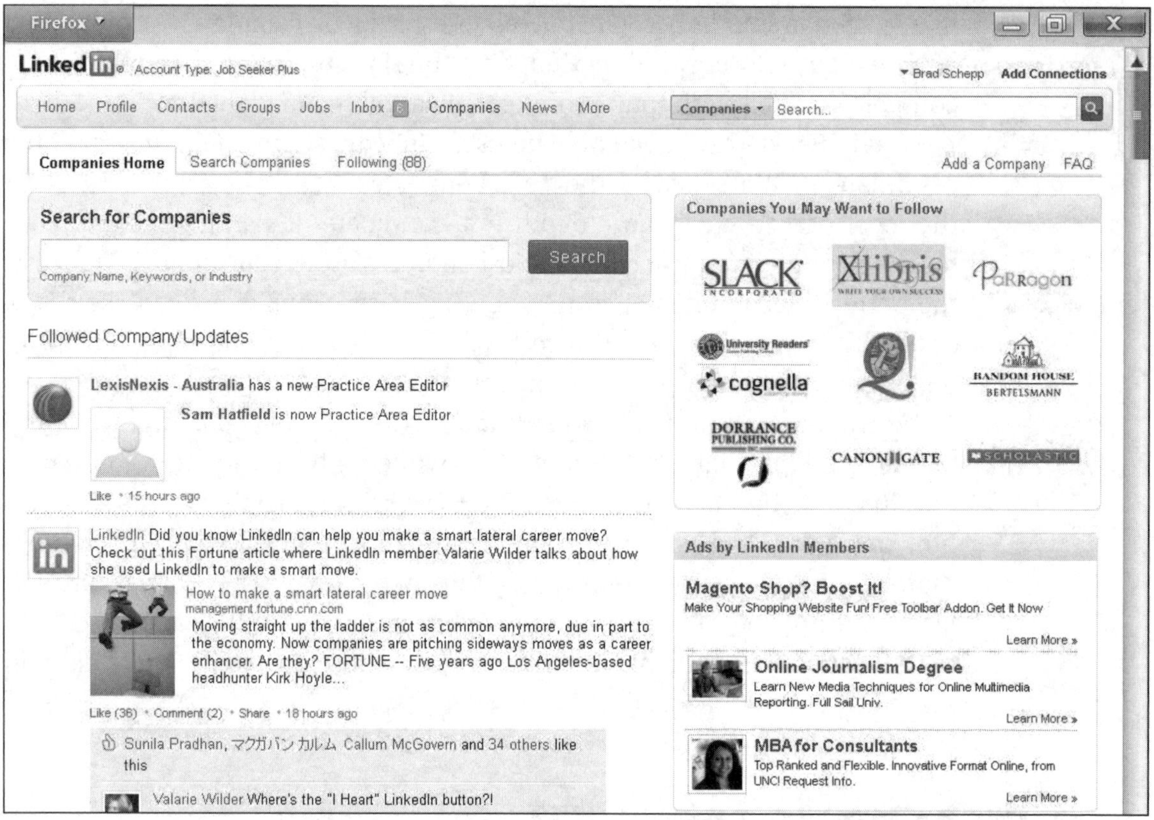

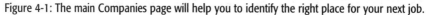

Figure 4-1: The main Companies page will help you to identify the right place for your next job.

own if you're an entrepreneur, for example—if there isn't currently a listing for it. To give you a head start, LinkedIn personalizes this area by showing you the latest updates from the companies you are following (see the "Company Follow" sidebar).

Let's use the profile for Google, shown in Figure 4-2, to illustrate in more detail some of the valuable information company profiles provide. Next to the company name, you'll find a lot of the same information that you would find in other directories, but with more of an insider's perspective. But this is where the standard directory-type information ends. Scroll down the page, and you may see photos of Google employees who are connected to you in some way. By default, you will see employees who are in your network, such as 1st or 2nd degree connections or members of one or more of the groups you belong to. Note the tab "Your College Alumni." Click on this,

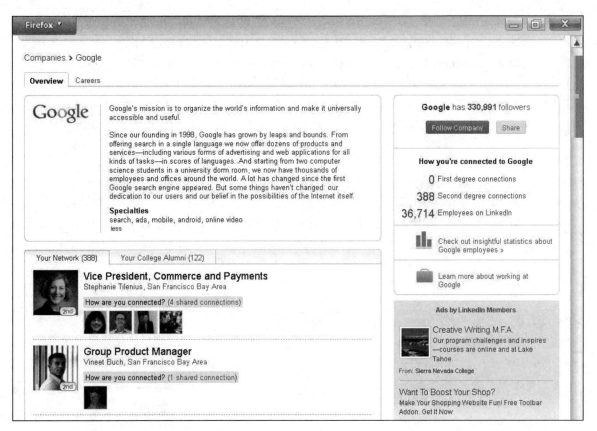

Figure 4-2: Part of Google's LinkedIn company profile.

and you will see Google employees who graduated from the same school you did. Between the employees who were already part of your network and those who went to your school, you should have several opportunities to find people who could help you out if you found a job at Google that interested you.

To the right of the information about how you're connected to Google employees, you'll see a box with several categories of information. First, you'll see how many people on LinkedIn are following Google so that they can receive updates about new hires, people who left the company, new products, or other news. Below that is a box with statistics on how you are connected to Google. If you were to click on the link that says "Check out insightful statistics about Google employees," you would see the chart in Figure 4-3. Just look at all the information you can glean from this one chart! Initially, you'll see the percentage of Google employees working in various types of jobs and how those percentages compare with the percentages of employees at similar companies. Click on the "Years Experience" tab, and you're shown data about the number of years of work experience Google employees have and, once again, how that compares with similar companies. Other tabs provide information on the types of degrees Google employees hold and, finally, the top universities Google employees attended.

Below the chart is another chart showing you the company's annual growth by month, as measured by number of LinkedIn member profiles. Roll over the "Filter by" box on the right, click on the arrow to see the pull-down menu, and you'll see various ways by which you can filter that

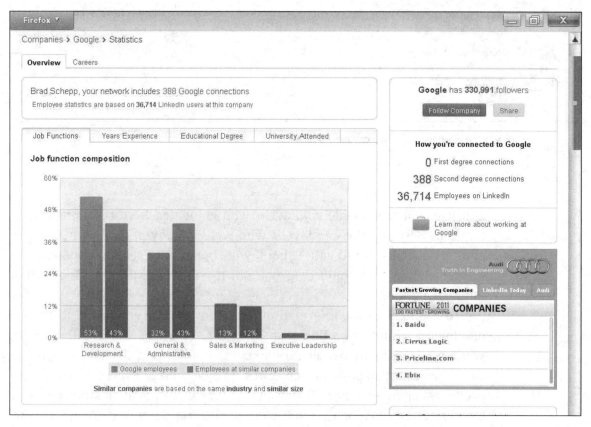

Figure 4-3: The information that's available when you click "Check out insightful statistics about Google employees."

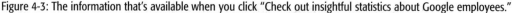

information. Scroll down a bit further, and you're shown the other companies viewed by people who looked at Google's company profile, for example, Apple, Microsoft, and Facebook. Click on the "Employee's connections" link, and you're shown the companies to which Google employees are most connected. Further down there's a chart showing the percentage of employees who have changed their title month by month. Further down you can view Google employees with new titles, those who have left the company recently, and the most viewed Google profiles. Finally, there's a chart showing, in graph form, the number of connections you have at Google.

If you'd like even more Google stats, head over to the column on the right again. The information there includes the top companies Google employees worked for before coming to Google. This is excellent information for all job seekers, but especially for those who may be freshly out of school and wondering just how it is you get to be a software engineer at Google, for example. You also can see the top companies Google employees went to after working there. There's also information about the cities or areas where Google employees live. Finally, you will see information about who in Google has the most recommendations on LinkedIn. As you can see, this is an incredible amount of information that probably would have taken you days to compile (if you were able to gather all that information at all) just a few short years ago.

Company Follow

LinkedIn has made it very easy for you to keep track of news and developments from the companies that interest you. Once you've found a company's profile on LinkedIn, you can elect to follow that company. It couldn't be easier. Simply click the "Follow Company" button on the upper right side of the page. Now you'll receive automatic updates of news and happenings relevant to the companies you choose to follow. These updates become part of your routine LinkedIn update stream. Here you'll receive news that includes new hires, departures, and products, just to name a few.

Even if you are not actively job hunting, following the most dynamic companies within your industry will keep you up to date about trends and developments as they happen.

We're not done with Google's company page yet. In fact, we're coming to the best part. Look at Figure 4-3 again. Notice that the default setting under statistics is Overview. Click on the "Careers" link, and you will get a quick snapshot of what it's like to work at Google, as well as information on specific jobs in which you might be interested. On the right side of the page is information about employee benefits and other sites where you can learn more about Google careers, including YouTube, Twitter, and Facebook.

"Go see who's been hired recently, and trace them back to their old companies,"
recommended career and life coach Anne Pryor. "Then you can see if their old
jobs are still open."

Now let's talk a little bit about how you can put this research into action. Once you've identified new hires, for example, Anne Pryor also recommends that you reach out to them for information interviews. "Approach new hires, because in the first month they'll have the time and inclination to be willing to talk," she advised. What if you find a contact who isn't a recent hire? Well, as long as you have a connection to that person, you've got an opportunity to touch base and explore the company for opportunities. Reach out to request an information-only interview. Anne shared some language you can use to approach an employee who may not be the hiring manager:

It's great to see you on LinkedIn. I hope you like your position at [this company]. I see there's an opening. Can we meet and talk about the culture, the work, and who might be the hiring manager?

Then, always end with the phrase, "Can I do anything for you today?"

If you include an invitation to lunch, you're very likely to get the chance to talk and get an insider's perspective about life at this particular company. In addition, now that you've made that person-to-person connection, your contact is a lot more likely to speak with the hiring manager on your behalf. Relationships lead to jobs, and you've enhanced this relationship fairly quickly and easily. Or equally important, you'll find out that the company you're thinking of isn't right for you.

An editor friend of ours once enthusiastically went after a job with a New Jersey publisher. He actually got the offer and was evaluating it in terms of salary, career-building potential, and the disruption his family would suffer by moving several hundred miles from their home. In those pre-LinkedIn days, he scoured the web for information about the publisher and, fortunately, learned that the owners of this publishing company were known as "the worst bosses in New Jersey." Now that's a bad boss! Luckily, he was savvy enough and dedicated enough to do this research on his own. Today, it would have taken only a few e-mails to LinkedIn connections to learn exactly the same thing and also confirm it with others.

Chris Perry Used Company Research to Land a Job

Chris Perry wears more than one hat. He works full time as associate brand manager for Reckitt Benckiser, and he is also the founder of Career Rocketeer. He frequently writes, speaks, and consults on LinkedIn for both individuals and businesses, and he gladly shared the story of how he landed his job through LinkedIn.

> I did land my current full-time job through LinkedIn, thanks to multiple personal branding and networking efforts. I have had recruiters and employers reach out to me after viewing my profile, but in this case, I took a more active approach. I was dead-set on a career in brand management. I initially used the LinkedIn Companies area to identify companies of interest, in addition to those I had already chosen to target. It was, in fact, thanks to this company directory that I came across my current company.

> I used LinkedIn People search, LinkedIn Companies, and LinkedIn Groups to identify brand managers in these target companies, and I requested information interviews to initiate career conversations. The great thing was that by joining a number of brand management and marketing-related LinkedIn Groups, I was able to direct message these brand managers. I would send/forward them a request for a few minutes of their time to discuss their careers, their companies' cultures, etc.

> I would never ask them for a job. I simply asked them to talk about themselves. In these conversations you naturally will have the opportunity to talk about yourself, and it's these opportunities that allow you to make a connection and share your job search efforts. At the end, I would ask how they broke into their

Chris Perry landed his current job by following classic job-hunting advice but fine-tuned for life on LinkedIn.

careers or if they had any advice for someone trying to break into that career or company. I had multiple people share advice and even offer to help.

One of these interviews led to the official interview for my current job. I also suggest asking these managers if they know anyone else in their organization or in the industry that you can talk to in order to learn more about this specific career. This helps you build a network of people who now know you and may contact you when an opportunity comes up. You can also then use LinkedIn Introductions through the person you just spoke to in order to connect with the next person.

LinkedIn not only helped me solidify my list of target companies, but it also both helped me identify and gain access to target network contacts and allowed those contacts to see my profile in the informational interview request process.

Now it's been decades since career counselors began counseling job hunters to request informational interviews. But here you've just read the first-person account of someone who not only followed that job-hunting advice, but also followed it directly to the job he was hoping to have when he started out on his LinkedIn journey.

THE "JOBS" LINK

For job hunters, the "Jobs" link at the top of your homepage is the path to millions of job possibilities, stretching far beyond those that LinkedIn members have posted on the site. If you were to mouse over to the "Jobs" link, you would see a pull-down menu. Click on the first item, "Find Jobs." You'll then see the page shown in Figure 4-4. The "Search for Jobs" box right at top of the page is tempting, and yes, we're going to devote a lot of coverage to that. But let's first go down the page a bit to the section called "Jobs you may be interested in." The jobs listed there, as we discussed earlier, are based on information you provided in your profile. Through the links to the right, you can choose to create an e-mail alert to receive notices

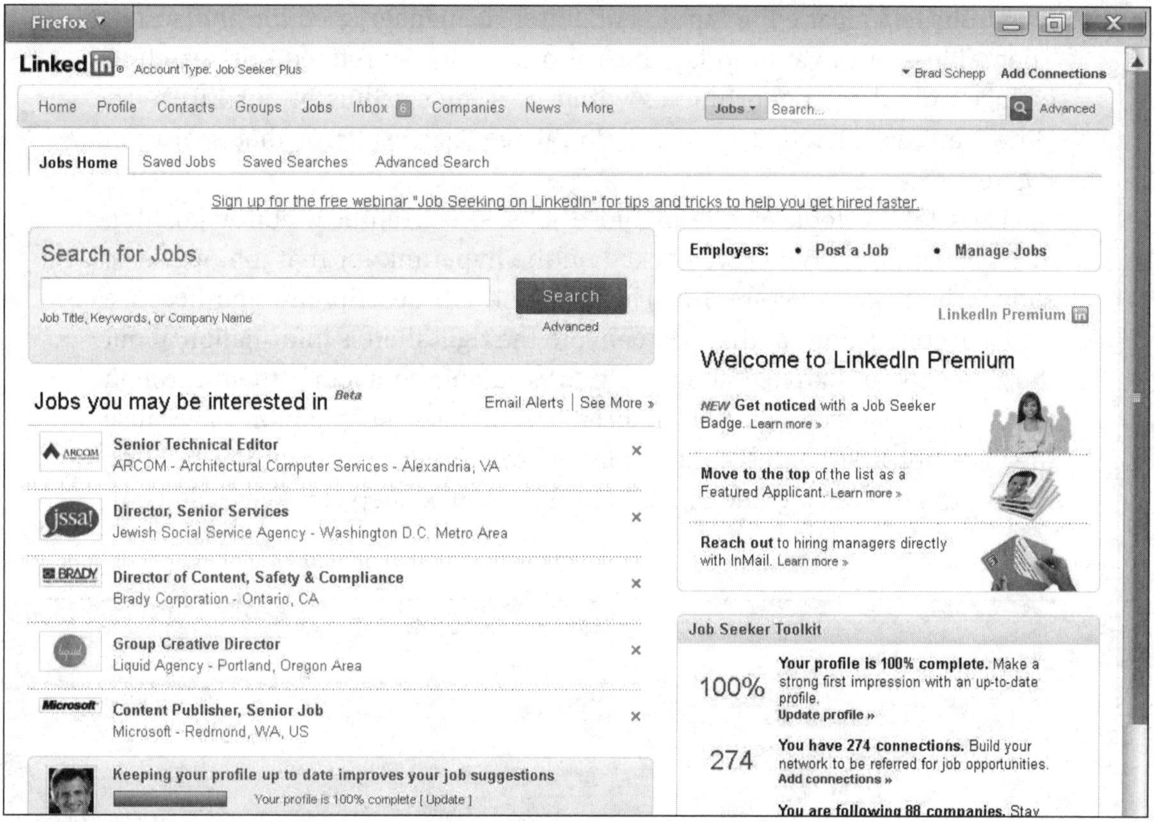

Figure 4-4: The page that appears after you click on the "Find Jobs" link under LinkedIn's "Jobs" tab.

of these kinds of jobs either daily or weekly. You also can choose to see additional jobs you may be interested in.

Let's get to that search bar now. Just enter some keywords, and immediately LinkedIn will present you with some job openings to consider. See Figure 4-5. Notice that LinkedIn lets you know how many people in your network work at the company listing the job posted (the last line for each job description). If you were to click on one of those links, you would be shown the people in your network who can assist you, including details about the type of connection they are.

Let's do a sample Advanced Search now just to show you what information you can retrieve. We clicked on the "Advanced Search" link shown near the top in Figure 4-5. We entered the keyword "editor" without refining the search in any way. That search resulted in 241 matches for a variety of jobs from technical editor to digital editor to managing editor and so on. Then, filling in the appropriate boxes to the left, we refined our search to include only those opportunities within a 50-mile radius of our ZIP code. Now we have 11 jobs to review. You'll see the results of that search in Figure 4-6.

Let's take a look at one of those jobs—the technical editor position available at SAIC. When we clicked on the hyperlink for that job, we were shown the page in Figure 4-7. There's a full job description, and because we have connections at that company, to the right there's information about those people and advice about how to go about contacting them through LinkedIn. In our example, we will need to send those people InMails because they are not first-degree connections. Now, if we were truly job hunting rather than writing a guide to job hunting, our next step clearly would be to

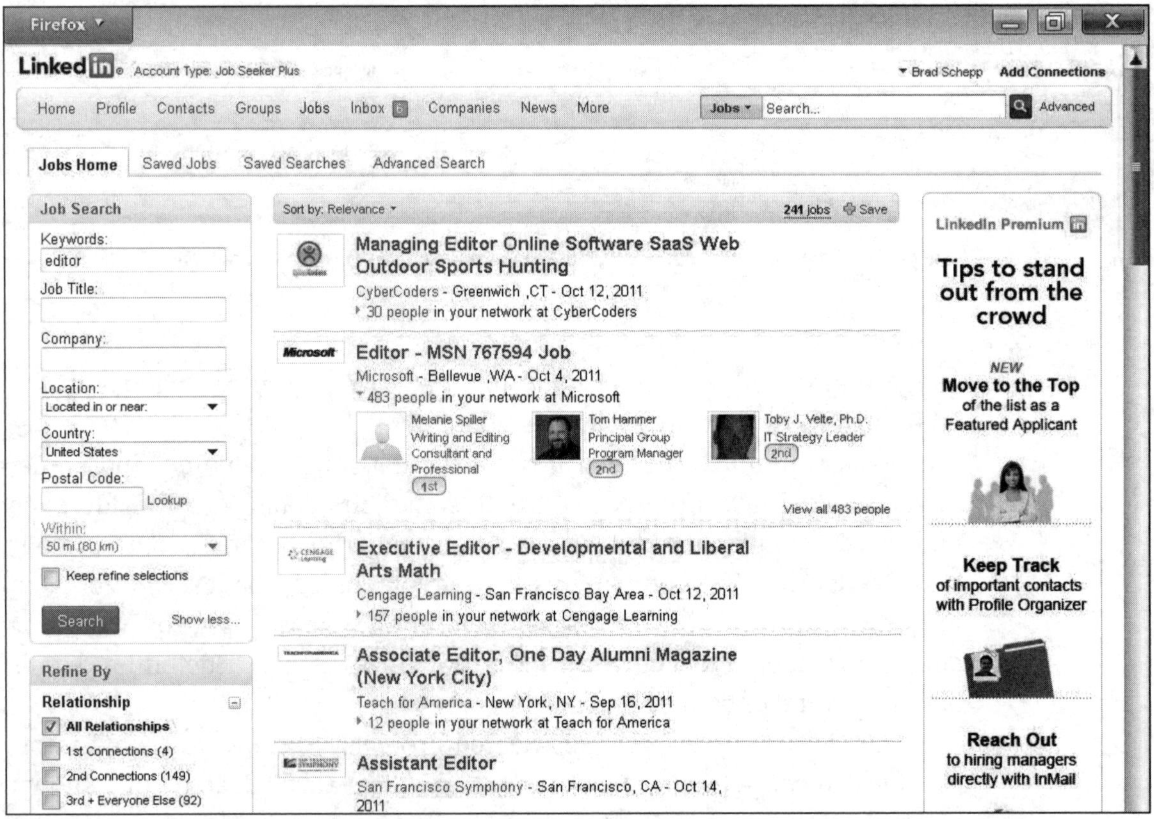

Figure 4-5: The Job Search Results page of the Advanced Job Search feature provides a wealth of information about companies looking to hire people like you.

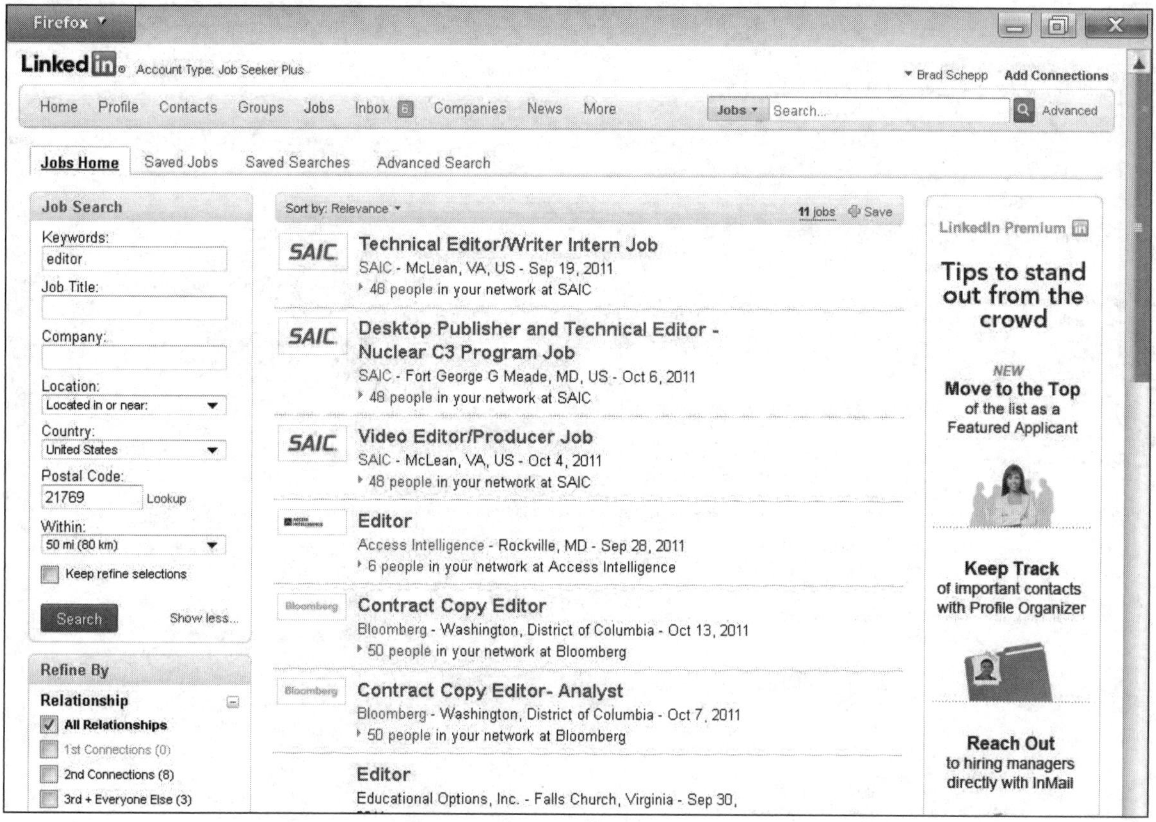

Figure 4-6: Editor jobs located within 50 miles of our ZIP code.

work through our connections to get introductions to people at the company in a position to know more about the job.

Don't concern yourself with getting a direct link to the hiring manager when approaching people in your network. That manager may not appreciate being contacted in this way. Remember how many job listings include words to the effect, "Please, no calls." Random e-mails out of the blue, even from LinkedIn members, may not be welcome either, which is why you should work through your connections to get an introduction to the person if she is not a direct contact.

The Jobs Tab Within Your Groups

Many of the groups you join will include posts for jobs available targeted to the subject of the group. Once you open the page for a group you've joined,

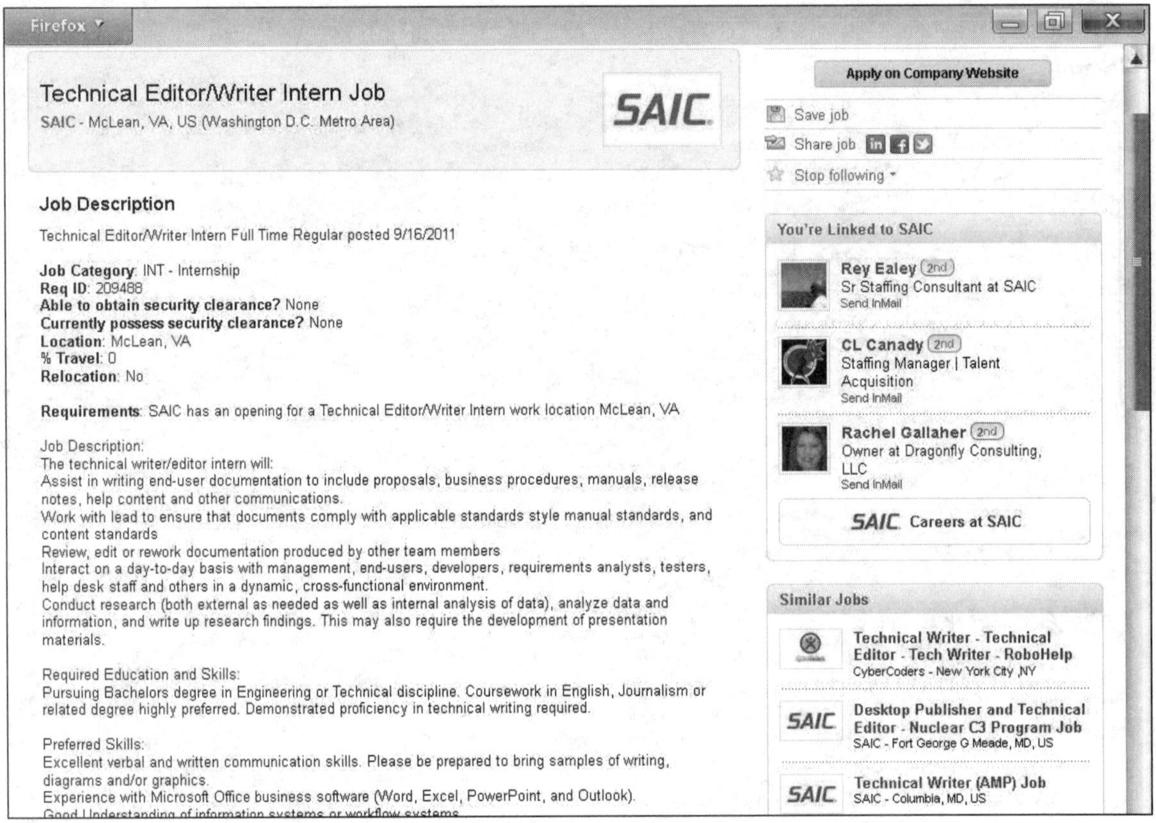

Figure 4-7: The ad for a technical editor showing how we're connected to the company that posted the position.

you'll often see another tab for "Jobs." Click this, and you can find and share jobs within your industry. You'll also get a link to show you how many people in your network either work for the company or have a business relationship with it. You also can click the "Share" link to post the job to other social networks such as Facebook or Twitter or send the job listing to your LinkedIn network, your groups, or individuals you think might find it interesting.

Get Simply Hired

No, this is not hype suggesting that getting hired through LinkedIn will be simple. Simply Hired is a job-search site that's been partnered with LinkedIn since 2005. Simply Hired describes itself as the biggest, smartest job-search engine on the web. The company currently "indexes" more than 5 million

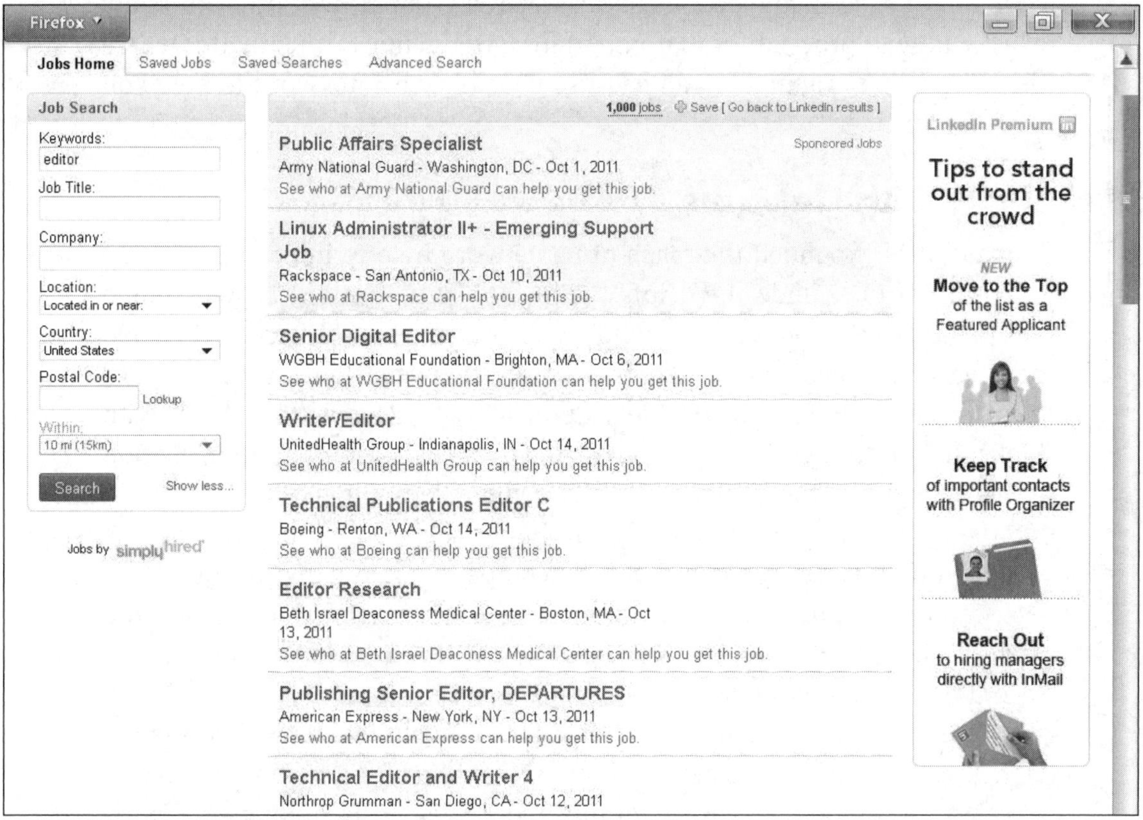

Figure 4-8: The Job Search Results page that appears through the "Simply Hired" tab includes hyperlinks allowing you to see if there are people in your network who can help.

jobs internationally, approximately 3 million of which are U.S.-based. These jobs are culled from thousands of job boards, newspaper classified ads, and even company websites.

Here's how the two sites work together: When you search for a job through LinkedIn, you'll be shown matches that appear on LinkedIn first. At the bottom of your search results, you'll see a link that says "See more jobs from Simply Hired that fit these criteria." Now here is how LinkedIn and Simply Hired work together: As part of your Simply Hired search results (Figure 4-8), you can click the link that says "See who at [name of company] can help you get this job." LinkedIn scours your network to see if you have a direct or indirect connection within the company to help you learn more about the job and bring you closer to getting hired. Your contacts will appear, starting, of course, with your 1st degree connections. Also included is information about what you have in common with them (number of shared connections and/or shared groups). By now, you know exactly how to proceed for that important introduction. So no matter where the job posting originated, you can use your LinkedIn network to help you land the job.

Apply with LinkedIn

LinkedIn has expanded the reach of its network by offering companies the opportunity to include the "Apply with LinkedIn" button in their online job postings. Now companies who decide to add this button to their job postings can receive your LinkedIn profile with a single click when you use this feature. Each time you decide to apply for a job through the "Apply with LinkedIn" button, you'll also be given the chance to tailor your information to the specifics of the company to which you are applying.

Using the "Apply with LinkedIn" button also will show you people within your network who work for the company you are approaching, and every job you apply for gets recorded in the "Saved Jobs" tab under the "Jobs" tab on LinkedIn. This provides you with an updated and ongoing record of your job hunt.

"One of the things LinkedIn is doing that's revolutionizing job searching is their new 'Apply with LinkedIn' button," said Mona Abdel-Halim, director of sales and marketing for Careerimp, Inc. "This really helps parse information so candidate information is never lost, which normally happens when a document is uploaded to large application systems used by job boards and corporate career sites. We've seen that around 40 percent of content is usually lost. The only downside of this new way of applying is that most job seekers have incomplete LinkedIn profiles." But, of course, that does not apply to you!

RECRUIT THOSE RECRUITERS FOR HELP!

Recruiters, headhunters, executive placement firms, whatever you want to call them—if you're looking for work, you want to embrace them as part of your job-search strategy. Recruiters love LinkedIn, and many are members who actively use the site every day. A recent survey by Jobvite, a company offering recruiting software and services, found that 87 percent of U.S. companies report using LinkedIn for recruiting. It's no wonder that recruiters love LinkedIn. Recruiters, by nature and profession, tend to be active networkers. Having access to a large group of contacts improves their chances of earning money, after all.

Use LinkedIn to find recruiters active in your own industry, and introduce yourself. The search technique is quite simple. Go to the Advanced People Search screen, and select your industry. Then plug in "recruiter" as a keyword. When we did this, selecting publishing as the industry, we found 495 recruiters. Just reviewing the list of names gave us ideas for people we could approach and new opportunities we might consider.

Elizabeth Garzarelli Shares Her Expertise as a Recruiter

Elizabeth Garzarelli is a principal with Ligature Partners, Inc. Her firm specializes in placing publishing professionals, and she generously shared her recruiter's perspective with us.

Every morning, I look at my 1st degree LinkedIn connections. Often I find interesting new people within the industries that I recruit, which include educational technology, digital media, K–20 educational publishing, consumer publishing, academic publishing, and entertainment. When trying to fill a specific position, I go to Advanced People Search and put in endless combinations of job titles, geographic areas, industry specialties, and keywords. For instance, "VP Marketing in the Publishing Industry, located within 35 miles of Boston," with the keyword "higher education." Or perhaps, "Director, in the e-Learning Industry, located anywhere in the nation," with the keywords "strategy" and "product management." Then I pull up a list of matches and start clicking on profiles of people who look interesting for some reason (usually because of their title, current company, or geographic location).

Once I identify someone who either looks like a fit or looks like they could refer candidates, I send them an InMail with a brief summary of what I'm looking for and an offer to send them the full position description if they're interested in hearing more about it. If they respond, I send them the position description and then follow up a few days later with a phone call or another e-mail. I have them send me a résumé, phone interview them, and hopefully proceed to a face-to-face interview.

Sometimes I'm looking for candidates, but sometimes I'm checking to see if what people put on their résumés matches up with what they put on LinkedIn. If it

Elizabeth Garzarelli is a recruiter based in North Carolina.

doesn't, that's a red flag. Some of the positions that I've found people for using LinkedIn include CEO, SVP publisher, VP of content, SVP global strategic alliances, VP business development, director of product management, and VP of marketing. Of 36 retained searches that I've completed over the last 18 months, approximately half of the final candidates were people that I originally found on LinkedIn.

I normally spend about an hour and a half to two hours a day looking for candidates on LinkedIn. I have contacted approximately 600 people about nonadvertised executive-level positions using LinkedIn over the past 10 months. Hundreds have responded, and dozens have turned into qualified candidates. Several have been placed successfully.

Here's one last piece of advice: If a recruiter contacts you about a position that's not right for you, respond anyway. Tell them why it's not a fit. Always refer others if you can. At least you'll be building a relationship, and the recruiter will be very grateful for any help you can offer. That recruiter will be more likely to remember you and contact you again in the future.

Elizabeth can speak with the voice of an insider, but hers is not the only success story we found when LinkedIn and recruiters come together. Her advice emphasizes the need to make sure that your profile is keyword-rich so that your credentials will appear when recruiters go searching. Even if you aren't currently looking for a job, it's a good idea to at least entertain opportunities brought to you through a recruiter. Stephen Weinstein of Cooper Power Systems was quite happy in his previous job when a recruiter approached him. He had been on LinkedIn for about three years when he received an InMail from a recruiter. He told her that he wasn't looking for a new job, but she encouraged him to take the information anyway. She was thinking that perhaps someone else in his network would be a good fit. Once Stephen got the details of the job she was seeking to fill, he decided to apply for it after all.

FREE VERSUS PREMIUM LINKEDIN SUBSCRIPTIONS FOR JOB HUNTERS

Once you find yourself looking for a new job, especially if you've been laid off from your former position, the temptation exists to do whatever possibly can be done to find a new professional home. You may be tempted to upgrade your LinkedIn membership by choosing a paid subscription instead of sticking with the version of the site that's free to use. With the free personal account, you can create a robust professional profile and build a network of connections from among LinkedIn's user base of 135 million people. Plus, you have access to all of LinkedIn's other great features, such as the Groups and the Answers area. More specifically, you'll be able to have five Introduction requests open at a time, and you can view 100 results per search. However, if you want to contact people who are not in your network through InMails, you'll need to buy credits at $10 per InMail. You are also able to view the number of people who have viewed your profile recently, but you won't have access to many details about those people. If you want more information about them, you'll have to pay for a premium account which includes the Profile Stats Pro component. A premium account also will allow you to view more than the minimum number of search results at one time and move to the top of the list of search results.

Recruiters and other business professionals using LinkedIn for research purposes as part of their jobs probably can justify paying for a premium account. More details on premium accounts are included in Chapter 6. For now it's enough to know that these accounts provide powerful tools for sifting through and organizing profiles of interest from LinkedIn's huge database. These surcharged (and expensive!) accounts may make sense for businesspeople whose companies may be footing the bill. But what should a job hunter do? It's clear that when you're looking for work, you may be watching your expenses more closely than ever. And many of the dozens of people with whom we spoke as we researched this book never went beyond the free account.

But it's also true that you may have to spend money to make money. Work with the free personal account for a while to see if it is truly meeting your job-hunting needs, but do consider upgrading to one of the premium accounts just for job hunters (discussed shortly) if you find yourself constrained by the limits of the free account. The more robust site offerings may justify the cost of the upgraded account. The second item under the "Jobs" pull-down menu is the "Job Seeker Premium" link. Click this link, and you'll see the screen shown in Figure 4-9. Here, you'll find three types of account upgrades. There's no need for us to go into detail about every feature offered through these accounts because the information is readily available on the site. However, we do want to mention some of the things that we think are especially valuable about these premium accounts for job seekers. We'll focus on the Job Seeker Basic account, which is available for $15.95 per month prepaid per year or monthly at a fee of $19.95.

The first thing listed in the chart describing the premium account features is the Job Seeker Badge, which account holders may include on their profiles to alert hiring managers and recruiters that they are actively in the job market. Frankly, we're not sure of the value of this badge, and it's

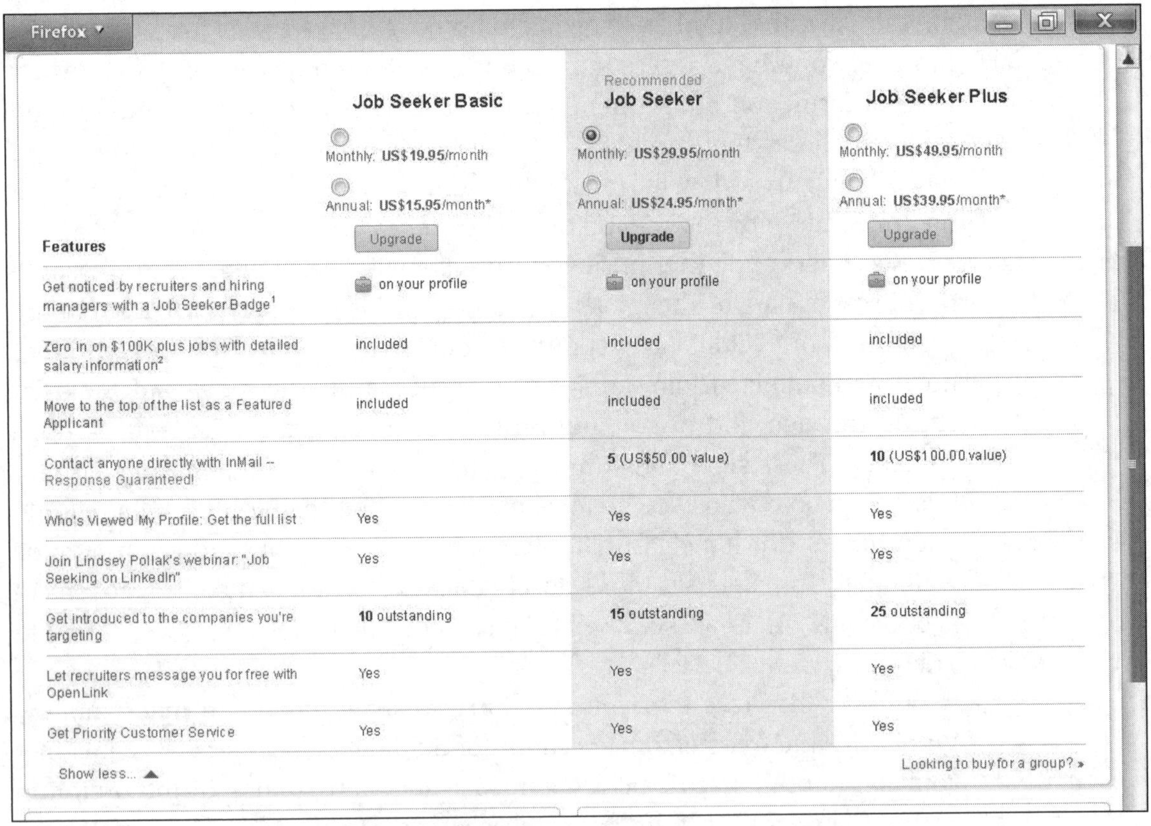

Features	Job Seeker Basic	Recommended Job Seeker	Job Seeker Plus
	Monthly: US$19.95/month	Monthly: US$29.95/month	Monthly: US$49.95/month
	Annual: US$15.95/month*	Annual: US$24.95/month*	Annual: US$39.95/month*
	Upgrade	Upgrade	Upgrade
Get noticed by recruiters and hiring managers with a Job Seeker Badge[1]	on your profile	on your profile	on your profile
Zero in on $100K plus jobs with detailed salary information[2]	included	included	included
Move to the top of the list as a Featured Applicant	included	included	included
Contact anyone directly with InMail -- Response Guaranteed!		5 (US$50.00 value)	10 (US$100.00 value)
Who's Viewed My Profile: Get the full list	Yes	Yes	Yes
Join Lindsey Pollak's webinar: "Job Seeking on LinkedIn"	Yes	Yes	Yes
Get introduced to the companies you're targeting	10 outstanding	15 outstanding	25 outstanding
Let recruiters message you for free with OpenLink	Yes	Yes	Yes
Get Priority Customer Service	Yes	Yes	Yes
Show less... ▲			Looking to buy for a group? »

Figure 4-9: Details on LinkedIn's Job Seeker premium accounts.

possible that it even can work against you if the hiring manager or recruiter is thinking she would prefer to hire someone who is not actively looking for a job. The badge is reminiscent of the waving hands in a classroom that say, "Pick me, pick me!" Then again, some recruiters like the fact that people include these badges because they then know for sure that they're in the market. However, just because you sign up for one of the Job Seeker premium accounts does not mean that the badge is automatically posted to your profile. It's always your choice, and in fact, it's set to off by default.

Another premium feature allows you to move to the top of a search results list as a "Featured Applicant." This is probably worthwhile because anything that separates you from the pack when someone is reviewing possibly extensive search results can be a good thing. You also will gain the more detailed information about who has viewed your profile, and this also can be a worthwhile feature. The Job Seeker Basic account also provides access to a webinar called "Job Seeking on LinkedIn." We have taken this webinar and found it worthwhile. In fact, here are some of the action items we compiled after our session:

- Check LinkedIn.com/today—a new feature and news aggregator.
- Search for local jobs. Use Advanced Search also.
- Recheck profile to make sure that all the necessary keywords are included.
- Make sure that you have a unique URL (public profile).
- Profile summary—keep paragraphs short, lots of white space.
- Fill specialties area with keywords. Check the profiles of people with jobs you want for keywords, groups they belong to, and more.
- Check Groups because they can become part of your personal branding.
- Don't overdo listing skills and certifications.
- Drive people to your profile by adding your LinkedIn URL to your e-mail signature.
- Strategically update your status one to three times per week.
- Consider InMails as cover letters. Use them to reach out to decision makers.
- See learn.linkedin.com—LinkedIn's Learning Center.
- Apply for jobs through LinkedIn so that your profile is included.

S. E. Day: Author and Spokesman

S. E. Day is the author of *How to Legally Steal Your Next Vehicle and Save $1,000s.* He is also the host of the *Legally Steal* radio show. He is an auto industry insider with nearly two decades of negotiating experience. He used his LinkedIn network to identify and solidify a five-figure book contract and a permanent position as a corporate spokesman. Here's how he put his LinkedIn network to work.

I used LinkedIn to research the right person to contact at Grow Financial Credit Union. I reviewed the vice president of marketing's profile on LinkedIn, which gave me selling points. With this inside information in my pocket, I was prepared to make a targeted proposal. I contacted the VP through LinkedIn and pitched a request for an interview. The VP's profile had enough information in it to give me the selling points I needed to pitch the proposal in a winning manner. I was granted the interview, and they were blown away with my proposal. Mind you, this proposal was not even a consideration at the credit union before I pitched it.

S. E. Day used his LinkedIn network to gain both a book contract and a spokesman position.

The name of the book is *The Negotiating Experience, Your Car Deal Your Way!* This happy and prosperous partnership is still going strong, and all because I knew how to work LinkedIn to the mutual benefit of my business and that of my client.

Programmer

Tim Kassouf is one of the many recruiters who turn to LinkedIn every day to do his job. That's nothing unusual. What is unusual is the person he was able to find through the site to meet a client's very specific requirements.

I work for G.1440, an IT [information technology] staffing firm in Baltimore, MD. We recently had a unique job requirement come in. They were looking for a developer versed in a rare and outdated programming language—it was so rare that no one in our candidate database of tens of thousands met the requirements. [*Note:*

The client was hired to do project work for the federal government and needed a specialist with a Plone/Python programming background.] In search of this rare skillset, I performed a quick search of my network on LinkedIn. I found three people with the necessary expertise, two of whom were willing to apply for the job we had available. The client interviewed both and hired one. They've been a client of ours ever since.

LOOKING AHEAD

As you've seen in this chapter, providing proven evidence of your accomplishments and professional experience is an important part of getting noticed by your next employer. Chapter 5 will give you a look at LinkedIn's Answers area. You'll be hard pressed to find a better, more efficient route toward building a fine reputation on the site and within your industry than by being an active contributor to this part of LinkedIn. Every time you post a question or an answer, you bring recognition and exposure to your profile and your background. By the time you get to Chapter 6, you'll be so busy building your reputation and enjoying the results that you may just forget that you once thought of this process as work.

CHAPTER 5

Questions? LinkedIn Has Answers. Answers? LinkedIn Has Questions.

n a winter afternoon otherwise darkened by cold, clouds, and a "wintry mix," as we call the dreary intermittent snow and freezing rain that plagues the Northeast, warm sunshine eventually broke through the day. No, the weather had not taken a sudden turn for the better. It happened within two hours of posting a question to LinkedIn for this book. In just that brief time, we received 12 excellent answers and were off and running despite the weather! Here is the question:

What are the best ways to use LinkedIn on the job? I'm working on a book for McGraw-Hill and was wondering about LinkedIn's value for those happily employed. There's no disputing that LinkedIn can be a big help if you're looking for work, but what if you have a good job and aren't really prospecting for something else? How can LinkedIn be of value to you? If you have anything to share on that score, especially personal accounts, I'd love to hear your thoughts and possibly include them in the book.

The answers? You'll find that wisdom spread throughout this book, particularly in Chapter 6. But this experience proved once again that for anyone who needs relevant, high-quality answers quickly, LinkedIn is the best tool since e-mail. If you're a reporter, market researcher, writer, product or brand manager, or just about anyone who has business-related questions, LinkedIn is a gold mine. Where else could you so quickly get input from such high-caliber worldwide experts? Not only that, the information they provide is free.

This chapter covers not only asking questions on LinkedIn but answering them, too. As you'll see, answering questions has its own rewards. For example, if you do it skillfully, you may impress someone in a position to help your career. But, whether you're on the asking or the answering end of a question, LinkedIn's Answers section is one of the most valuable parts of the site. As a matter of fact, it alone justifies the time and effort you'll put into using LinkedIn.

THAT 80/20 RULE

When you discover the ability to get timely, expert information from LinkedIn members, it's only natural to be like a kid with a great new toy and fire away whenever you have a question. But this is a community where karma counts, and for the community to really work, you must give as well as receive. This means that you should plan to answer questions and not just ask them. More than one LinkedIn expert advised that members abide by the 80/20 rule and answer four questions for every one asked. You may not have to be quite so exacting about it, actually keeping a score of each question asked and answered, but answering more questions than you ask is definitely the way to be a valued LinkedIn neighbor.

Looking for Work?

The Answers section is not the place to announce to the world that you're looking for a new job. If you do post such a question (for example, "I'm looking for a job in pharmaceutical sales. Can anyone help?"), you may well get flamed by more experienced LinkedIn members who resent that you posted your personal query so publicly. Or they can flag your question as inappropriate, and LinkedIn may well remove your question. Ooops!

As you saw in Chapter 4, you'll have much greater success job hunting by clicking on the "Find Jobs" link and searching from there. Now, once you have a job, take full advantage of the Answers section to show your boss how smart she was for hiring you. "LinkedIn is a site that your boss doesn't mind you being on," said Krista Canfield. With the first-rate information and advice available through the "Answers" link, you'll quickly agree.

THE "ANSWERS" LINK

Okay, it's time to open the lid to that treasure chest. Simply roll over the "More" link at the top of any LinkedIn page. The first link you'll see on the dropdown menu is "Answers." Click on that, and you'll see the screen shown in Figure 5-1. As you can see, the options across the top of the page are

Answers Home. Here, you'll find some current questions from your network up for consideration. You'll also be able to see the degree of separation between you and the questioner.

Advanced Answers Search. From here, you can search the huge database of questions and answers already posed on LinkedIn to see what may be of use to you. You'll find a wealth of information here with no need to reinvent the wheel. You can choose whether you want to view just open questions or all questions, including those that are closed to new responses. By default, your results are sorted by date, with the newest first. You also can sort by how many degrees away from you the questioner is or by relevance. Finally, you can refine your search by category or keyword.

My Q+A. This is your personal repository of the questions that you've asked and answered. Having complete and concise access to this information here is valuable because it allows you to easily keep it well organized for retrieval when you need it.

Ask a Question. This takes you to the form you use to craft a question and designate who will receive it.

Answer Questions. Click this tab to go to the pages that list open questions you can answer. The questions are presented in order of how many degrees the poster is away from you. You also can sort them by date.

You may be wondering why people would go to the trouble of answering questions from complete strangers. Some LinkedIn members answer hundreds of questions a week! Part of the motivation to do this rests in the

Home   Profile   Contacts   Groups   Jobs   Inbox **6**   Companies   News   More   **Answers ▾**

Answers Home   Advanced Answers Search   My Q&A   Ask a Question   Answer Questions

Ask a Question

Thousands of professionals are available to give you an answer.

[Next]

Answer Questions

Recommended categories for you:

- Job Search
- Freelancing and Contracting
- Writing and Editing
- Staffing and Recruiting
- Education and Schools

New Questions From Your Network

?   • **"It's not what you make but what you keep!" -- looking for real life examples and similar quotes?**

14 answers | Asked by Steven Burda, MBA (1st) | 1 day ago in Wealth Management, Personal Debt Management

?   **When working and concentrating really hard at work, and you're creativity is interrupted, do you welcome the break or feel very irritated?**

1 answer | Asked by Chris Barton (2nd) | 24 minutes ago in Work-life Balance

?   **Why is there not a single European or Japanese brand in the Interbrand Best Global Brands Top 10**

2 answers | Asked by Dr Vikram Venkateswaran (2nd) | 1 hour ago in Branding

?   **Is there anyone who experienced logistics supplier's M&As?**

0 answers | Asked by Junichi Kato (2nd) | 1 hour ago in Supply Chain Management

?   **What is fundamentally wrong with Europe? Is it the demographic shift or a shifting of**

Figure 5-1: Your choices in the Answers area of LinkedIn are displayed along the top of the "Answers Home" tab.

philosophy behind LinkedIn, the idea that you have to give more than you receive. "The more you give, the more that comes back to you in different ways," said Gary Unger, author, public speaker, and advertising consultant. "Normally, consultants would hesitate to give too much information away, but I always give advice," he added.

Another, perhaps less altruistic reason to answer questions is, in a word, exposure. Each time you answer a question on LinkedIn, you get the chance to display what you know in an area that may be aligned with your livelihood. Right next to your answers will appear your name, title, and hyperlinks to other answers you've provided. Your name actually is a hyperlink to your LinkedIn profile. So don't be reluctant to post questions. People are glad to answer them. It's good for you, and it's also good for them.

Susan Shwartz, Ph.D., Is Available to Answer Your Questions

Susan Shwartz is very generous with her time and energy in the Answers section of LinkedIn. She was equally generous with our request to help us understand the best ways to approach asking and answering questions and in explaining her motivation for doing so. She has a doctorate degree in English from Harvard and a long list of books and stories published. In addition, she's currently working as a financial writer on Wall Street. Despite all these tasks that lay before her, she was kind enough to help us explain how newcomers can get started on LinkedIn. We'll share with you our questions and her answers:

Why do you choose to answer so many questions on LinkedIn? For you, what's the payoff, considering the time you put into it?

I have been on the Internet for more than 20 years, starting with the bulletin boards and Usenet. I enjoy the ongoing conversations of online communities. On LinkedIn, the questions are fascinating because they come from people who are well advanced in careers in so many different areas and geographies. I've got a lot of curiosity, and I love participating.

How do you recommend those who are new to answering questions proceed? Any advice to share?

First, I think they should complete their profiles to whatever extent is possible. Many of us check profiles before answering a question or after reading an answer to understand how a person's background and experience have informed what they've written. Newcomers really do want to create a context that gives them credibility. Then I think they ought to read some questions and answers, perhaps check out the profiles of people who have a lot of expertise points, and then answer their first questions in fields of which they're very sure. I wouldn't start by being flippant. You can get away with more once you're online "friends" with people.

In actual fact, I organized my profile first, saw the questions, realized that they were really interesting, and jumped right in. The "scream and leap" approach has its drawbacks, but it's a lot of fun.

How have you been able to leverage your LinkedIn status as someone with so much earned expertise? Do people tend to contact you more as a result?

More people do tend to contact me as a result. I find this very satisfying. What, frankly, I find the best of all is the custom on LinkedIn that you reply, at least to say thank you, to everyone who answers a question that you've put up. I've made some of my best connections through those dialogues because I go back, check their profiles, and realize that there are synergies between the two of us. Then, usually, one or the other of us will ask to connect.

GOT A QUESTION? GLAD YOU ASKED!

First off, LinkedIn recommends that you ask questions that call for one of three things: knowledge, experience, or opinion. That said, click on "Answers" from the "More" link, and you'll see the "Ask a Question" box. You then can use that form (shown in Figure 5-2) to craft your question. The first box you fill in will become your question's headline and is the most important one you'll complete. Once you have filled in the headline, you would click "Next" at the bottom of the box. On the next page, you will have the option of adding details. These details are important. In fact, those details and the way you phrase them have a lot to do with the quantity and quality of the answers you will receive. Provide the information and details needed for people to really understand your question and be enticed to answer it. Next, categorize your question by clicking on the category that best describes it.

There are more than 20 categories of questions, including several quite relevant to job hunters (shown in Table 5-1). Once you select a category, you may be shown a number of subcategories to further refine your question's topic. For example, if you were to select Career and Education, the following subcategories appear in the next box: Certification and Licenses,

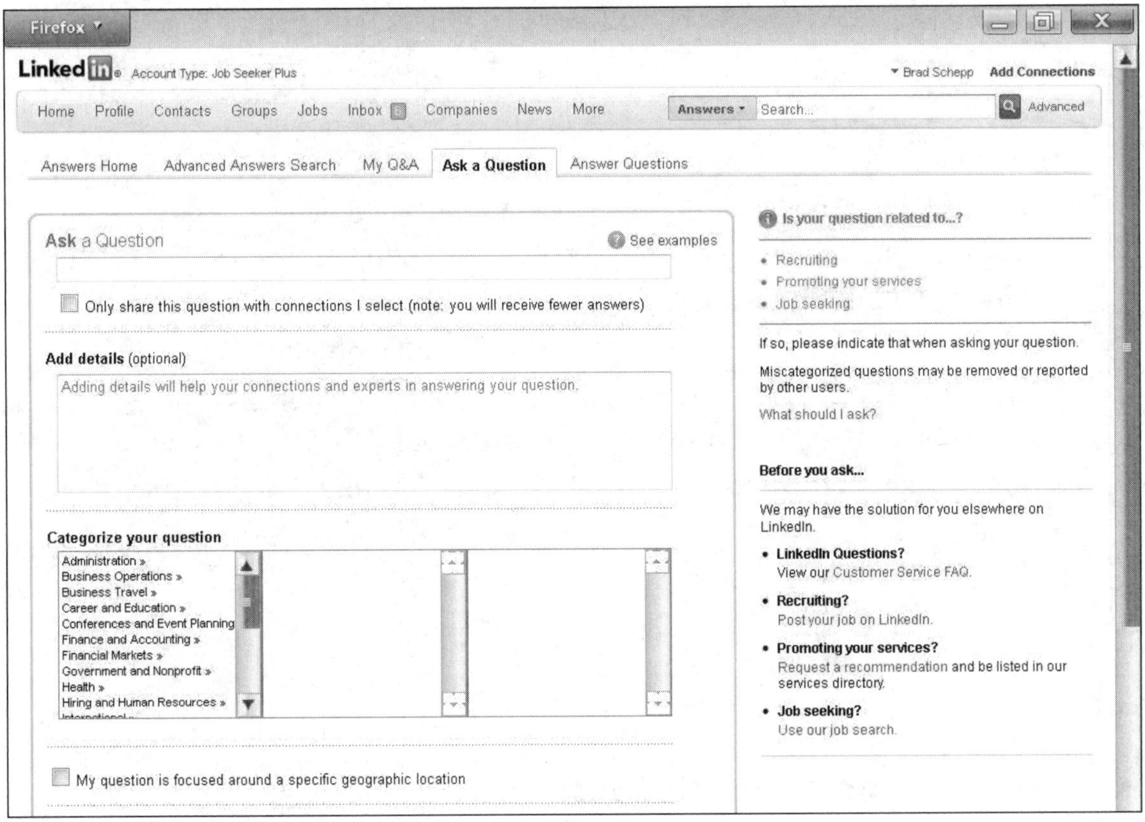

Figure 5-2: The form you'll use to pose your questions on LinkedIn.

Education and Schools, Freelancing and Contracting, Job Search, Mentoring, Occupational Training, and Résumé Writing.

Once you post a question, it remains open for seven days; then it closes, meaning that you will no longer receive responses. You can close it yourself sooner than that if you find that your question is answered sufficiently or it's apparent that LinkedIn's members aren't going to help you with your dilemma of the moment. After that seven-day period, you can reopen a question if you'd like. Just click on the "Answers" hyperlink, and then click the "My Q&A" link. The questions you have asked will be hyperlinked. Click on the one you want to reopen, and then click "Reopen this question to answers."

Table 5-1 Categories of Questions

Question Categories

- Administration
- Business Operations
- Business Travel
- Career and Education
- Conferences and Event Planning
- Finance and Accounting
- Financial Markets
- Government and Nonprofit
- Health
- Hiring and Human Resources
- International
- Law and Legal
- Management
- Marketing and Sales
- Nonprofit
- Personal Finance
- Product Management
- Professional Development
- Startups and Small Businesses
- Sustainability
- Technology
- Using LinkedIn

Use Advanced Search First

Before asking your question, it makes sense to search the Answers section to see if similar questions have been asked before, how they were answered, and when. The information you need may already be there. However, if the question hasn't been asked for a while, or if you are seeking other information, go ahead and ask the question again. No one will mind.

Further, you can use the Advanced Search feature to keep up to date with your own particular industry. "Use advanced answers search to see what's going on in your area of interest," said Krista Canfield. "It helps you to keep current. Questions pop up with relevance sorting. The numbers can tell you what's hot in that particular field," she added.

Examples of Good Questions

All kinds of questions are posted on LinkedIn, and you'll see that some can get 50 or more responses, whereas some only get one or two. Why the variation? There are many reasons. One may be just how provocative and timely the question happens to be. Another may reflect the effort the questioner took in crafting the question.

Let's start with the obvious. If it's apparent that you just fired off a question without giving it much forethought, rambling on perhaps, you've made the task more difficult for the experts who may consider answering your question. Frame your question concisely. Make sure that you've actually asked a question and not just stated something that you want people to respond to. Remember, you have the ear now of a brain trust that's 135 million strong, so don't waste your opportunity. Besides, people who ask good questions are viewed in a positive light among the LinkedIn community. Of course, be sure that your question is free of grammatical or typographic mistakes. This shows that you took the time to think and proofread your question. If you don't show this level of interest in your question, why would others be interested in spending their time creating an answer? Finally, if you're at all unsure of how best to proceed, review questions that have been asked before to see which of those received a lot of on-target responses. Once again, this will take you back to the Advanced Search function.

Here are some examples of actual questions that produced a lot of good answers. You'll see that they're all in the form of a question, they invite discussion, and they're challenging to people with the expertise to answer them. No one had to try to figure out just what these people were asking. With so many questions posted, you can't afford to make the expert's job too difficult.

- What constitutes professional status updates?
- How would you advise the incoming U.S. president to use YouTube?
- What is dragging the growth of environment-friendly solar energy in the United States?

Just for fun, here are some examples of questions that produced many responses, even though they may not seem as buttoned down as the preceding examples:

- Mind teaching me something new today? (193 answers)
- Do thoughts produce reality? (78 answers)
- What is the funniest word you know? (35 answers)

There Really Is Such a Thing as a Bad Question

It's only fair that we also provide examples of bad questions. These are courtesy of LinkedIn:

- Data about consumers contacting magazines and big company customer service departments.

- What is a home equity line of credit (HELOC), where can I get it, and what are the advantages and disadvantages?

- What are the three best companies?

Why I Answer Questions on LinkedIn

Joshua C. Chernin, director of operations for Boston's Web Industries, Inc., has answered dozens of LinkedIn questions, having achieved expertise in more than 20 areas! (You achieve an expertise point when the person who asked the question selects your answer as the "best" answer.) We asked Joshua why he spends so much of his valuable time helping people on LinkedIn. In answering our question, he once again proved how generous he is in sharing his time and expertise:

I am first and foremost just fascinated with the possibilities that the Internet and sites such as LinkedIn present to all of us. How else could one ask a question and get informed, diverse answers from 135 million people all over the world—in hours? How cool is that? I just love to be a tiny part of this process.

Second, I learn a tremendous amount from the Q&A on LinkedIn. I have wide interests, and there are some great Q&As on a kaleidoscope of issues on LinkedIn. Often, with a question that I'm interested in but don't have the expertise to answer, I just read.

Third, I like to contribute. I really believe in the "pay-it-forward" concept. I have seen it in action too many times to mention. I especially like to answer questions from people who are truly trying to figure something out and are genuinely asking for help ("I need help rewriting my résumé" or "I need help figuring out how to manage a project") rather than the opinion-type questions ("What do you think of the budget deficit?"), although I also answer the interesting ones of this genre too. I skip the weird ones and the ones that are just advertising fronts, although on the latter, I'm not beyond flagging them either. I believe that the users have to take responsibility for maintaining the integrity and the purpose of the site.

I try to contribute something new. I don't repeat what others have said, and if someone has already offered the answer that I would have added, I skip it. Sometimes I'll amplify an answer already given or reference it in my answer to give credit, and once in a while, just to be provocative and stir the pot, I'll play devil's advocate. It's fun! I try to keep my answers short, punchy, and concise—a couple paragraphs. I think that is more useful, and brevity of writing breeds focus of mind.

Determining Who Sees Your Question

You can either share your question with the entire LinkedIn network or specify that only members of your network will see it (up to 200 members) or both. After you've created your question, you'll see that below the text box you can check a box that says "Only share this question with connections I select." Questions open to everyone are deemed *public*; those only intended for your network are termed *private*.

We've tried posting questions both ways—allowing them to be visible to everyone and specifying that they go only to our direct connections. We've found that if your network of direct connections is large enough and chosen carefully enough, there are advantages to sending a question just to your network. You may receive answers sooner because the question is directly e-mailed to your connections. Also, because your network members know you, they may do a more complete job of answering and even tailor the answer to you. They have a connection to you beyond the overall LinkedIn community and are motivated even more to help you out.

Most often you will want to open your questions up to everyone. After all, you don't know who among LinkedIn's 135 million members may have just the information you need. Despite your best efforts to create an A+ network, it's likely that there are many people who are outside your direct connections with something of value to share. Give them the chance to do so.

Hiding Embarrassing Questions

Okay, confession time—it's good for the soul. The first question that one of your authors (no names, but this one takes out the trash and shovels the snow) ever posed on LinkedIn was a request for job leads. It was definitely a LinkedIn faux pas. Happily, if you also make a mistake, your mistake does not have to glow in cyberspace forever. We learned from that early experience that LinkedIn allows you to "hide" a question. To do this, you must first close it. Then, from the "My Q&A" tab, choose the question you want to hide. Once you are actually on the screen that shows you the question, you'll find a hyperlink box on the left that includes the option to "Completely Hide Question." Of course, then you may want to resist the urge to write a book with your wife, who will happily reveal your little social slip to everyone!

How Job Seekers Can Use the Answers Section

While it's against LinkedIn protocol to ask for job leads outright, there's no reason why you can't use the Answers section to get advice about conducting your search. As we mentioned earlier, the Career and Education category includes many subcategories of questions that would interest job seekers. Here are some examples of excellent actual questions posted in the Career and Education category that would provide food for thought for many job seekers:

- I'm a graduating MBA student. How can I get recruiters from major brands to notice me? (24 answers)

- What is the best business advice you have ever received? (187 answers)

- What should I include in an "elevator pitch" about myself? (9 answers)

- Is it worth it to have your résumé professionally written? (24 answers)

Of course, another way job seekers can use the Answers area is to increase their visibility and skillfully advertise their availability. A LinkedIn member asked the following question: *Do you "actively participate" in LinkedIn Groups? Why or why not?*

Trenton Willson was one of the members who responded. He was job hunting at the time, and we thought he made good use of the Answers section to demonstrate his expertise as well as promote himself to his network (see Figure 5-3). Notice that Trenton not only answered the question well, he also went the extra mile and suggested helpful articles (from his own blog, thus further promoting himself) and LinkedIn experts who he thought would have something of value to say on the topic. Someone in the market for an employee with his skills might well take a look at his profile because his response was so helpful. After all, we did. "Questions and group discussions

Trenton Willson (2nd)
JOB SEEKER/ACCOUNTANT
/INNOVATOR
see all my answers

⭐ Best Answers in:
Using LinkedIn (2)... see more

I find **groups** to be one of the best ways to project your brand as well as your expertise. If you can get a good discussion going **in** a group, you become known **in** the group as a subject matter expert. Your answers to other discussions can do the same. You become a thought leader.

The **groups** I am part of but don't **participate actively** are there for resource if I have time, but mainly they project my interests and create a brand statement to others looking at my profile. I value every group I am part of.

I have added a couple blogs I have written that express better my thoughts on branding and being a thought leader.

Links:
http://trentonpipelinedevco.blogspot.com/2011/06/ancestor-of-every-action-i...
http://trentonpipelinedevco.blogspot.com/2011/06/moab-swoosh-and-boilers-wh...

Trenton Willson also suggests these experts on this topic:
• Jason Alba
• Jennifer Armitstead

posted 1 month ago | Report answer as...

Kenneth Larson
Retired Aerospace Contracts Manager,
MicroMentor Volunteer and Founder
"Smalltofeds"
see all my answers

⭐ Best Answers in:
Small Business (42)... see more

I belong to no **groups** here, finding them boring, non-productive and too focused on limited objectives. It is preferable for me to take the larger, longer view from the main menu.

posted 1 month ago | Report answer as...

Lisa Nofzinger
Temporary Telephone Operator
see all my answers

⭐ Best Answers in:
Using LinkedIn (19)... see more

Yes, I do, but I'm only very active **in** 2 of them and less active **in** the others. I like my **groups** because we can have discussions based on a common profession or spirituality.

posted 1 month ago | Report answer as...

Figure 5-3: Trenton Willson's response to a question gave him favorable exposure on LinkedIn.

are great ways to share your expertise," Trenton told us. "My intention is to help people with real, meaningful answers from my book of experience. I try to be a thought leader and ask and answer meaningful questions."

Choosing Good/Best Answers

As a good member of the LinkedIn community, you'll want to rate the quality of the answers you receive. You should do this after you've received enough answers to give you the information you need or sufficient time has passed (say, a week). We like to reward any answer with a good rating as long as the person who answered it actually added something of value. And we always choose a "best" answer.

Does Posing a Question Result in Actionable Information?

We think LinkedIn's Answers feature is brilliant, but don't just take our word for it. Robin Wolaner, author and founder of the social networking company TeeBeeDee, checked the history of all the questions she had asked on LinkedIn for us. "Every one of them got helpful business answers for me in starting my company," she said. Here are some of the results she achieved from the questions she posted:

- *Can you write a better tagline?* (49 answers, in Writing and Editing)
- *Does anyone have a great employee handbook?* (11 answers, in Personnel Policies)
- *Do ComScore ratings generally overstate, understate, or roughly reflect companies' own logs of their web traffic?* (10 answers, in Web Development, Starting Up)
- *Do you know someone who can paint our logo on the interior wall of our new office? Cheap?* (6 answers, in Starting Up)
- *What is an ergonomic chair that is also affordable?* (12 answers, in Facilities Management)

ANSWERING QUESTIONS

The payoff you receive when you ask questions is apparent. Hopefully, the information you get in response will be useful to you whether you're looking for a new job or just trying to solve a task or research challenge for your current job. But, answering questions also has its rewards, as we've said. The two main ones are

- Every time you answer a question, your name and contact information appear next to it. Free advertising! The answers also become part of your profile.
- It feels good to help other people out. And answering questions on LinkedIn is a great way to share the knowledge you've accumulated.

Finding Questions to Answer

Once again, roll over the "More" link, and then click the "Answers" link. You'll then see the "Answer Questions" link. Click that, and first off you're shown the latest questions posed by people in your own network. It's more than likely that you'll be able to answer one or more of these questions because people in your network share your interests. Plus, since you know them, you're likely to understand more clearly the information that would be most useful to them. It's a great place to start.

By default, the questions are presented according to how many degrees away from you the person who asked the question is. You also can choose to sort the questions by the date they were posted. Also, to the right, there are open questions you can browse by category.

Now, while you're at it, please don't answer questions just for the sake of getting your name on the site. If you don't have anything of value to contribute, move on to another question. We've actually seen people respond, "That's a good question, but I don't know the answer." Hmmm, then why did they bother responding? Quite likely, just for the exposure, but the exposure in this case is not the kind of exposure you want. If you prowl the boards enough, these kinds of opportunists become known to you. You don't want to be one of them.

Gaining Expertise

If someone chooses your answer as a "best" answer, you have cause to celebrate. You will have earned "expertise" in the area of that question, and that fact will be displayed on your profile and on the form you use every time you answer a question in the future. You can see what this looks like in Figure 5-4. The ability to earn expertise and then have that displayed for the entire world to see is one of the things that makes LinkedIn so valuable to business professionals. The expertise serves as proof that someone else has found you knowledgeable in a given area, and this can't help but give your future answers and your profile as a whole more weight. If your profile notes that you have expertise in solar architecture, for example, your answers are going to carry more weight among people interested in green energy or even in other alternative-energy categories. From then on, when you reach out to a potential client on LinkedIn, you have more than your profile to attest to your expertise. You have put yourself ahead of the pack should someone be looking to hire an expert. Your answers demonstrate the knowledge your profile describes. So by all means, answer questions with an eye toward putting your best work out on the site.

Sahar Andrade, MB.BCh (1st)
Diversity&Inclusion| Leadership
Training| Social Media Marketing|
Employee Engagement|Public
Speaker|Cultural Competence
see all my answers

⭐ Best Answers in:
Using LinkedIn (719), Professional
Networking (19), Business Development
(17), Event Marketing and Promotions (13),
Career Management (13), Staffing and
Recruiting (10), Internet Marketing (10),
Job Search (9), Communication and Public
Speaking (9), Public Relations (8),
Organizational Development (8),
Advertising (7), Ethics (7), Small Business
(7), Starting Up (6), Hotels (5), Mentoring
(5), Blogging (5), Business Dining and
Entertainment (4), Travel Tools (4), Writing
and Editing (4), Wireless (4), Education
and Schools (3), Exporting/Importing (3),
Events Marketing (3), Viral Marketing (3),
Sales Techniques (3), Search Marketing
(3), Planning (3), Professional Books and
Resources (3), Computer Networking (3),
Air Travel (2), Freelancing and Contracting
(2), Occupational Training (2), Conference

Figure 5-4: The LinkedIn proof of your expertise that will follow you on the site.

Business development and marketing professional John S. Rajeski is a
LinkedIn Q&A guru. He has earned expertise in 44 areas, including Business
Plans, Professional Networking, Internet Marketing, and Green Business.
Here are three simple rules he's shared to help you make a great impression
on this part of the site:

Be brief in your reply.

Be as specific as possible regarding whatever information you're posting.

Be sincere and have a genuine interest in assisting others. Towards that end,
I subscribe to the "pay it forward" model regarding networking.

Wallace Jackson: A LinkedIn Answers Expert

Wallace "Walls" Jackson is the number two all-time question answerer on LinkedIn. He's answered more 34,000 questions! (Figure 5-5 shows the top LinkedIn experts.) He also has achieved more than 100 "best" answers in dozens of categories. We didn't think Walls would mind if we asked him just one more: "How do you find the time to answer so many questions?" (By his own estimate, he answers three to four an hour—*every* day.)

Walls blends answering questions with the other work he does. He is a multimedia producer and i3D programmer operating his own business, MindTaffy Design. As a programmer, he does a lot of "compiling and rendering." Basically, this involves "setting everything up and then having the computer do what computers do," he explained. So Walls has downtime while he waits for the computer, and one way he makes use of it is by answering questions on LinkedIn.

He has 10 windows open on his desk at any one time, so he's ready to jump on a question at a moment's notice. He also keeps his answers very concise, condensing his response down to a line, sometimes a single word. "Many people appreciate not having to wade through a lot of verbiage, so I get my share of thanks," he said.

But all this work isn't just for sport. Answering so many questions, and doing it so well, explains how Walls now ranks as LinkedIn's number two expert, and that's number two out of more than 135 million. "It's like having a degree from Harvard. People assume because I'm LinkedIn's number two expert that I can deliver," he said. To prove his credentials, Walls shares this link with people: http://tinyurl.com/6kvws6c (which is Figure 5-5). Of course, this not only proves his mettle, but it also gives curious newcomers a direct link to his profile.

Not surprisingly, answering all these questions has brought Walls a lot of opportunity and solid work. His company produces storybooks, hip hop albums, e-books, and cutting-edge websites. His clients have included familiar names such Samsung and Sony. People from Oracle found him on LinkedIn when they searched for experts in the JavaFX programming language. "They told me I was coming up 'number one on all their searches for JavaFX,'" he said

"In a down economy, LinkedIn has saved me," said Walls. While some bigger companies are watching and waiting for a better economic climate, Walls uses LinkedIn to attract business from smaller companies. Keeping this

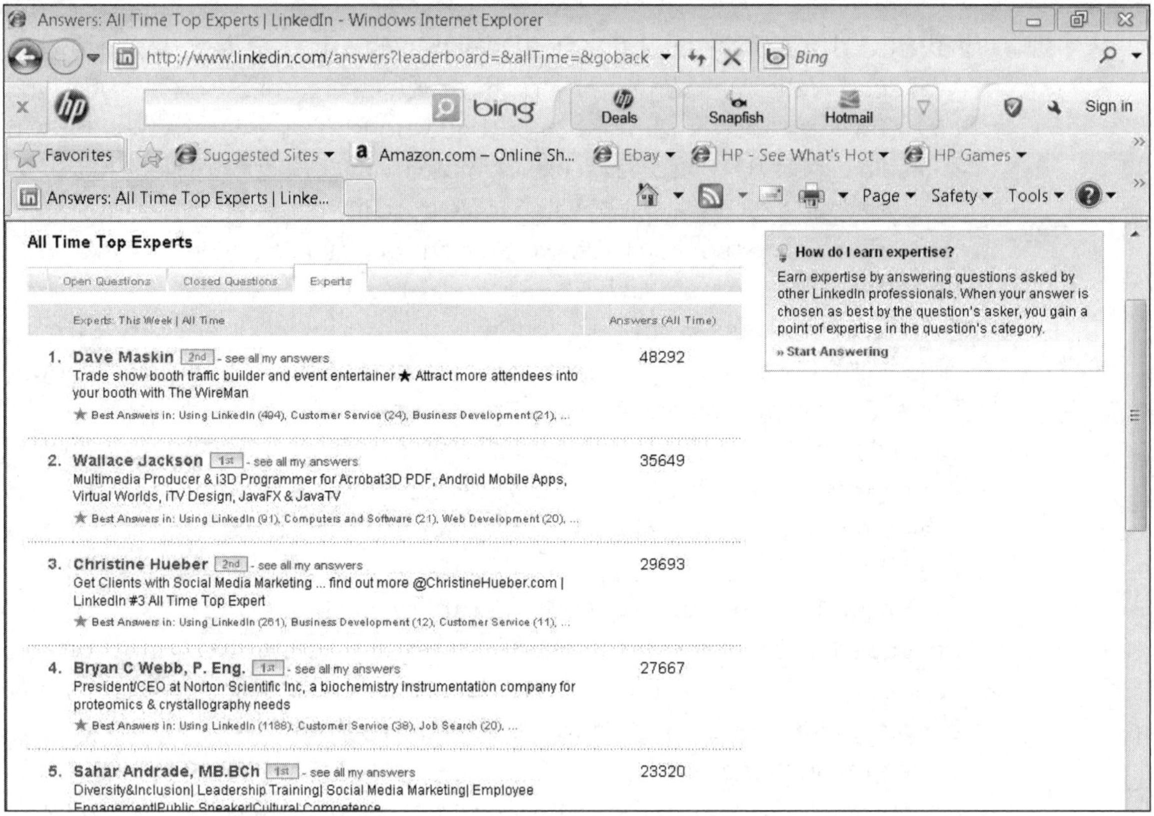

Figure 5-5: LinkedIn's top experts, based on number of answers provided.

steady workflow also helps him to build and protect his brand. His company, MindTaffy Design, stands out each time he earns expertise points. He calls what he does "positioning." Walls works hard to stand out among key people by proving what he knows and demonstrating the expertise that makes him unique.

He's putting himself out there and "getting in good" with people he hopes to work with later, when the economy turns around. It's not about short-term client stuff—it's about long-term business building. So, at the same time that he's cultivating smaller clients, he is also planting seeds within his industry that he expects will blossom when the economy improves and everyone is looking to expand.

RSS Feeds Your Brain

If there are categories of answers that you find yourself checking regularly, set up an RSS feed. As we discussed in Chapter 3, RSS most commonly refers to Really Simple Syndication, and once you set up an RSS feed, information is sent to you automatically, without your having to do anything to retrieve it. In the case of the Answers area, you can set up a feed to new questions in your category of interest.

To set up an RSS feed for Answers, follow these steps:

Go to your LinkedIn homepage.

Scroll down to the All Updates section.

Roll over to the "More" hyperlink, and you'll see the "RSS" hyperlink in the dropdown menu box that appears. Click on it

On the right side of the page that appears next, choose an Answers category.

Click on the RSS reader of your choice, or click on the "RSS" icon.

Now you'll receive a steady stream of new questions to answer, which will make it that much easier to help your fellow LinkedIn members and establish your expertise.

Stephen Weinstein: From LinkedIn to the National Theatre of London

Marketing communications guru Stephen Weinstein not only landed his latest job through LinkedIn, but he also was able to arrange an internship for his daughter at the National Theatre of London. Stephen uses LinkedIn's Answers section a lot, posting and answering dozens of questions. His questions range from business-related queries to more philosophical ones. He posts these questions not just for himself but also for other people. On behalf of a podiatrist friend, for example, he asked whether a referring physician was due a commission for referring a patient to another doctor. He got 36 replies!

Stephen Weinstein has become an expert at answering LinkedIn questions and more, too.

When Stephen receives a helpful response, he reaches out to the person who answered, inviting him or her to be a part of his network. On one occasion, he connected with someone who had a connection at the National Theatre of London. He asked his new connection if she would send an Introduction for him, and the rest is LinkedIn magic. Once Stephen was connected to that person, he mentioned his daughter, a student at Carnegie Mellon, and her need for an internship. His newfound contact encouraged him to have his daughter get in touch. From there, she landed her internship at the National Theatre of London!

I GOT A JOB ON LINKEDIN

 Sharon Delay: Career/Business Coach

Sharon DeLay is a small-business owner who, like many people in her position, must balance generating revenue (actually doing work for a client) with marketing her business.

> I find LinkedIn to be a critical tool to marketing my business, Boldy Go Coaching, and reaching new customers. As a matter of fact, it has been so successful for me that I actually teach other small-business owners how to use the tool to do just that (I started just teaching my career clients how to use it to find a job). I spent 20 minutes on LinkedIn one day answering questions and ended up getting two clients from that, which could be calculated at an approximate 500 percent return on investment. Granted, my price points are lower than something like a GE giant, but for just me, it's a great motivator and example.

 Sahar Andrade: Founder of Sahar Consulting, LLC

Sahar Andrade operates a consulting firm dedicated to diversity and global marketing. She started her business in 2010 with, as she told us, "a zero budget for advertising." She had begun building her business idea several years earlier, putting the structure in place that allowed her to launch. Here, in her own

Sahar Andrade used LinkedIn questions to build her business when advertising dollars were scarce.

words, is the story of how she built a thriving consulting firm by using LinkedIn.

I started using LinkedIn in 2007, but I really got involved with Questions and Answers late in 2008. I have used LinkedIn as a marketing and business-development tool. I answered as many questions as I could every day, bartering my time as soft dollars versus paying for advertising.

I was able to build a brand and increase visibility and credibility in what I do as well as create an awareness for my services and public speaking abilities. LinkedIn didn't fail me, and to date, it is still my best marketing tool.

Your challenge is the time it takes and to keep the quality you establish. I use LinkedIn any time of the day because I control my own time.

LOOKING AHEAD

Now you know how valuable LinkedIn's Answers section can be, whether you're looking for a new job or just trying to get insider, expert information relevant to the job you have. But there are many other ways LinkedIn can help you to shine at work or win that next promotion. Turn the page to Chapter 6, and you'll see the many different ways your life on LinkedIn can help you to increase your efficiency and performance, no matter what your job status.

CHAPTER 6

Using LinkedIn on the Job

"Linkedln seems to have a reputation of being somewhat of a job-hunting board," said digital marketing consultant Susan Emmens. "I can't recall a time I've ever used it that way. And yet, I'm on it at least an hour a day." Undoubtedly, LinkedIn is a fantastic resource for job hunters, but you may be surprised at how frequently you'll use it as an invaluable tool once you have a job. Even with high unemployment rates of 9 percent or higher, which is where they hover as we write this, the unemployment rate among those with bachelor's degrees or above is only 5 percent, according to the latest U.S. Bureau of Labor Statistics reports. And even though that number may not reflect the so-called discouraged and underemployed workers, it's fair to say that many of the people who use LinkedIn are currently employed.

In this chapter you'll learn some very creative answers to the question, How can LinkedIn help me with my job? We're happy to say that the site can be invaluable in making you more effective and productive with nearly any aspect of your job, and this holds true for nearly any kind of job you may have.

Here are some suggested ways for using LinkedIn at work, which we'll explore in detail in this chapter:

- Using LinkedIn to locate vendors
- Doing market research, including online focus groups
- Locating industry experts
- Tracking sales leads
- Supporting purchasing decisions
- Staying current with your industry
- Scouting for possible new hires
- Conducting reference checks
- Finding other recent hires once you've joined a company

Of course, exactly how useful LinkedIn is to you initially may vary with the industry you're in. Unquestionably, people in media, marketing, e-commerce, human resources and recruiting, high technology, consulting, and related fields are especially well represented on the site. But this doesn't mean that you won't find people from other industries there as well. All told, representatives from more than 150 industries are on LinkedIn.

BEHIND THE "COMPANIES" TAB

A good place to get a feel for how LinkedIn can help you at work is the Companies area that you've already learned so much about in support of a job search. As you know, this unique resource provides information on more than 2 million companies.

This is information that you simply will not find elsewhere. To create it, LinkedIn started with the companies that have the greatest number of employees. It spoke with representatives there to determine the information that would be useful for both LinkedIn users and the companies themselves.

We did a search for our publisher, McGraw-Hill, and found the page of information shown in Figure 6-1. This figure is from midway down the page, and it shows you McGraw-Hill's activity on LinkedIn at the time. This is great information for job applicants, of course, but it's also valuable to competitors seeking clues about where the company is putting its resources right now. Note that the people who show up there are present LinkedIn members only, and as a result, the information isn't complete. Not every recent hire, for example, appears there. The ones who are there appear because they noted on their LinkedIn profiles that they recently started

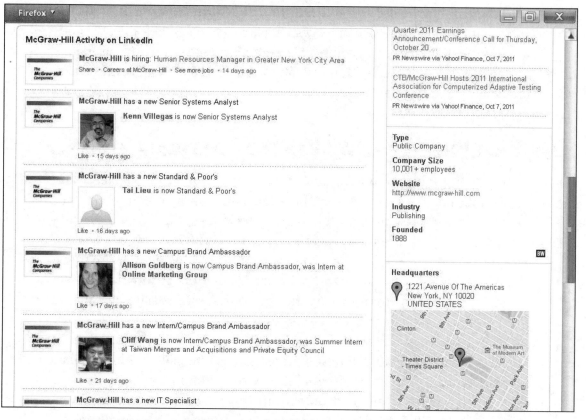

Figure 6-1: Information from McGraw-Hill's company profile, one of 2 million such profiles on LinkedIn.

working at McGraw-Hill. Other categories of employees are those recently promoted and those who have changed jobs within the company.

If you were to search for your own new employer, you could use the company's LinkedIn profile to see who else has been hired recently. This is especially helpful when you join a large company where new hires may be spread among a large population and lots of different departments. The information along the right-hand side of the profile is a blend of what's likely to be in similar directories (for example, related companies and details on the industry of which McGraw-Hill is a part) and insightful information that's unique to LinkedIn. As we've mentioned elsewhere, the Companies area includes information in two main sections. There is an "Overview" tab and a "Careers" tab. If you were to click on the "Careers" tab and then to the right click on the link that says "Check out insightful statistics about

McGraw-Hill employees," you'll find lots of information about McGraw-Hill's workforce, including employees who have changed their titles. There's also information about the company's annual growth. In many cases, this information is compared with information from "similar" companies based on industry and company size.

USE LINKEDIN TO LOCATE VENDORS AND EMPLOYEES

Now let's put the shoe on the other foot for a moment. In Chapter 4 and throughout this book you've seen how LinkedIn can help you to get your next job or work assignment. But you may be in a position yourself to hire someone using the site to prospect for talent. Recruiters know this all too well, but so do managers. "I've also seen people use it when they are trying to fill a position," said Jan Brandt, vice chair emeritus at America Online. "A recommendation from a friend or close business associate has always yielded great candidates for me," she said.

The same goes for vendors you're thinking of doing business with. While there are many directories of professionals that can be tremendously helpful, they also can be costly. And if they're not online, you can imagine how quickly they're outdated. For Scott Rogers, however, an executive with McGraw-Hill, "LinkedIn is, increasingly, a great way to find professional colleagues and/or look up the background of a potential business partner." Scott went on to note that the information on LinkedIn is often more detailed than what you're likely to find through other resources. "Typically, [other resources] provide only partial information, and you must be a paid subscriber to access information—making LinkedIn the better choice."

Megan Montplaisir is the director of social media for Nology, a Seattle-based social media strategy and content company. Megan handles a lot of the company's hiring and "loves LinkedIn for recruiting because it is the one social network where everyone has their business hat on." She added: "When people are using LinkedIn, they are looking for a change in life, and as an employer, you are getting potential candidates at the right time. You can check them out before scheduling an interview. It also allows the candidate to check out the company so that neither party is wasting time."

Wallace Jackson, who we profiled in Chapter 5, will conduct "talent searches" on LinkedIn in a hunt for contract production employees he can hire for projects he's working on. He uses Advanced Search to "data mine."

His search results yield many candidates, he says, because his network is so deep. "The bigger your network, the more connected you are."

Prospect for Sales Leads

Michael Jansma, owner of online jewelry retailer Egems, Inc., uses LinkedIn to make introductions or get introductions. "Say, for instance, I want to meet a buyer at Home Shopping Network," he explained to us. "I can visit their site, get his or her name, then put that name in LinkedIn, and most times, I know someone who knows that person. Then I can send my friend an e-mail saying, 'Hey, can you introduce me to so and so?' You can dig deeply into people's backgrounds to locate very specific resources—get in front of the decision makers who can aid you."

Jennifer Murphy, a salesperson for an employment screening service, also finds LinkedIn useful for digging up contacts and leads. "LinkedIn is a great tool for networking and for introductions to potential clients," she explained to us. "I do a lot of cold calling in my line of work, and often times I can at least get a name from LinkedIn as a starting point."

David Becker of the branding and packaging firm PhillipeBecker is a LinkedIn maestro when it comes to using the site for tracking down sales leads and conducting market research.

"I'd go into Advanced Search functionality and type in 'Gardenburger' (as a keyword) and see who has that on their résumé," David said. "We want to get in front of the marketers. We also want to be in front of brand managers and creative people. I could search for all brand managers of Stanley Tools, for example. That's very valuable information. There are services that provide this, but they're very expensive. You might have to spend $50 per name." This strategy may work even with very large companies. "Proctor & Gamble is a huge company with hundreds of brands," David said. "I could hire someone to find all the brand managers, but I can go to LinkedIn and do it for free. It's a huge time and money saver."

David is also using LinkedIn to keep track of the product and brand managers he has worked with, no matter where their careers may take them. He uses status updates to keep track of his contacts as they move from one company to another. Once a contact moves to a new company, David has the opportunity to contact him and find out what his current needs may be. It's likely the contact will be in a similar job or even a more senior position. David estimates that half his contacts have changed jobs within the last five years. He prefers to contact them because he is sensitive to the fact that they may find it unseemly to seek out his services for their new employer after working with him for their previous company. This may be a gray area in terms of noncompete clauses, for example. But, as soon as the contacts update their LinkedIn status, David is notified, and he can reach out to them. The result is likely a new project with a trusted client.

Wallace Jackson also plays the site like a maestro. To prospect, Walls will communicate with members of the many Groups to which he belongs. "Invariably, almost half the people I'm trying to connect with share a group with me," he says. Anything can spark a search. He may hear something on the radio, and then he'll be off and running, firing off keywords—say, "Quiznos and marketing" or "Quiznos and branding." He also will use LinkedIn to connect with the head people at ad agencies so that when they sign clients, they can keep him in mind. He finds LinkedIn so effective that he doesn't spend time on other social networks—just on LinkedIn.

If he wants to connect with someone and that someone is not in a group, he'll go see if she has asked any questions. If she has, and the question is still open, he'll furnish an answer. Once you answer someone's question, you can send them a private note at the same time. And so he connects in that way.

Aside from potential clients, Walls will connect with all kinds of people, knowing that their networks may lead to gold. "I'll connect with an orthopedic surgeon because I know that not everyone in his network will be an orthopedic surgeon," he said. "Maybe the vice president of branding for Quiznos is in his network." These people then become part of Walls' network.

Check Those References!

One of the greatest benefits of LinkedIn is that you can easily locate people who worked at a particular company at the same time your job candidate or potential business partner worked there. What an improvement this is from the old-school route you used to have to take to check someone's references. You no longer need to be satisfied calling a company's human resources department and getting just the most basic of facts. To locate potential references, from your home page, click Advanced to the right of the search box at the top of the page. On the page that appears next, you'll see four

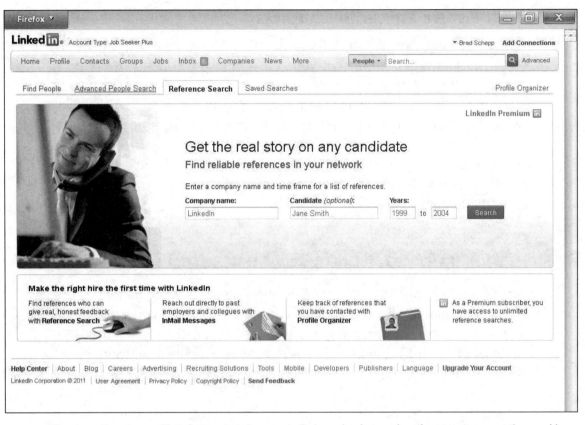

Figure 6-2: You can use this Reference Search screen to find people who may have known your prospective new hire or business partner from a previous company.

tabs right below the hyperlinks near the top of the page. Notice that "Reference Search" is one of those. Click on that, and you'll see the screen that appears in Figure 6-2. Enter your candidate's name, the company name, and then the years during which your candidate or potential business partner worked there. The next screen that appears will list the names of people in your network who also worked at that company sometime during the time span you specified. Viola! You now have the names of people you can contact for impressions of that person's work. Remember, though, while you're checking out vendors and potential new hires on LinkedIn, they may be doing the same for you! So, once again, keep that profile up to date and complete so that it's as positive a reflection of you as possible.

Your Future LinkedIn Contacts

Just a reminder: Never forget that LinkedIn is at least a two-way street. Once you join a new company, you should view your new coworkers as possible future references. Cultivate them. Get to know them. They may be your future LinkedIn contacts, and you may need them sooner than you think. The next time a prospective employer goes looking for the people who worked with you, you'll want them to find fellow employees who will speak well of you when they pop up in your reference search. Everything about your LinkedIn profile should be a real-time résumé that reflects your up-to-the-minute status.

ENTREPRENEURS EAT WELL ON LINKEDIN

No one works harder than the small-business owner. When you're the boss, this means that you do everything from prospecting for work to handling human resources to accounting to advertising and marketing, and this list could go on. At the same time, you also have to actually produce the work you're finding. LinkedIn is an entrepreneur's treasure trove of research and resources.

Through Answers, you can get current information about subjects ranging from accounting advice to vendor recommendations and everything in between. You can get up-to-the-minute recommendations for branding your business. We've already seen how LinkedIn can allow you to freely spread the word about your work and identify prospects and contacts. Now we'll look at some specific ways that LinkedIn enriches the lives of small-business owners.

John G. Herndon: Training the Next Generation of Venture-Capital Professionals

Every now and again we each meet that one teacher who opens our eyes to possibility in a way no one else has done previously. John Herndon, a lecturer in the Accounting and Finance Department at California State University, East Bay, is just such a teacher. In addition to his teaching position, John is also a consultant in accounting, finance, tax issues, and venture-capital generation. Rather than set out to teach his class in the usual lecture, reading, and testing

John G. Herndon used LinkedIn to help his students gain real-world experience in business development.

manner we all know so well, John structured a course for his graduate students that allowed them to have real-world experience. This experience also afforded fledgling companies the opportunity to explore sources of some cold, hard cash.

John used LinkedIn to identify local startup companies that might be interested in working with his students to prepare the materials necessary to approach venture capitalists and fund their businesses. He was careful to concretely detail the steps his students would take to help the companies selected.

Here is the message he posted to many groups on LinkedIn:

I am a prof of Acctg and Fin for undergrad & grad level & consultant in the field of Acctg & Fin. I am teaching a grad course in Jan 2011 & would like to send teams to help companies raise capital. Here is the goal and construct of the class and my objectives:

Concepts and practices of financing and financial management of a new venture or expansion of an existing growth business. Valuation, financial planning, corporate structuring, exit strategies, private placement, initial public offerings, venture capital, etc.

Objectives: Provide targeted experience for the students in assisting small to medium-sized companies with free help raising capital.

I intend to send teams with the intention of developing financial plans and/or strategies. I will oversee both the teams and the work product, having gone through the exercise myself. The companies will not incur any expenses and have the benefit of professional graduate educated finance/accounting professionals to help them meet their expansion goals.

The message resulted in John having 35 potential companies to offer his students. He whittled the list down to the nine firms the students actually would help. Of course, in the meantime, he'd taught his class what they'd need to know in order to attract investors for the companies. They learned how to write business plans, analyze markets and industries, and became familiar with the language CEOs and CFOs use to converse.

By the end of the class, one firm had secured $525,000 from an investor! All the students had gained real-world experience and will graduate with first-hand knowledge they can put into practice to either build their own companies or help other budding entrepreneurs.

Promote Yourself as a Freelancer or Consultant

It's the rare consultant or full-time freelancer who doesn't have her own website these days. The only challenge with a website is making sure that people can find it. Of course, you can give current contacts your web address, but what about people who are just prospecting for someone with your background and skills? Unless you become a search engine optimization (SEO) pro, prospective customers may or may not come across your site when using a search engine such as Google. However, if you have a LinkedIn profile, LinkedIn does the advertising for you and leads people, if not to your front door, then certainly to the neighborhood that includes you. Because you made your profile keyword-rich, that profile will attract clients and employers. Once they find you, there's no better way to showcase your work and therefore get more business than through LinkedIn. Including LinkedIn applications such as Portfolio Display makes demonstrating your skills and prior achievements even easier.

As freelancers ourselves, we use LinkedIn all the time, and not just because we're working on a book about it! Through our LinkedIn profiles, we can describe what we've done before and what we can offer new clients. But we also use LinkedIn to research prospective clients, to pose questions and answer them, and to stay on top of the publishing industry.

Boost Your Marketability

It's easy to get mired in your own little world when you work in an office by yourself most of the time, as many freelancers and consultants do. Try as you might to stay on top of trends, it's challenging, even with the Internet. In fact, the Internet can make your task seem more daunting because there's just so much information available through general websites, blogs, and social networking sites that the noise can drown out the music that's truly worth "listening" to. Once again, LinkedIn comes to the rescue. "I think it has given me tremendous insight into what clients need from consultants such as me," consultant Susan Emmens told us. "People like us are good at what we do, but how can we be great? What kinds of issues do people commonly run into when they try to find people who offer my services? It gives me great insight into habits or things I might take for granted that leave clients confused or uncomfortable in any realm."

For example, as a digital marketing consultant, Susan Emmens has learned that a lot of clients have questions about SEO. "SEO is a very technical and complicated field when you really get into it," she said, "and customers know they need it for rankings, but they didn't really get what they were paying for. SEO can get very pricey, but there seemed to be a lot of mystery around why and what exactly was being done to their website for that kind of cost." In addition, Susan has learned that it's not just clients who are misinformed about SEO. "On the flip side, I think a lot of consultants in this particular field take for granted that consumers 'get it.' When anyone would approach me about their SEO, I never did package prices because ultimately it was important that we had a conversation. They needed to understand what kind of time goes into things like keyword research, website page name changes, etc. I get the sense that most clients ask an SEO firm for help, get a complicated document about their recommended changes and a price, but they might as well be speaking Latin."

The Answers area, discussed fully in Chapter 5, is a great way to get a feel for what the hot buttons are in your field and what the current thinking is toward them. As you know, you can pick the brains of experts worldwide through the Answers area. It's quite common for those answering questions to post links to helpful articles as part of their responses. For example, we posed a question about Google + and its potential usefulness for job hunters. In responding, someone posted a link to a just-published article from *PC Magazine* that we had not yet uncovered. This sort of thing happens all the time on LinkedIn.

You also can stay abreast of what's going on through LinkedIn Today, discussed in Chapter 1. As mentioned there, through LinkedIn Today, you can track not only the hot stories being shared by LinkedIn members but also stories reflecting your areas of interest, as suggested by who makes up your network.

Here's another way to get market intelligence through LinkedIn. Go to your Groups area (the link is along the top of your homepage). Choose one of your Groups (you have signed up for some, right?), and click on the "Discussions" tab right under the Group name. Check out what people in your Groups are discussing. To keep things simple, you're shown the most popular discussions first. While there will be the usual Internet noise ("Wishing you a Happy New Year"), you also may find discussions about other companies in the industry, helpful software tools, and industry-rattling events. Also, you'll find members posting articles in the Discussion area. The articles are often very well targeted and presumably helpful to other Group members.

USING LINKEDIN'S APPLICATIONS ON THE JOB

We discussed LinkedIn's applications in Chapter 2. Many of these applications are especially useful to people on the job. For example, if you'd like to monitor Twitter for the latest tweets about your industry or your other professional interests, you should check out the Tweets application Once you install that application, you can access recent tweets from the people and companies you are following on that site. You even can send tweets, reply to tweets, and retweet right from your LinkedIn homepage. If you don't want your own tweets to appear on your LinkedIn profile, be sure to uncheck the box for that on the application signup page. Other applications you might want to use include Polls, where you can survey members of your network (no charge) and then share your results through LinkedIn's Twitter and Facebook integrations or even embed the module for voting right on your own blog or website. Projects and Teamspaces, Huddle Workspaces, and SlideShare are also good tools to use as a way to collaborate on projects and share information. Be sure to read LinkedIn's terms of use before adding these applications because the information collaborators provide can be displayed publicly.

But Don't Just Take Our Word for It!

We used LinkedIn's Answers to see exactly how real people were using the site on the job. As we've come to expect, the answers were quick and abundant. We've pulled some together to share with you so that you can clearly see what's possible for the happily employed on LinkedIn.

David, branding manager: "We also use LinkedIn to screen people and learn more about potential contacts. For example, if I meet someone at a business mixer, the first thing I'll do later on is look at their LinkedIn profile, and I imagine he's doing the same for me. As far as potential employees are concerned, if you're not on LinkedIn, you really are not in the job market."

Cara, senior acquisitions editor: "It is definitely useful to those happily employed. The articles keep us in the loop regarding other publishing companies, and professionals can share information, such as recommending agents. It is also helpful when publishers are actually looking for freelancers because freelancers often post when they are looking for work."

Dick, professor of broadcast sales and management: "LinkedIn allows me to stay connected to professionals in the field as well as poll folks outside the field on issues related to broadcasting, to get the lay person's viewpoint. I pose questions that elicit written responses. Things I've asked about are HD radio, Internet radio, indecency before the Supreme Court, and so on. Responses are insightful for sometimes realizing how little folks pay attention to these things. It kind of brings your feet back to the ground.

Susan, digital marketing executive and social media enthusiast: "I've found that a lot of value comes from the Answers section here. Frequently, people who are in the position of finding vendors and need recommendations, input, or what they should look for regarding certain services comes up. For example, am I overpaying on my SEO? My design firm is using an open-source checkout process; are there any pitfalls? Things like that."

Dennis, founder at KareerKit: "Sites like LinkedIn definitely help happily employed people, and if you aren't using these networking sites, you should be. Here are some benefits: (1) maintaining relationships with existing contacts in your field, (2) making new contacts in your line of work, (3) creating an online identity that brands your professional expertise, (4) keeping up to date on the latest developments in your field, and (5) having a dedicated forum from which to seek advice on challenging issues."

Jennifer, sales at a background investigation bureau: "LinkedIn is a great tool for networking and for introductions to potential clients. I do a lot of cold calling in my line of work, and often times I can at least get a name from LinkedIn as a starting point!"

Christopher, content strategist, network building: "I belong to a number of LinkedIn groups and find them useful on many levels. I get a feel for what others are doing in my field. I sometimes read about opportunities or alliances that can be created. I also post replies to group discussions to contribute something to the industry I'm in, but also to get the name of my company out there a bit. I've had more than a few connections and business relationships come from my participation in the groups."

Julie, marketing consultant: "I've been inspired by other people's questions and answers and have actually gotten ideas on how to do my job more proficiently. I've been exposed to ideas that I would have never thought of. It is also good to connect to people in your area and invite them to events such as workshops that we hold at my place of work."

Zachary, information technology (IT) technician: "Personally, I am using LinkedIn to learn about the IT field. I'm still in college and plan to start a career in computer networking once I get my degree. I use LinkedIn to meet other people who are already working in the IT field. By talking with these people, I can learn what my future job environment may be like, hiring and salary trends, what skills are most in demand, generally just what I can expect as an entry-level network technician. I've learned a lot about my future career from LinkedIn. For the time being, I'm a self-employed computer technician, so I'm not using LinkedIn to try to find work, but to learn about my future career and better prepare for it."

FREE VERSUS PREMIUM ACCOUNTS

LinkedIn refers to its standard free account as a Basic account. As we mentioned in Chapter 4, free accounts let you to do all the things we've described in this book, including build and maintain a profile, ask for recommendations, use the Answers area, perform company research, and take full advantage of the Groups area. You also can build a network, although you will require introductions through your first-degree contacts to reach out to those who are within their networks but outside your own. In Chapter 4 we also first brought up the subject of premium accounts, when we discussed the Job Seeker accounts available for from $15.95 per month.

Here we discuss the other types of premium accounts that are available. These accounts fall into two categories: accounts for business professionals, such as those in marketing, competitive analysis, brand management, and so on, and those who use LinkedIn for heavy-duty recruiting purposes, primarily so-called headhunters, executive recruiters, and human resources (HR) professionals.

It's time now to explore just what you get when you pay for these types of upgraded accounts and whether doing so may be worth it for you. If you're willing to pay for a premium account, then you will have the ability not only to receive but also to send InMails (the quantity will vary with the account), retrieve additional results for each network search that you do, and save more searches than you otherwise could so that you can repeat them easily. In addition, these accounts include tools that help you to organize profiles or your "candidate pipeline." You also will receive upgraded customer service. Premium accounts also include a feature called Profile Stats Pro, which provides deeper insights into how popular your profile is, showing you, for example, a complete list of those who have viewed your profile recently. These are people who have shown an interest in you, and it might well pay for you to check these people out. Profile Stats Pro, first mentioned in Chapter 4, also gives you stats on how many times you have appeared in search results and the top keywords people used to search for you, as well as the geographic locations of those viewers. Finally, you can track viewers by industry.

Figure 6-3 compares the three premium business accounts. These range in cost from $19.95 to $74.95 monthly, for those who make an annual commitment. Figure 6-4 compares premium accounts for those who use LinkedIn primarily for recruiting purposes. These accounts range from $39.95 per month to $399.95 per month, with annual subscriptions. These accounts enable recruiters to better pinpoint candidates for positions they are trying to fill. They help recruiters zero in on people who may not be actively looking for jobs, so-called passive candidates. Recruiters also can receive alerts for when new candidates matching your preset criteria have joined LinkedIn.

For recruiter Elizabeth Garzarelli, for example, such a paid account is worth the expense. "I have a paid membership because it allows me to contact people immediately and directly with InMails," Elizabeth told us. "Asking for and then waiting for an Introduction takes too much time in my line of work." She said that paid subscribers should be part of OpenLink, which allows them to receive an unlimited number of direct contacts from LinkedIn members. (You opt in for OpenLink by rolling over your name on your homepage, clicking the "Settings" hyperlink, and proceeding from there.)

We agree with Elizabeth, who feels that "for your average user, a free membership is quite sufficient." In fact, even those who use LinkedIn often to prospect for valuable sales leads and conduct market research may find that a free account is all they need. "I've found thousands of leads," said PhilippeBecker's David Becker. As you've seen, David uses his free account to track down prospects to approach, to keep up with his industry, and to

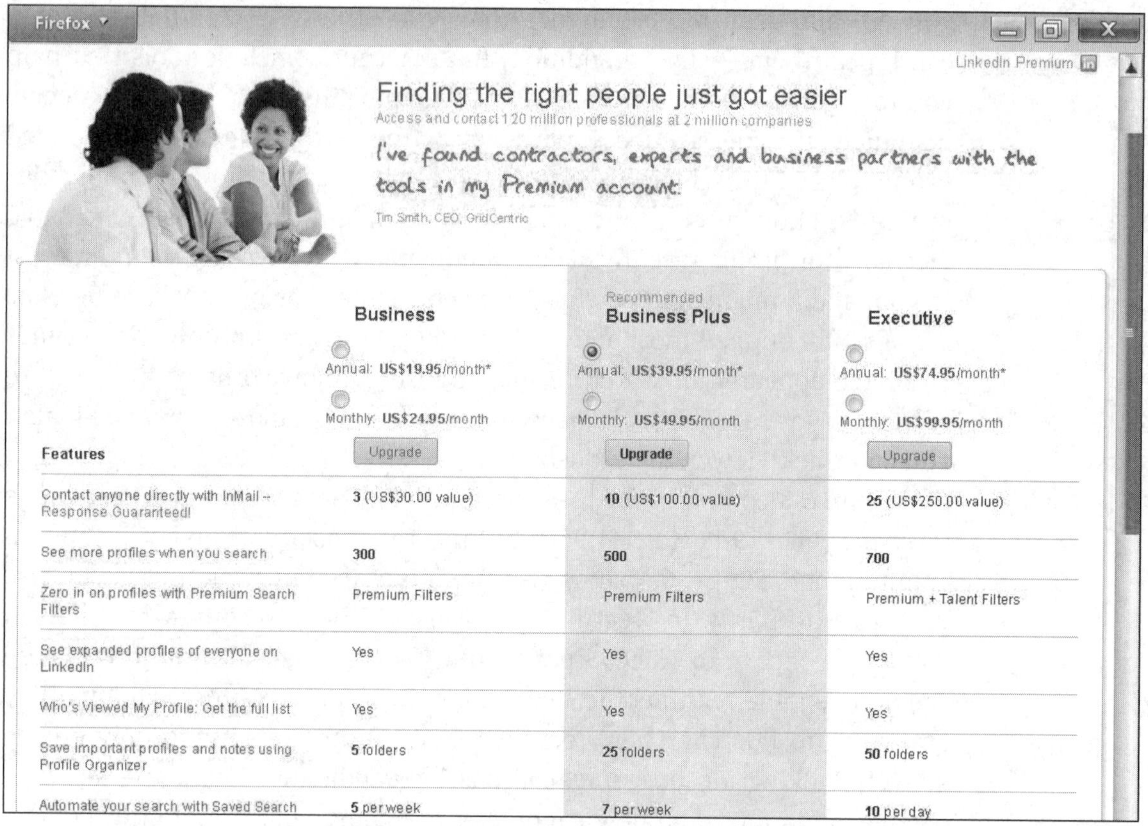

Features	Business	Recommended Business Plus	Executive
	Annual: US$19.95/month* Monthly: US$24.95/month Upgrade	Annual: US$39.95/month* Monthly: US$49.95/month Upgrade	Annual: US$74.95/month* Monthly: US$99.95/month Upgrade
Contact anyone directly with InMail -- Response Guaranteed!	3 (US$30.00 value)	10 (US$100.00 value)	25 (US$250.00 value)
See more profiles when you search	300	500	700
Zero in on profiles with Premium Search Filters	Premium Filters	Premium Filters	Premium + Talent Filters
See expanded profiles of everyone on LinkedIn	Yes	Yes	Yes
Who's Viewed My Profile: Get the full list	Yes	Yes	Yes
Save important profiles and notes using Profile Organizer	5 folders	25 folders	50 folders
Automate your search with Saved Search	5 per week	7 per week	10 per day

Figure 6-3: The types of premium LinkedIn accounts for business that are available and what each one offers.

conduct extensive market research. He even conducts online focus groups. To check further into premium accounts, click the "Upgrade Your Account" link at the bottom right of your homepage.

LOOKING AHEAD

You've seen now just how powerful LinkedIn is for finding job opportunities, sharing expertise, and building your personal brand. But LinkedIn isn't just for those of us who have been spending many years building careers. LinkedIn is a valuable resource for building a career path no matter how freshly minted that diploma may be. For example, young graduates just starting out can use the job histories of the long employed to plot their

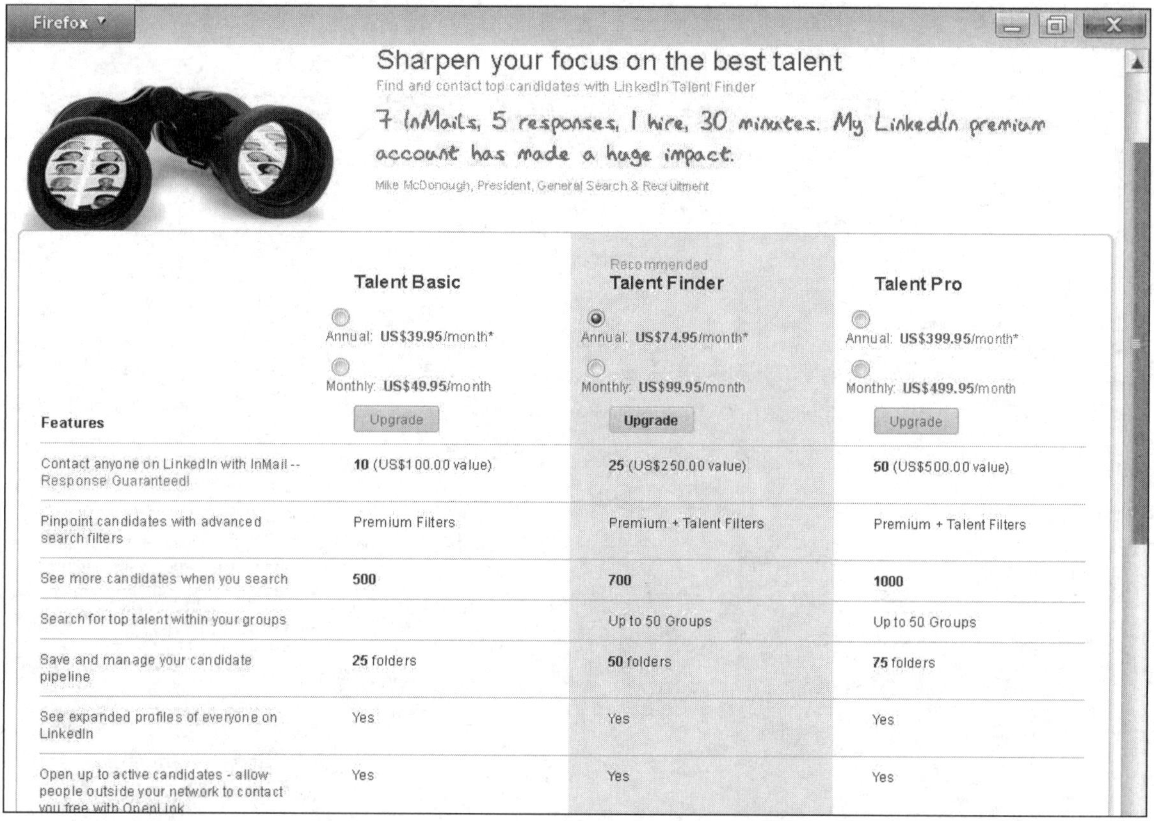

Figure 6-4: The various types of premium LinkedIn accounts available for recruiters and what each one offers.

own courses. Krista Canfield gave us some great advice to help those just starting out.

"Go to Advanced Search and search for your dream job title," she said. "Then you can see how the people who have that job got there." What were their educational backgrounds? Which companies gave them the biggest boost? Is there a pattern in terms of where these professionals started and how they progressed? You may not follow along the exact path, but at least, as a newly minted graduate, you'll have a roadmap of sorts to lead you in the right direction.

Turn the page and find an entire chapter devoted to those newly minted graduates. They're young, but they also have a facility with these tools that their elders have had to work hard to gain. In showing them some great job-hunting tricks, we might just learn a few more for ourselves.

CHAPTER 7

LinkedIn Makes the Grade for Students and New Grads

tarting out in your career in the worst economic climate since your great grandparents were working is a daunting prospect. As we write this, unemployment is at an all-time high for recent graduates. Every new headline makes Mom and Dad's sofa look like an inviting alternate lifestyle. We know that finding a job is going to be hard, but we've also learned that when times get tough, it's a good idea to take stock of your advantages. Graduates at the dawn of the twenty-first century's second decade have a huge advantage. You've grown up using social networking. You have an ingrained sense of power and comfort with these tools that older workers had to develop. Yes, your lack of work experience is a challenge, but you have considerable advantages, too. Let's take a look at the many ways you can put the power of LinkedIn and other networks to work for you as you get your career off to a solid start.

We feel very confident in taking you through the steps you'll follow. Before we were authors, we were college students together. We graduated at a time of terrible economic troubles with majors that weren't in great demand. We struggled, for sure, but we also found our way without the advantages of Internet access. Plus, in the last five years, we've personally watched four college students turn into fully employed adults. We know what you face, and we're here to say that you can feel positive about what's ahead of you. There is a place for each of you in the world of work!

YOUR PROFILE

Your LinkedIn profile will be a living, breathing reflection of who you've been as a student and who you hope to be as a professional. Here's your chance to put your best face forward. Yes, we know, you've had a Facebook profile for eons. You, no doubt, have a more robust Facebook profile than both of us combined. We'll talk about that in a bit, but LinkedIn is going to be different. Think of your profile as you would prepare for career day on campus when you know a representative from your dream company will be there, and you'll have just a few minutes to make a great impression. With this in mind, you'll know what to include and how to position yourself. LinkedIn was very generous in sharing with us some profile-building advice directed specifically to students. Plus, we've got some advice of our own to share.

TIP

Before we go any further, and as soon as you start to build your profile, claim your own unique URL. This is going to be www.linkedin.com/in/yourname. Also set your privacy settings to make your profile public. LinkedIn is really good at Search Engine Optimization (SEO), so your profile is likely to appear near the top when someone does a search for you. But your own URL definitely will help to ensure this. You also can include it as part of your e-mail signature. That alone proves your professionalism to prospective employers because they see straight out how seriously you take your budding career.

Your Photo

Okay, here's a throw-away: You know your LinkedIn profile needs a photo to be 100 percent complete, and you know better than to include one from last spring's trip to Cancun. No kidding, right? Choose instead a photo of you alone. If you have a head shot, that's great, but don't worry if you don't have one. Get an image of you in clothes appropriate for business, and make sure that it's clear and of good resolution, focusing mostly on your face. You don't have to wear a suit or display a briefcase. Just use an image that shows your friendly, self-confident, open personality. Don't settle until you've got one that says, "This looks like a nice and dependable person I'd like to work with." Remember, you're not just looking for a job; you're looking for a group of people to join, and those people want to bring on someone who looks bright, confident, and agreeable. In other words, they want someone who will "fit in."

Your Headline

It's difficult to feel confident when you stand on the brink of a new chapter in your life, but your headline is a great place to start showing that confidence, even if you don't quite feel it. LinkedIn advises that you think of your profile headline as the slogan for your professional brand, for example, "Student, national university" or "Recent honors graduate seeking marketing position." You'll find inspiration by searching for other graduates or alumni you admire to see how they've described themselves. If you've already read Chapter 4, you know that we don't encourage most LinkedIn members to overtly state "I'm looking for a job" as a headline. You are the exception. Everyone expects a recent or soon-to-be graduate to be job hunting, so you can feel confident in stating that as part of your headline.

Your Summary

Your summary statement should be concise but full of details about who you are and what you can do. Focus on your goals and qualifications. Be sure to include relevant internships, volunteer work, and extracurricular activities. These show you to be well rounded and enthusiastic about not only your education but also the rest of your life. If you speak another language, say so. Present this information in short bursts so that a visitor to your profile gets one pop of information about you after another. Don't hesitate to use bullet points if you think they will be a good way to highlight what you've done. Beginning with your summary, be sure to include keywords relevant to the field you'd like to be a part of. This is how you'll increase your chances of turning up in search results when employers and recruiters are looking for workers like you.

Katie Lorenz: An Attention-Getting Keyword-Rich Profile

Katie is the communications director for the American Lung Association in the organization's Chicago office. She is also a former Miss America contestant who went on to receive her MBA. Through her keyword-rich LinkedIn profile, she gained important exposure for both her career and her organization. Thanks to those keywords, a *Bloomberg* reporter found her on LinkedIn and asked to feature her in an article the magazine was preparing about beauty pageant contestants who also earned MBA degrees. Katie shared her experience and advice for other recent grads about using social networking sites to gain opportunities and get noticed. First, we asked her why the reporter looked for her on LinkedIn rather than turn to the Miss America organization to find people to interview.

Katie Lorenz's keyword-rich profile grabbed attention.

"I think it's faster and easier for a reporter to do a LinkedIn search," she explained. It's a more direct route to the exact person a reporter would like to contact. "Why go through a middleman when you can go directly to the source?"

Katie's coursework at Loyola Graduate School of Business often called on the students to use social media, and now her job with the American Lung Association includes updating the organization's Twitter and Facebook pages as part of her job description. "Social media is a great way for nonprofits to stay in touch with donors and event and program participants," she explained. She estimates that she updates these accounts weekly. "We also post job openings, volunteer opportunities, event and programming opportunities, and advocacy calls to action to keep our constituents updated on the latest news," she said. "We use LinkedIn for networking purposes and have groups to encourage our board members to get to know each other professionally. LinkedIn provides a natural 'ice breaker' that allows our volunteers to see who they know in common and how they can work together to support our cause," Katie explained.

When we asked her to advise other recent grads about using LinkedIn, she was quick with her recommendations. "Make it public! Unlike Facebook, it's to your advantage to have a public LinkedIn profile," she said. "Recruiters and HR managers use LinkedIn to find potential candidates; alums of various groups you're involved with provide volunteer, speaking, and networking opportunities; and the more people who know you're looking for work (especially as a recent grad), the greater your web to catch potential opportunities."

Finally, we couldn't resist asking her what it was like to be a contestant in the Miss America pageant. "It was a dream come true!" she replied. "I've wanted to compete for Miss America since I was seven years old, and this was one of the few childhood dreams I was able to pursue and achieve."

Your Education

Okay, here's your chance to shine. Our culture disdains braggers, but if what you're saying is true, it's not bragging—it's simply building your brand based on your strengths. Since your work experience is likely to be modest, make the most of the work you have been doing all these years. Include all the schools you've attended. Include your major and minor areas of study and brief statements about why you selected them. Don't forget to include study abroad experience, summer institutes, and internships. All these show your abilities outside the classroom as well as inside.

Profile Sections that Highlight Your Strengths

LinkedIn has added sections you can select to customize your profile. Some of these are especially useful for students. You'll find the link for selecting these sections just above your Summary. Click to open that new section menu (shown in Figure 7-1), and decide which sections will be best for you. Here are some examples:

• *Projects:* You couldn't have received your degree without having worked on special projects, whether those were your senior thesis or group efforts requiring teamwork. You may not think of that work as relevant to the working world, but your abilities to work as a team member, meet deadlines, and present the work you've completed to a group are all transferrable skills, so be sure to include them.

• *Honors & Awards:* Not every graduate made the dean's list semester after semester. We were not all honors graduates, and we did not all receive

Figure 7-1: LinkedIn's new options for sections you can add to beef up that profile!

awards recognizing our accomplishments. If you did, then you have not only subjective information about your abilities but also objective proof. Be sure to feature it!

- *Test scores:* If you did exceptionally well on standardized tests or you have a knockout grade point average (GPA), let prospective employers know about it. With your next career move, that information becomes less relevant, but with your first job, such quantitative information can make you stand out.

- *Courses:* If you consistently took upper-level classes, say so. Everyone works for that diploma, but if you spent your time at school taking the most challenging courses you could, then you've proven yourself to be a hard worker dedicated to getting the most of your opportunities. Employers will notice.

Your Work Experience

Just because you've been hitting the books doesn't mean that you don't have work experience worth mentioning. You may not think that your stint as a waiter or your time behind the counter of your campus coffee shop counts, but it does. Working while going to school takes dedication and drive. Your summer jobs gave you a set of skills you would not have had if you'd spent those months just hanging around with your friends. So sure, don't describe these jobs in throw-away terms, but consider what skills you gained from them, and include them in your profile.

Recommendations

You'll need three recommendations before your profile is considered complete. Of course, your faculty adviser would be a strong candidate, but many students leave school with a close bond with special professors. Don't forget any supervisors you worked for at jobs or internships. Even colleagues who worked with you on projects can add a dimension to your recommendation list. Just be careful not to make it obvious that you made a deal with someone to write a recommendation for you if you'd do the same for them. Such a quid pro quo arrangement is apparent to steely-eyed LinkedIn recruiters who have seen it all.

Profile Details

Your LinkedIn profile isn't the same as your résumé. It gives you the opportunity to show how you're constantly gaining experience and expertise in ways something as static as a résumé can't even approach. Here, you'll find some details you may want to add to keep your profile current.

LinkedIn Applications

You'll find a robust offering of applications you can add to your profile to make it more interesting. For example, Reading List by Amazon will allow you to review books you've read. Keeping these on a professional level is great, but don't hesitate to sprinkle in a few non-work-related titles. That will present you as a well-rounded individual. Also, you can add projects you've completed. These can include PowerPoint presentations or Google Docs. And assuming that they're "professional," include your blog and Twitter link.

Collect LinkedIn Group Badges

We'll discuss LinkedIn Groups soon, but for now, know that your profile will be more professional and dynamic as you add group badges identifying you as a member. These show your connectedness to the LinkedIn community.

Update Your Status Frequently

With your profile complete, you'll begin really building your network. You'll want to be a vibrant part of that network, and posting frequent status updates can help you to do that. As you know, LinkedIn isn't Twitter, so those updates should be 100 percent professional. At least once a week, tell your network about work-related events you're attending, major projects you've completed, and professional books you're enjoying. If you find an interesting blog posting or journal article, share it. Every time you update your status, your entire network gets a little announcement about what you're doing—and that matters.

LinkedIn Tools for Students and New Grads

LinkedIn offers some tools that people new to the workforce may find especially useful. Here are two that we like:

- *LinkedIn Jobs Portal.* Here is a corner of the site for students and recent graduates who are looking for jobs and internships. Simply go to www.linkedin.com/studentjobs and begin searching for openings in specific industries and geographic areas. You'll find entry-level jobs and internships that may be just right for you as you are starting out. When we searched for writing/editing jobs, we found 76 positions advertised throughout the country. "Use the Jobs function on LinkedIn," recommends Trenton Willson, a recent job hunter and savvy LinkedIn user. "Companies pay a premium for posting jobs, expecting a higher-quality field of candidates," he explained. "LinkedIn may be the only place the job is posted."

- *LinkedIn Résumé Builder.* As we write this, the LinkedIn Résumé Builder is part of LinkedIn Labs. You'll find it at resume.linkedinlabs.com/. After you provide your LinkedIn account details, your profile information is presented to you in 11 different formats. Some will be more suitable for your experience than others. This is a quick way to get a résumé that includes all the information you worked so carefully to include in your LinkedIn profile.

- *LinkedIn Answers.* Chapter 5 gives you all the information you'll need to navigate the LinkedIn Answers section. We mention it here because as newcomers to the site and the career world, we thought you might benefit from some specific advice. When you visit the Answers section, you'll find a wealth of practical information posted by people who are actively involved in the careers you're currently hoping for. We encourage you to jump into the conversation. Just because you lack experience doesn't mean that you don't have much to contribute. You may have just studied the subject someone posted a question about or read an interesting article on the matter. If you'd like to ask a question, search through the answers first to see if your particular question has been discussed already. If you don't see a discussion within the last three months or so, go ahead and ask your question. You aren't just asking for insight. You're also giving people the opportunity to share their expertise and display their own professional acumen. People on LinkedIn are remarkably eager to help, so let them.

BUILDING AND WORKING YOUR NETWORK

Chapter 3 provided a lot of good, solid advice about how to build a vibrant network on LinkedIn. We don't intend to repeat that advice here. Much of it applies to those starting out, as well as more established workers. Here, we'll really zero in on ways that students and recent grads can begin building their networks.

First, we want to remind you that just because you may be light on work history, this doesn't mean that you have nothing to offer the LinkedIn community. What you may lack in experience, you can more than make up for with your energy, your expertise in social networking, and your eagerness to take your place in the working world. Many recruiters are quite eager to hire talented, dedicated, and enthusiastic grads seeking their first real jobs. You can join an organization without preconceived ideas of how things are done. One recent grad we spoke with said that his new boss told him straight out, "I saw something in you, and I want to cultivate that in keeping with our own company culture." So you may be inexperienced, but you have every reason to approach building your network with confidence that no matter what field you're pursuing, managers are looking for people just like you—vibrant and worthy employees.

Where Do We Begin?

When you sign on to LinkedIn, you'll be asked to provide access to your e-mail address books. Some of your connections will be people you'll want to make a part of your network; others not so much. But start there anyway. Then begin to think about the people in your life who already have an investment in seeing you succeed. Consider your professors. Many of them will be happy to link with you. Your bosses, coworkers, mentors, dormmates, and resident advisors also make for potentially good connections. Next, think about the people who are important to you outside of school and work. Send invitations to members of your faith community, family members, your parents' friends, and your neighbors. If you've done volunteer work, seek out the people who shared your devotion to those organizations. Every time you meet someone through your job-hunting efforts, for example, at a job fair, send an invitation to connect. This doesn't mean that you should be a promiscuous networker. Build your network with people you have things in common with, and who would have an interest in helping you further your professional goals (for example, a favorite professor, a former boss, that well-connected close family friend, and so on).

When you send invitations to connect, be sure to customize them. Offer your new connection a reason to be part of her network. It can be as simple as noting that you met earlier in the day at a job fair and found your conversation to be thought-provoking. Sending the standard impersonal LinkedIn invitation may send the message that you are only interested in building your network for your own advantage. Remember the 80/20 rule that applies to social networking, and end each invitation with an offer to help or support your new contact.

Join Groups

Here is a fast and targeted way to expand your network. First, search the Groups area for your alumni group. You're bound to find yours—there are currently nearly 20,000 alumni groups on LinkedIn. Now that school is over, you'll find alumni of every age and professional background still devoted to the schools they attended. Soon (trust us on this) you will see the treasured place your alma mater holds in your heart and life history. Others have the same allegiance to your alma mater, and they'll be more than happy to welcome you into the group. Of course, once you're a member of any LinkedIn group, you have automatic and free access to all the other members of that group.

If you belonged to a fraternity or sorority, be sure to check LinkedIn for a group devoted to that organization. The same is true for any nonprofits you support. Of course, seek out groups devoted to the profession you are trying to build and also search for groups targeted toward students and recent grads. When we searched Groups using the keyword "student," there were more than 40,000 listed. These included alumni groups, but it still gives you more than 20,000 others that are not just for graduates of specific colleges and universities. Finally, don't hesitate to include a group or two that simply reflects your passions. If you are devoted to a sport or hobby, you're likely to find groups on LinkedIn where other people feel the same way. For example, we found nearly 400 groups devoted to lacrosse. Who knows where in your network your next job lead will come from?

Alex Parks: Turning His Alumni Group into a Great Career Move

Alex Parks graduated from Brandeis University summa cum laude in May 2010. He had BAs in economics and philosophy. He had studied as a visiting student at Oxford University for a year, and he had completed two internships in marketing before he received his diploma. Despite his stellar academic record, Alex found himself struggling to find a job. When we spoke, he'd been working for the previous six months as an associate for Fresh Ground, Inc., a public relations firm. "Things are going very well," he told us. But that's not the way his story began.

Alex Parks reached out to Brandeis alumni through LinkedIn's Groups area.

"During my senior year, I applied for marketing jobs that were listed on Indeed.com, Idealist.org, or Craigslist," he said. "Although I had many interviews with companies such as Compete, Vistaprint, Meltwater News, Adverplex, and Edhance, nothing panned out." Soon after he graduated, Alex took job as a specialist at an Apple store while he continued to search for a job.

"In June 2010, I decided to begin an aggressive outreach campaign to Brandeis alum involved in marketing, public relations (PR), or sales through LinkedIn's Brandeis Alumni Group," he recalled. Over the course of five months, I sent messages to over 60 Brandeis alumni titled, 'Note from a Recent Brandeis Grad.' Although the notes varied in context and length, they all had a standard three-paragraph format. I briefly introduced myself, explained my work/life situation, and said why I wanted to meet them. I also uploaded my résumé to Google Docs and added a link to my résumé for each note," Alex explained.

"Of the 60 or so messages I sent out, I had about 20 responses. Of the 20 responses, I had approximately 8 phone information interviews and 5 in-person meetings. Of these 13 meetings, 5 resulted in genuine friendships with other alum, and 1 of them resulted in a job offer," he said. "Chuck Tanowitz, principal of Fresh Ground, Inc., decided to take me on as an associate. Chuck took a big chance on me. I honestly don't think Chuck would have ever hired me if we didn't go to the same college," Alex said. Never underestimate the power of networking!

SCRUB YOUR FACEBOOK AND OTHER FACTS OF LIFE ON SOCIAL NETWORKS

Of course, LinkedIn isn't the only place where you'll find opportunities for job leads and professional networking. Facebook and Twitter are invaluable business tools, and Google+ is promising to be the same. The rest of this book is devoted to helping you navigate those sites as you build your career.

You don't need us to tell you how to use Facebook or Twitter. These are tools of your generation, and you probably are quite adept at using them. Still, it's sometimes easy to overlook the details of something that's so familiar. Although we're not Mom and Dad (well, actually we are, but just to other recent grads), we still hope you'll take our advice and be very careful about what you and your friends post on all your social networks.

We asked David Becker of PhillipeBecker, a marketing and branding company, how he and his firm use social networking sites when looking for candidates. "We have used [them] . . . to screen people," he said. "When we're looking at candidates, we'll use [them] . . . to see how they've presented themselves and to see if what they've said is reality. We see who they are connected with. For the most part, [such sites] . . . give more depth to a candidate. It's interesting to see how people interact."

Other hiring managers agree. We recently attended a meeting where a library branch administrator explained her use of social networking. "Three librarians conduct the interview, one taking notes on a laptop computer," she explained. "When I'm the note taker, I always check out the candidate on social networks to see if what he's telling us holds up." So it's very true that what you do online follows you, no matter.

This may be the bad news, but the good side of this is that recruiters are all using LinkedIn, Facebook, Twitter, and more to find great candidates. As long as you manage your online reputation carefully, and you'll be doing that for the rest of your life, you're a lot more likely to gain benefits from using these sites than you are to suffer detriments.

LOOKING AHEAD

Speaking of other social networks, the rest of this book is devoted to Facebook, Twitter, and Google +. LinkedIn is the most professional and business-oriented of the social networking sites, but these other sites offer plenty of real work, connection, and job opportunities. When you're looking to catch a big fish, you might as well use a big net. We'll show you how you can use all these sites as you advance your career goals.

PART 2

Facebook, Twitter, and Google+

CHAPTER 8

Facebook: Not Just for Networking Socially

A re you on Facebook? Chances are that you are and so are your friends, your coworkers, your neighbors, and many others from every corner of both your working and nonworking life. With *Time Magazine* naming Facebook president and CEO Mark Zuckerberg "Person of the Year" in 2010, a movie (*The Social Network*) all about how his company got started released, and 800 million worldwide users, Facebook just may be the best-known company on earth. But even with all its acclaim, you may not associate Facebook with business networking. We're here to make that association crystal clear.

We understand if you associate Facebook more with musings from friends, weather updates, vacation pictures, links to cool YouTube videos, or even virtual gifting, poking, and other things that have nothing to do with serious business networking, let alone job hunting. Bryan Webb, one of LinkedIn's most connected LinkedIn Open Networkers (LIONs), when asked about his use of Facebook, had a response typical of many of the "LinkedIn people" we spoke with. "I'm on Facebook," he said, "but not that much because I'm too busy to be a social butterfly." Another LION, Steven Burda, was even more specific in describing the line between LinkedIn and

Facebook. "I keep Facebook just for my friends and pictures of my wedding and my baby," he said. It has "nothing to do with my professional life."

While we agree that many people use Facebook mostly for personal or social networking (Figure 8-1), that perception of Facebook as only the world's biggest multimedia bulletin board is old school. As you'll soon see, there is also a lot of business being done through the site. And the face of the Facebook community is changing quickly, with "older" demographics among the fastest-growing groups. According to the website socialmediatoday, "Facebook is used primarily by adults of both sexes, but significantly female, in the prime of their active professional careers for social interaction." So pigeonholing Facebook as just a place for casually keeping up with friends would be a mistake.

In the fall of 2011, Facebook announced massive changes to the way its site looks. Now, if you've been on Facebook for any length of time, you know that the company frequently and seemingly capriciously makes changes to the site. Very often these changes are met with ire from the

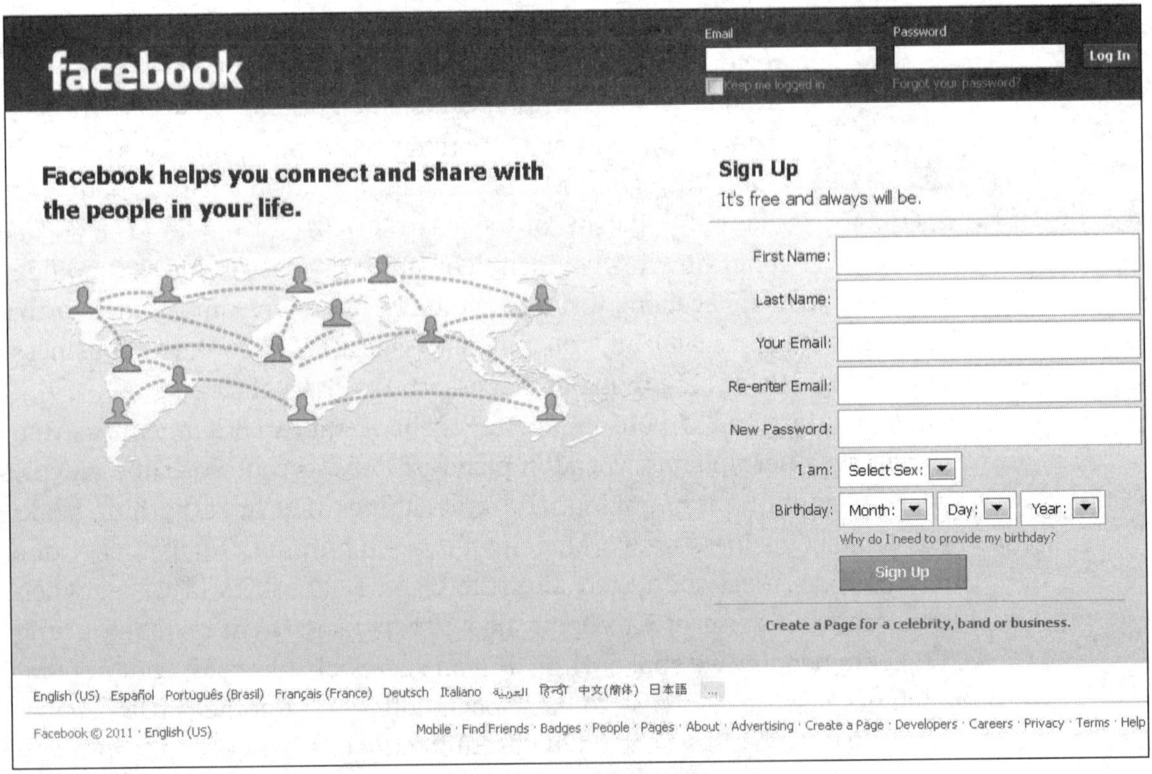

Figure 8-1: Facebook's homepage, where you'll soon find lots of connections.

more than 800 million users worldwide. But the changes announced in 2011 dramatically alter the functionality of the site and promise to make it more effective as a business and professional tool. With this in mind, please remember that things as we describe them in writing here today may appear somewhat differently to you when you read them in our future, which is actually your present.

FACEBOOK *IS* FOR JOB HUNTERS

People *are* finding real jobs through Facebook, jobs that support families and lives. In this chapter you'll learn about how others are using Facebook to find new work and how you can do the same. We'll include profiles of people who discuss, in their own words, the new jobs they found thanks to Facebook.

In mid-2011, JobVite, a company that provides software to allow companies to recruit effectively on the Internet, published the results of its 2011 Social Recruiting Survey. Now, you would expect that LinkedIn would fare quite well in such a survey, and it did. A full 95 percent of companies using "social recruiting" said that they had hired successfully through LinkedIn. But Facebook came in second at nearly 25 percent! Not only this, more than half the companies surveyed are now using Facebook to recruit. No, Facebook isn't LinkedIn, but it still has tremendous value for job hunting.

Building Your Facebook Network

By now you know how easy it is for LinkedIn to connect you with people you already know. It's the same for Facebook, only more so. After you sign up, one of the first things Facebook prompts you for are your e-mail addresses and passwords so that it can search your address books for people you might want to connect with.

You also can search through Facebook's member base yourself to find people you may know. You start this process by clicking on the "Find Friends" link along the left side of your page under the top heading "Favorites." From there, you can search Facebook for friends by

- Clicking on or entering your e-mail host. *Note:* While Facebook will allow you to import contacts from AOL, Yahoo, Hotmail, Comcast, MSN, and many other e-mail service providers, Gmail isn't one of them.

Google has blocked Facebook from having access to that data. There apparently are workarounds, such as exporting all your Gmail contacts to .csv format and then using Facebook's Other Tools to import a contact file. Obviously, this is a bit convoluted and hopefully something that will have changed by the time you read this.

- Clicking on "Other Tools" to upload contacts from a desktop-based mail client such as Microsoft Outlook.

- Clicking on one of the hyperlinks Facebook has provided based on your profile to find friends at a company at which you may have worked, a school you may have attended, or even the town in which you live.

- Reviewing Facebook's People You May Know Suggestions (many of whom share mutual friends).

Of course you can always use the Search bar at the top to search for friends who haven't shown up yet through one of the other options we described. No matter how you locate potential Facebook friends, once you do, inviting them is as easy as clicking the "Add Friend" button next to their names.

Facebook Lists Your Friends—and So Can You

As part of the site changes announced as we write, Facebook has added a List feature for organizing your connections. Smart Lists get created automatically and include people identified through your shared profile information. For example, your current coworkers who have listed their workplace will appear automatically in a list once you identify your employer. Every time you add a friend who also identifies himself as an employee of your company, his name will be added to your list. Generic Smart Lists include Work, School, Family, and City.

You also can create your own lists and populate them as you see fit. You may have a list of friends from a charitable organization you serve or friends from your neighborhood. You then can send updates and links to just your friends on those specific lists without having them appear on your public wall.

Lists can be especially useful as you job hunt on the site. With your friends and family members organized in specific categories, you can post things to your Lists without concern that your prospective employers or their staff members will find them. You can create lists specific to the companies you are approaching. Then, when you want to interact with those connections, you can, but if you want to share something more personal with just your family members, you can access them through your Family list.

Getting Help on Facebook

If you ever need help, Facebook's "Help" hyperlink is at the bottom right of any page, or you can access it from the drop-down arrow at the top right corner of your homepage. Just click on that link, and you'll wind up at Facebook's Help Center (*www.facebook.com/help*), shown in Figure 8-2. From there, you can search the Help Center by entering keywords in the search bar at the top of the page next to "Home." Or, along the left you'll find quick links to about every part of the site. You also can search for answers by looking for relevant discussions in groups. Also check out Facebook's blog (blog.facebook.com), which is especially helpful if you're interested in new features.

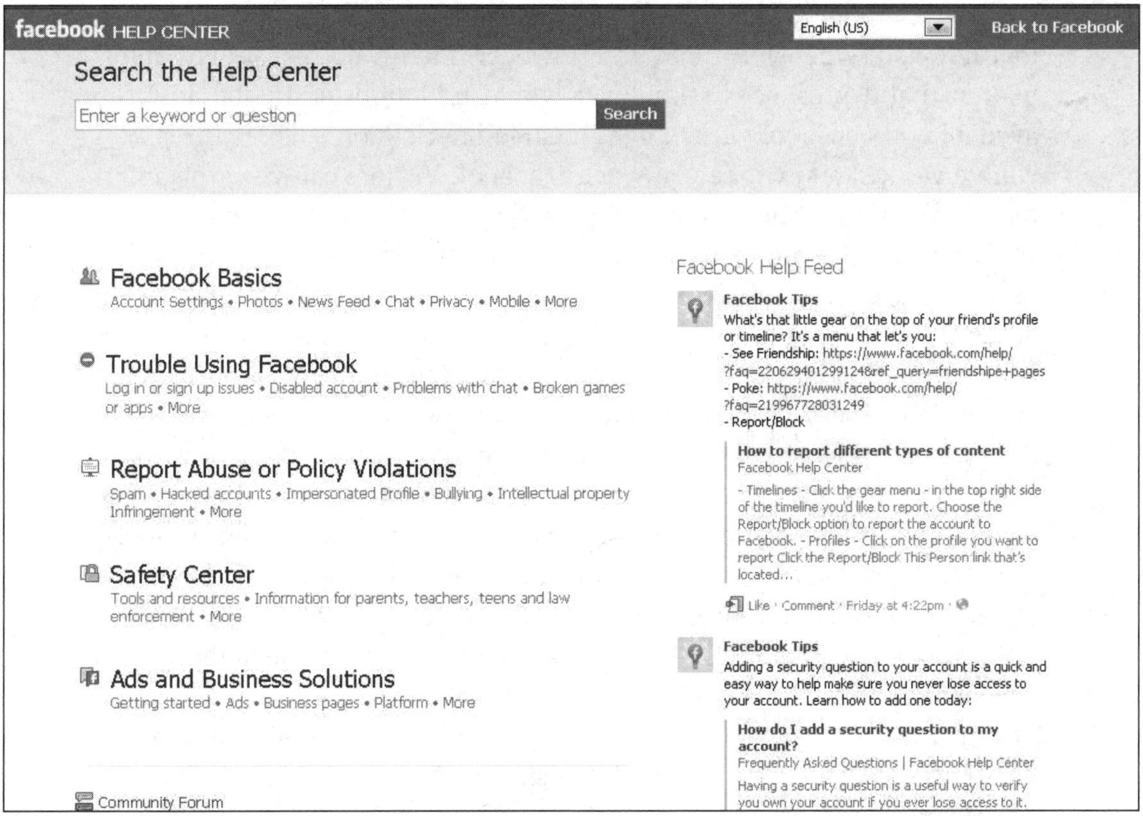

facebook HELP CENTER | English (US) | Back to Facebook

Search the Help Center

Enter a keyword or question | Search

Facebook Help Feed

Facebook Basics
Account Settings • Photos • News Feed • Chat • Privacy • Mobile • More

Facebook Tips
What's that little gear on the top of your friend's profile or timeline? It's a menu that let's you:
- See Friendship: https://www.facebook.com/help/?faq=220629401299124&ref_query=friendshipe+pages
- Poke: https://www.facebook.com/help/?faq=219967728031249
- Report/Block

Trouble Using Facebook
Log in or sign up issues • Disabled account • Problems with chat • Broken games or apps • More

How to report different types of content
Facebook Help Center
- Timelines - Click the gear menu - in the top right side of the timeline you'd like to report. Choose the Report/Block option to report the account to Facebook. - Profiles - Click on the profile you want to report Click the Report/Block This Person link that's located...

Report Abuse or Policy Violations
Spam • Hacked accounts • Impersonated Profile • Bullying • Intellectual property Infringement • More

Like • Comment • Friday at 4:22pm •

Safety Center
Tools and resources • Information for parents, teachers, teens and law enforcement • More

Facebook Tips
Adding a security question to your account is a quick and easy way to help make sure you never lose access to your account. Learn how to add one today:

Ads and Business Solutions
Getting started • Ads • Business pages • Platform • More

How do I add a security question to my account?
Frequently Asked Questions | Facebook Help Center
Having a security question is a useful way to verify you own your account if you ever lose access to it.

Community Forum

Figure 8-2: Facebook's Help Center shows just how easily you can find help while working on Facebook.

A FACEBOOK PROFILE FOR BUSINESS

Facebook is a place for being you, connecting with friends, sharing thoughts and events, and otherwise being social. But you're planning to go to Facebook now in search of a job or new work assignments. Your profile needs to reflect this. Yet, at the same time, you still want to make people glad that they stopped by. Facebook is a great place to let your own personality sparkle a bit. After all, visitors to your page have almost endless choices of where to go on the site. They may have 500 Facebook friends. They may belong to 50 groups. If you're boring them or depressing them, they can just move on. Wouldn't you?

What Your Page Says about You

It's true that Facebook is more casual than LinkedIn, and your page should reflect that. People go to different places with different expectations, and on Facebook, no one wants to hear or even think about how much you need that new job, whatever it may be. However, there's no reason why information that a prospective employer would be interested in shouldn't be available on Facebook. This might include information such as the places you've worked and where you went to school. Visitors can view this information when they click on the "Info" hyperlink on your main page.

Let's consider how you can use this real estate to showcase why you'd be such a great catch for any company. Just click on the "Edit Profile" button at the top right of your page to get started. The areas under which you can add information appear along the right. The "Education and Work" option is especially relevant. Fill these areas in fully. Be sure to take advantage of the "Add a Project" option under each employer so that you can work in details about your accomplishments. For the About Me part of the profile page, think in terms of elevator pitches for a building with a lot of floors. (So you'll get not 15 seconds but maybe 30 seconds worth of facts.) This would be more apt for Facebook. Write down your answer to the question "What do you do?" until you have a cogent, interesting statement that would appeal to potential employers, as well as friends who may be in a position to help you land a new job or new gigs of some sort. Beyond that, think of your Facebook page as a billboard that shows you as a person, yes, but specifically what makes you a great catch for a company.

Whenever you post something to your wall, you have another opportunity to showcase why you'd be such a fine fit at XYZ company. Some things to include, then, might be

- Links to articles you've written, such as a thought-provoking blog entry. For example, on his Facebook page, consultant Terry Seamon had a link to an article called "Refreshing Advice for the Job Hunt." Now that got our attention.
- Links to videos showing you speaking before a group.
- News about interesting projects you're working on.
- Short blurbs about the books you're reading or the movies you're watching. (Adding information like this should be very simple by the time you read this as Facebook forges more relationships with partners such as Netflix and the *Wall Street Journal*.)
- Photos of your life that get people thinking. For example, University of Maryland student Laurel Hughes studied abroad in Spain during the spring semester of her junior year. The pictures she posted from that trip and the blog she wrote might well intrigue those considering her for various internships.

At the very least, don't forget a photo of yourself. It doesn't have to be as business-like as your LinkedIn photo, so pull off that necktie or kick off those heels—and be sure to smile. You want to come across as someone an employer would want to add to an already existing team. Think business casual.

Finally, use the Update Status area (at the top of your page) to let people know that you're in the job market, but do it in a "look what Company X is missing" sort of way. For example, Chris Schlieter, a former marketing executive looking to reenter the field, wrote " . . . is happy to work for a privately held company that still wants to grow." This shouldn't make anyone feel uncomfortable and may just make the right person take a second look at Chris's page.

Content That's Pertinent

Let's narrow the focus just a bit. If you're on Facebook, your page should feature some content that's *relevant to how you earn your living*. Artistic people will have more to explore about this in the upcoming multimedia section, but for here, let's use the example of a person with a background in marketing. You would want to include items that validate your knowledge and interests as someone who knows how to put products into people's hands. Good things to feature on your page would be links to advertising campaigns you've created, relevant articles, and especially articles you have written yourself.

Dr. Scott Testa, professor of marketing at St. Joseph's University in Philadelphia, feels that recent grads should display their interests as well as their knowledge. In other words, when he reviews someone's Facebook page, he wants to see evidence of genuine interest in the profession affiliated with that person's field. He believes that having these things on your page gives you an advantage over people who don't include that context.

But all this content can present a double-edged sword. Consider Facebook's new Timeline feature, just announced (and not yet available) as we write this. According to Facebook, Timeline will allow for "reimaging of your profile" so that you can create an online scrapbook of your life, pulling in all the information you've ever posted on Facebook—the comments, photos, videos, links, profile information, everything. Add in the many applications that Facebook is bringing to the site (so that you can share news of movies you're watching, books you're reading, music you're listening to), and your Timeline becomes not only historic but also real time. In essence, Facebook lets you create a real-time multimedia book all about *you*, available for anyone to see. This includes the person who might be your next boss.

Is all of this information you would want everyone to have access to? Of course not. That means as Facebook (or any social networking site) introduces new features, you'll need to take a look at your privacy settings again. Although the Timeline feature was in beta testing as we wrote this, we've read that, by default, your Timeline information will be publicly available. This is a setting that you'll need to change. Fortunately, as *PC Magazine* reported, each Timeline entry will have a drop-down menu next to it so that you'll be able to filter who may see the item. There's a saying in boxing: When boxers are in the ring, they're supposed to protect themselves at all times. It's the responsibility of boxers to make sure that they're safe, not the refs and certainly not their opponents. In this sense, the Internet is like a boxing ring. Once you step into it, you must protect yourself at all times. Not that you're likely to get knocked out, of course, but you could be knocked from the running for that job you really want. With so much information about you available in so many places on the web, you must protect yourself. Consider that there are companies now such as Social Intelligence (www.socialintel.com) that will pull information from Facebook, Twitter, and MySpace but then will go even deeper, scouring e-commerce sites, users groups, and blog postings and comments, too. All this information will then be presented to potential employers in an online dossier of you. These companies have received the government's okay to do this—it's legal. According to Social Intelligence, 70 percent of recruiters have rejected candidates because of information found online.

It's much more difficult to control online information about you once it's out there than it is to make sure that it's never put online in the first place. In the spirit of "protecting yourself at all times," Professor Testa had the following advice about Facebook for job hunters:

- Be careful of what you put on your Facebook page.
- Be careful of what others put on your wall.
- Don't post anything that you wouldn't want your mother to see.

Of course, once you start job hunting, you'll need to revisit your privacy settings on Facebook. You can't expect to attract people to your page if you've got everything tamped down so tightly that all they can learn about you is that you are on Facebook. Before you open your account to more public scrutiny, carefully scrub your Facebook page and hide or remove any items that may reflect poorly on you, even marginally. Send a message to your friends explaining your job-hunting status, and ask them to be wary of what they post to your wall. Finally, check Facebook several times a day to ensure that anything that does slip through gets taken down as quickly as possible.

Multimedia Content

Facebook gives you the ability to add to your page lots of multimedia content, including brief messages, "graffiti," videos, and pictures. If you're looking for a job and you have samples that would help to sell you (for example, you're a writer, a graphic designer, an illustrator, or even a musician), it's a real boon to be able to include such content right there on Facebook. Just be sure to share things that would appeal to employers you target, such as a portfolio, writing samples, music, scripts, and so on. And put that best foot forward by choosing your samples carefully! If you're in business for yourself, one thing that you can do is post videos showcasing your latest products to push people to a website where they can make an actual purchase.

Finessing Facebook's News Feed

Every time you log on to Facebook and check out your page, you will view your own customized news feed showing what the people in your network are up to. If you check Facebook frequently, these will be the postings added since your last visit. But, if you're checking in less frequently, Facebook will present your news feed according to the importance of the information presented. For example, a Facebook friend recently spent a week in the hospital while all her Facebook people posted get-well wishes and concern for her condition. The afternoon she returned home, her single-word status update "Home!" was the top news story of that day. Additionally, if you see an item that wasn't designated as "Top News," you can click the blue triangle in the left corner of the posting to mark it as such. Of course, it works both ways. People in your network also get to see what you've been up to. It's not often that you get to address such a diverse group of people, who may well know you and be interested in what you're doing. Use the items that people will see about you to your best advantage. This is your chance to show how clever and smart you are, not how mundane and ordinary life can be. We all have to feed our pets, eat, and deal with nasty weather, so, instead, tell your network about the incisive commentary you've just read, the mind-expanding video you saw, or even that you're looking forward to your next job interview with an ad agency in New York. In this way, your Facebook page boosts your own personal stock.

Facebook also has altered its standard news feed from the center of your homepage to a "ticker" that scrolls along the right side of your page. Here, you'll see the friends in your network as they comment, like, or repost the thoughts and observations of your connections. Simply scroll over the comments that interest you, and you'll see them expand to include a box that lets you add to the conversation directly in the ticker. The ticker makes it very easy to see what's going on in your network.

Be sure to use your privacy settings, shown in Figure 8-3, to control which items about you your Facebook contacts receive. As someone who

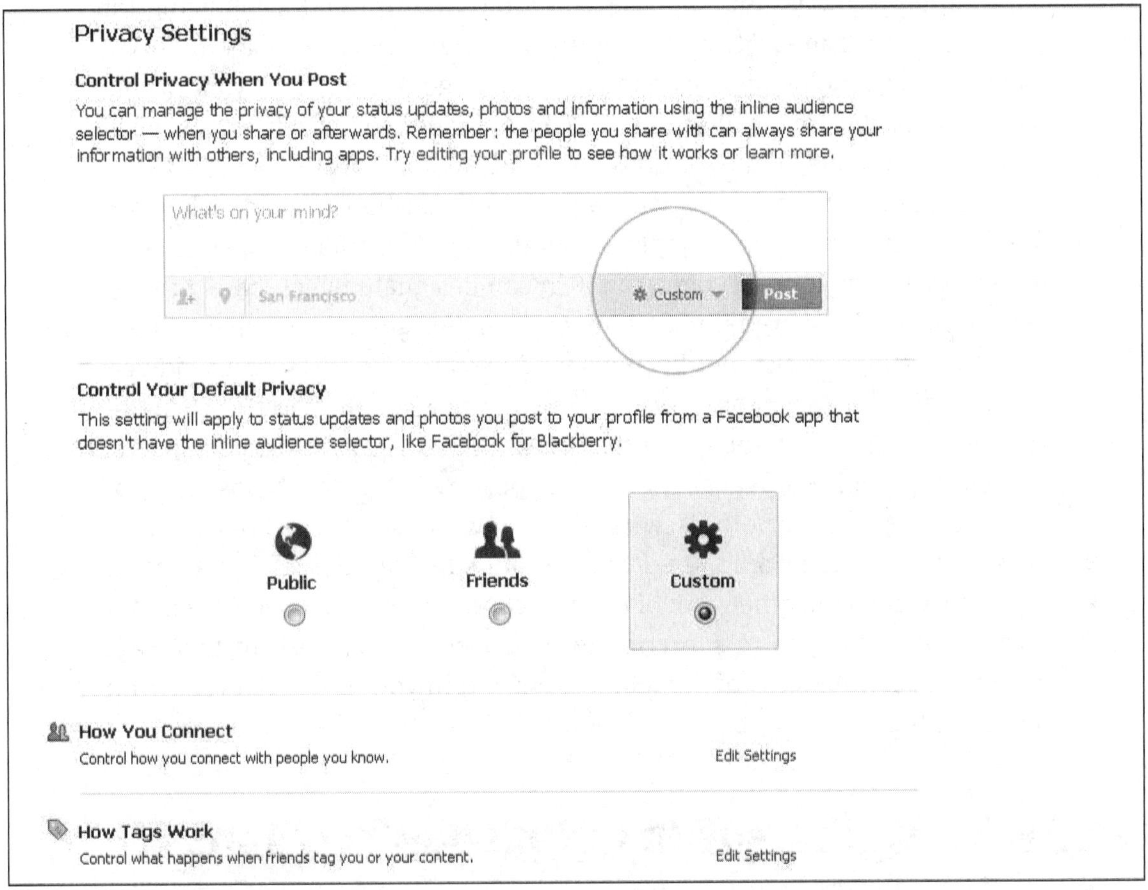
Privacy Settings
Control Privacy When You Post
You can manage the privacy of your status updates, photos and information using the inline audience selector — when you share or afterwards. Remember: the people you share with can always share your information with others, including apps. Try editing your profile to see how it works or learn more.
What's on your mind?
San Francisco
Custom
Post
Control Your Default Privacy
This setting will apply to status updates and photos you post to your profile from a Facebook app that doesn't have the inline audience selector, like Facebook for Blackberry.
Public
Friends
Custom
How You Connect
Control how you connect with people you know.
Edit Settings
How Tags Work
Control what happens when friends tag you or your content.
Edit Settings

Figure 8-3: The privacy settings you can control to make sure that your Facebook page is making the right impression. You'll find this page on the "Settings" drop-down menu at the top of any Facebook page.

is seeking a new job, you may want to adjust those settings for a while so that every time you write on a friend's wall, for example, that action isn't visible to everyone in your network. And if someone writes a comment on your wall that reflects poorly from a business point of view, use the "Hide Story" option to remove it. You'll find more specific suggestions along these lines in a moment.

To Subscribe or Not to Subscribe

Facebook now allows you to subscribe to other members' public news feeds and allows others to subscribe to yours, whether or not you share a network. Based on your privacy settings, your friends are subscribers to your public postings. But suppose you are trying to build a following for your blog. You can easily add a "Subscribe" button to your page that will allow your latest blog update announcement to go public. From your profile page, simply click the "Subscriptions" button under your picture. Now click "Allow Subscribers," and your posts will be made public.

You can fine-tune this by selecting who on Facebook can see what you post. You can keep access tamped down to only your friends, open it up to friends of friends, or everyone. You also can designate which parts of your news feed will be shared. In addition, you can designate who can comment on your postings, which notifications you'll receive, and who can send you friend requests. Facebook recommends that you keep this last setting at "Friends of Friends" to dissuade spammers.

Just as people can subscribe to your postings, you can choose to subscribe to the work of others who also allow subscriptions. If you have favorite bloggers, check to see if they permit subscriptions. If you attend a conference and enjoy the work of the guest speaker, go ahead and see if that person will allow you to subscribe to his Facebook postings. In this way, you can follow the work of thought leaders within your industry even if you never get the chance to befriend them.

NETWORKING FOR BUSINESS THROUGH FACEBOOK

Here's one of this chapter's top tips: One of the best ways to use Facebook is to search for people who can help you get a job once you have an interview or have pinpointed a company that interests you. But first use LinkedIn to pinpoint such people. Keep reading to see exactly how this can happen.

Let's say that you learn that there's a job available as a product manager for America Online (AOL). You have the job description, perhaps you e-mailed a résumé, and now you want to stand out from the pack of applicants. You know from previous chapters that you can use LinkedIn to search for people in the department at AOL that you're interested in or for others who seem in a position to shed light on the job or put in a good word for you. (Remember our discussion of Advanced People searches in Chapter 3 and Company searches in Chapter 4.) It's true that through LinkedIn you then could contact these people. But to do that you'd have to use InMails if those people aren't part of your network. InMails cost money. Try to contact those people on Facebook instead of LinkedIn, suggested Lorne Epstein, founder of the InSide Job website (myinsidejob.com). On Facebook, there's no cost to reach out to people. Plus, you can approach them on a site they probably check even more often than LinkedIn and at a time when they may be more receptive to what you have to say.

Here's an example of the note Lorne suggests you might send to a business contact on Facebook:

Hi Khalid,

I am scheduled to come in for an interview with your organization very soon and would like to learn more about your company to see if I am a good fit. What can you tell me? I appreciate your help in advance.

Sincerely yours,

Lorne

Jordan Harbinger: Writer and Entrepreneur

Jordan Harbinger is one of young cofounders of The Art of Charm, a New York– and Los Angeles–based startup company that teaches men "advanced social skills and dating science." In other words, these life coaches teach men how to meet, attract, and charm women and other people, too. The goal is to help men to be more socially competent in both their business and personal lives. The Art of Charm has been featured on the *Today Show*, in the *Huffington Post*, and on *Saturday Night Live*, as well as many other outlets.

Jordan Harbinger of The Art of Charm uses Facebook to befriend and connect with editors to enhance his freelance writing business.

As if his thriving company weren't enough to keep him busy, Jordan's also an aspiring writer. He didn't plan it that way. It's just that the articles he wrote to promote The Art of Charm were so popular that he started making good money on them—good enough to cover his rent. Web editors sometimes pay on a sliding scale based on how many views your article receives. Thanks to a large social media presence through Facebook (6,700 "likes"), Twitter (13,000 followers), and YouTube (where his videos have been viewed 70,000 times), he's able to drive a lot of people to his articles. This translates into better pay.

What's especially interesting from your perspective is how Jordan is able to get new writing assignments. We can say from experience that it's not always easy for a writer to get an editor's ear. So we were curious when we learned that Jordan was using social networks to pitch article ideas to editors. He'd start by thinking about which sites were the largest men's websites and how he could connect with the editors-in-chief of those sites. Through simple web searches, he found out who the editors were and then he looked for them on Facebook. He checked to see if they had any friends in common. If they did, he'd message his friend and say, "How do you know this editor? Would you mind making an introduction?" Even if they had no common friends, though, Jordan still would approach the editor. For example, he may get to know an editor for a while by following her on Twitter, and even on Facebook, Jordan has found that people usually will accept friend requests.

He never asked for a job (article assignment) immediately. Rather, he'd spend more time getting to know the editor through Facebook, for example, maybe sending messages back and forth. He might even offer some information to help the editor out. He let editors get to know him through the updates he posts on Facebook. He tries to make those very entertaining so that others can get a feel for his personality. "I also try to help them connect with people who can help them so that they realize I'm a value-giving guy," Jordan said. "Once I have an idea I'd like to pitch them, it's a snap because we're already friends, and they're happy to help me out in return." His strategy has worked out, and Jordan has gotten assignments with Examiner.com, Brobible.com, and Mademan.com.

He has also used his social networking savvy to help other people get jobs. A fan who enjoyed his podcasts got in touch with Jordan on Facebook. It turns out he was a private military contractor. At the same time, Jordan had military personnel going through his Art of Charm training, and one of the military guys mentioned to Jordan that he needed an assistant. Jordan introduced him to his Facebook fan, and his fan got the job. "That guy will remember me," Jordan said. "People want to reciprocate." The idea of giving before getting is the same pay-it-forward strategy we discussed earlier in the book, and Jordan is a charming master of it.

It's a Two-Way Street

You're reaching out to companies and their employees on Facebook, but others are checking you out, too. Depending on which study you read, anywhere from 10 to 50 percent or more of employers are already screening candidates through Facebook. And while employers may be more likely to use LinkedIn to check out a potential hire with experience, Facebook may be the network of choice when they are screening younger candidates. This only makes sense because kids right out of school are a lot less likely to have a LinkedIn profile than they are to have a Facebook presence stretching back several years. If you're under 30 especially, your prospective employer may even be *likely* to search for you on Facebook to see what can be learned about you, according to Professor Testa, the social marketing expert. If it's down to two or three candidates, he explained, a savvy human resources (HR) manager may visit candidate Facebook pages to help make a decision.

JOB POSTINGS ON FACEBOOK

Yes, there are actual job postings right on Facebook! This is just another piece of evidence in support of the blurring that is occurring between social and business networking on the Internet. On Facebook, three sources for possible job postings exist. These are third-party applications, Facebook Groups, and Company Pages.

Applications

There are thousands of third-party programs and websites that work in tandem with and on Facebook. Many of these are games such as Farmville, but others will be of great use to you as a job hunter. The advantage of using them on Facebook is that they are right there on the site; you don't have to go elsewhere on the web. Another advantage is that since they are integrated with Facebook, certain searches may bring up Facebook members you can approach for help. Checking out these pages should become part of your Facebook routine. Here's a look at three of them.

BranchOut

BranchOut is a Facebook application that allows you to submit your career and educational background to be viewed not only by your friends but also by your friends' connections, too. Just as you can scroll through your LinkedIn connections to get introduced to the people who may be able to help you locate a job or learn more about a particular company, BranchOut allows you to do the same with your Facebook connections. When you sign up for BranchOut, you'll create a separate professional profile with just your pertinent career information. You can share endorsements and career "badges" with members of your network to validate your credentials, but personal information, including photos and status updates, are not included. At the time of this writing, BranchOut's database included an estimated 3 million jobs and 20,000 internships. When you search for a company through this application, you'll get a list of your friends and the friends of your friends who may work there. Then you can work your way toward an introduction or a recommendation for a job. BranchOut is also available on Twitter.

CareerBuilder

CareerBuilder is an authorized Facebook reseller, and it has a presence on the site with many good features for job hunters. Now, we're not the biggest fans of sites such as Monster.com and CareerBuilder because they can be real wheel spinners. With so many résumés posted on them, the competition is fierce. But CareerBuilder is definitely worth your time to check out if you're on Facebook anyway.

Type "CareerBuilder" in the search bar at the top of your page, and notice all the job category icons. CareerBuilder has more than 30 different Facebook pages (reachable by clicking on your icon of choice) covering job categories such as engineering and health care. When you click on a category icon, you're taken to a page showing the most recent pertinent jobs. But be sure to click on the "See All Jobs" button at the bottom of the page. From there, you can search for jobs by subcategory (for example, nursing or administrative jobs within health care), as well as by location.

Finally, you can become a CareerBuilder fan by clicking the link to receive special promotions from the company. Just remember that doing so will place a CareerBuilder icon on your profile, so decide first of all if that's something you'd like.

Simply Hired

We've discussed Simply Hired before. These folks say that they operate the world's largest job-search engine, and we don't doubt it. On Facebook, just type "simplyhired" in the search box. You'll be taken to the page shown in Figure 8-4. From that page, you can search millions of jobs culled from thousands of different websites. Enter some keywords for job title or skills

Figure 8-4: Career site Simply Hired's Facebook page.

and location, and you're off and running. Once you're on the first page of actual job listings, you can refine your search in many ways, including by education, experience, and even "special filters" such as Fortune 500, Mom Friendly, or New Graduate. We also recommend that once you're on Simply Hired's main page, you click the "Info" link along the left. From there, you see useful links you can click on such as Simply Hired's blog, Twitter site, and more. As with CareerBuilder, you can become a Simply Hired fan.

Other Job Applications on Facebook

Other companies are joining CareerBuilder and Simply Hired by providing Facebook applications and leveraging the site to help job hunters. One is intheDoor, whose mission is "Job Search for the Facebook Generation." The company enables you to "work" your Facebook network to find jobs unobtrusively at your friends' companies. We don't know how well it actually does what it claims, but our research showed that it's definitely worth looking into. BeKnown is another Facebook app company. BeKnown enables you to transform your Facebook network into a "professional network," according to its website.

Facebook's Groups

Facebook isn't just about connecting individuals. It's also about connecting people who share common interests. One way Facebook does this is through the Groups area. Facebook overhauled its Groups area in 2010, and as a result, it may be less useful to job seekers. For example, there's no longer a Groups Directory, meaning that you have to use the search box to find Groups of interest. Facebook also streamlined the process of creating a group. Anyone can create a group right from their Facebook homepage. You're encouraged to create small groups of any type, such as one for your book club, college buddies, soccer team, people from your old neighborhood, and so on. It's no wonder that there are now 50 million groups (!) on Facebook.

Can you still find Groups dedicated to professional interests? We started typing "business" in the search bar at the top of our homepage and did find groups for business book writers, women in business, business success, and so on. They only had a few hundred members. The Official Facebook Public Relations Group, which we mentioned in the last edition of this book, is still alive, with more than 10,000 Facebook members. PR Job Watch, also mentioned in the last edition, is also still active on the site. But we only found those groups because we entered their exact names.

So you will need to experiment with the Groups area to see how useful it might be to you. Try pertinent keywords and see what pops up. If you do find groups that look promising, be sure to check out the discussions to see if you'd actually find them useful. And by all means join your alumni association. That may be your best use of the Groups area.

Company Pages

Individuals have profiles on Facebook, companies have pages. And it's those pages that can help you to reach out to a company in ways you wouldn't be able to otherwise. A company's page (originally called a "fan page") may describe new offers and discounts, provide links to videos and newsletters, enable you to access catalogs, and through its wall even let you interact with other customers and employees. All these things can help you to get a grasp for the company's priorities.

Obviously, if you have an interview coming up with a company, checking its Facebook page would be a smart thing to do. But what if you think that one day you might *want* an interview with a company? Can checking out its page help? Yes, and in fact, companies actually post openings on their pages. For example, Figure 8-5 shows the company page for The Voice of Your Consumer. According to company president Crystal Kendrick, The Voice of Your Consumer (a marketing and advertising research firm) hires from 20 to 30 people a year through Facebook. A sampling of other companies reported to hire through Facebook includes RazorFish, eBay, LexisNexis, and Waste Management.

Crystal Kendrick Hires Some Through LinkedIn but More Through Facebook

Crystal Kendrick is the president of the marketing and advertising firm The Voice of Your Consumer. The Cincinnati-based company specializes in market research, secret shopping, and media campaigns. She routinely uses LinkedIn and Facebook for recruiting staff, and she also uses Facebook to keep in close contact with clients, contractors, and prospective employees.

"In this tight job market, before using social media sites to recruit, our phones were ringing off the hooks," Crystal said. "We were swamped with résumés from overqualified candidates. For example, we received a résumé from the CFO of a midsized company when we ran an ad for a bookkeeper." Now that The Voice of Your Consumer uses both LinkedIn and Facebook to recruit and hire, it is saving the company lots of time. "We use LinkedIn more for hiring internal support people," Crystal told us. These positions may be in public relations, graphics support, and administrative roles. On LinkedIn, "I used to just post: Hey, I am hiring," Crystal says. "Now I search LinkedIn

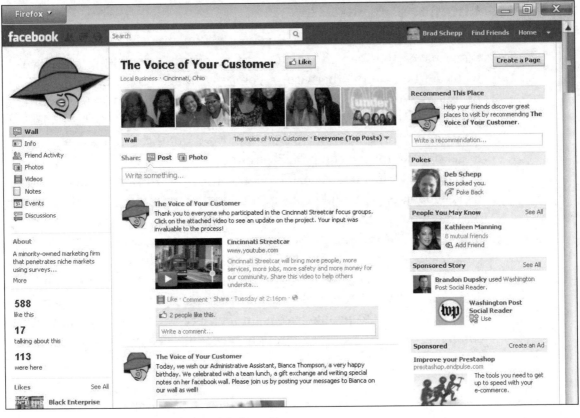

Figure 8-5: Company page for The Voice of Your Consumer.

using keywords relevant to the job, such as 'event planning,' 'Cincinnati,' and 'Microsoft Office.' Search results are presented to us ranked by the number of connections we have in common with the person. If we have a lot of connections in common, it's easier to check references." Interestingly, Crystal says that if a person's LinkedIn headline says "Job Seeker," that actually gives them an edge because she knows that this person is seeking work. Crystal's company prefers to use connections rather than recommendations to check people out. She finds that connections give them a more complete look at a person.

The Voice of Your Consumer uses Facebook more when it's seeking to hire contractors. According to Crystal, these people typically do not have LinkedIn profiles. "So we're more likely to find the kind of people we need to hire for short-term assignments, say, 8 to 10 weeks," she said. "We actually post the job announcements on our Facebook company page. We also encourage people

Crystal Kendrick, president of the marketing and advertising firm The Voice of Your Consumer, routinely recruits and hires market researchers she finds on Facebook.

to share the ads with their friends. When we hire people on Facebook, we're looking for people with experience in reaching out to others, who handle rejection well, and who have conducted research face to face, as well as people with direct sales experience."

In the average year, The Voice of Your Consumer hires 2 to 4 people through LinkedIn and 20 to 30 people through Facebook.

The Voice of Your Customer also uses Facebook to post articles and information with tags and links written by the staff, articles featuring the staff, and mentions of the company published in reputable business and industry media. These strategies reinforce the importance of the company's services, confirm the credentials of the staff and firm, and illustrate its regional and national reach and capabilities. Occasionally, The Voice of Your Customer also uses Facebook to post comments, pictures, and links to completed projects that engage the community and create awareness of the company's work.

Finally, The Voice of Your Customer routinely celebrates "Thank You Thursday," a weekly post with tags and links to thank and acknowledge staff, vendors, or customers. Employees are honored to be recognized by their employer. Vendors are thrilled to be recognized and endorsed on Facebook. Many of the company's customers are thankful for the exposure and the support of their initiatives.

Blue sky it. Make a list of the companies you think you might want to work for, and then check them out on Facebook. Be sure to "Like" them by clicking that button so that you're sent the latest news and possibly special offers. Just as following companies on LinkedIn may lead to the start of a something big, so may "liking" them on Facebook. Depending on your field, it also may make sense for you to try to get a dialog going with key personnel, not the manager you're trying to work for, but other influential people at the company. But let's put first things first: Before approaching anyone directly, work toward building a relationship with them. Don't be coy, just friendly and gently inquisitive. This shouldn't be as challenging as it may sound if you have a genuine interest in working for the company.

Nothing is quite as encouraging as reading about the success others have found through following the path you are taking yourself. Here are some inspiring tales of people who have used Facebook to recruit people or to land jobs themselves.

Jocelyn Wang: Information Architect/Business Analyst

Jocelyn Wang was celebrating her one-year anniversary at her job with speakTECH (a design and technology company) when we spoke, and she has a Facebook connection to thank for making it all possible. Her story is interesting because it reflects both the unique social environment of Facebook and its potential for bringing together people who never may have met otherwise.

Jocelyn Wang found her current position on Facebook almost without realizing it. (Photo by Arden Ash.)

I have been in my current job for one year now, and it was through a Facebook connection. At the time, I had joined Facebook for general networking opportunities; I was not specifically looking for a new job. I was contacted by a person I mistakenly thought was someone I knew from high school. In reality, he was simply someone connected to a friend of mine. He added me because he saw me on our mutual friend's list and thought I "looked interesting." We spoke over the course of several months, but what I didn't realize at the time was that he had been sizing me up for a specific position at his company. I thought he was simply being friendly when he asked me about work and also what I was doing in business school (I was in the process of getting my MBA at the time). About three months after we first began talking, he made a formal job interview request, and we continued the process until I was eventually hired.

Ruth-Ann Cooper: Freelance Web Consultant and Writer

Ruth-Ann Cooper now uses Facebook as her primary source of new assignments!

I am a freelance web consultant/writer/editor, and over the past year, I have had multiple leads that resulted in freelance jobs from connections on Facebook.

In fact, it has been my primary direct or indirect source of new work. The leads did not come from posting a status update that I was looking for work; they came from networking.

For example, I reconnected with an old college friend and looked up the company she worked for. Out of curiosity, I looked at the company's job openings. I ended up applying for a freelance position with the company and, using my friend as a reference, was hired for the position.

Freelancer Ruth-Ann Cooper keeps busy with work she's found on Facebook.

In another example, a Facebook friend from my college years saw that I was freelancing and heard of someone looking for a writer, so she connected us. She did that another time as well, and I have done repeat work with both the people she connected me with.

An example of indirect networking is that I became friends on Facebook with someone I knew from college, and when I was looking into joining the alumni board for my college, I saw that he was the head of it. After talking with him, I was able to join the board. Attending a board meeting, I met the new dean of the college and am now working on a couple of projects for him.

Another small project came in—creating a website for a friend on Facebook. In that case, I knew that she had her own business, and I soft pitched her on the idea of me helping her out.

I was contacted the other day by my former college roommate and a friend on Facebook about possibly helping her company with some writing for its website. I had sent her a soft-pitch message through Facebook as well.

Fabrice Calando: Account Manager

"Facebook helped me land a job at one of Canada's largest advertising agencies," said Fabrice Calando. "There was no job posting, but after a brief encounter, I learned that one of my old colleagues was now working there. We were friends on Facebook, so I reached out to her, sent her my CV, and one thing led to the next—I got a job as an account manager. How did that experience differ from using e-mail or the phone? Because we were friends, I was able to stay in touch with her easily. If I had had to rely on e-mail, I wouldn't have known how to reach out to her."

So Fabrice's advice to people who want to find work through Facebook is "become friends with fellow employees and people in your industry. It's less of a professional networking tool than LinkedIn, but you get to build more personal relationships, and who doesn't want to help out a friend in need?"

Erika Walker: Human Resources Manager

Erika Walker had received her MBA and was working as an assistant HR manager for a small transportation firm in Orlando, Florida, when the recession hit her hard, and she was laid off. Unemployed and living with her parents, she was frustrated by the lack of opportunities available in the summer of 2008.

"One evening I was chatting with my friend on Facebook about the horrific situation I found myself in while watching some of the videos he suggested to help me get over the first signs of depression," she said. "The videos were quite amusing, but I was not in the mood, so I briefly skimmed the whole page, looking for more interesting stuff. I came across an ad for an HR manager position. I did not take it seriously at first because I have never thought of Facebook as a place to advertise something. I had never even looked through those ads. But you can call it destiny if you want. I decided to see what it was all about and called the company the next day. I got the job with BestEssayHelp, and I am still working here, being more attentive to Facebook ads now!

Erika Walker found her job one evening while hanging out with a friend on Facebook.

"As an HR manager myself, I would say that it is possible to use Facebook as an advertising platform," Erika said. "One of my job responsibilities is to find and hire freelance writers to assist our clients." When we spoke with Erika, she was considering an advertising campaign to hire more freelance writers. "I think that Facebook will be one of the perfect search markets. As for the general Facebook advertising option, I would say that not all businesses or industries will profit from advertising on Facebook," she explained. "Freelance writing is kind of an informal position and is more likely to be noticed on Facebook."

LOOKING AHEAD

As you can see, it's quite possible to find work through Facebook, as the preceding accounts point out. Now it's your turn to get that profile in shape, start connecting, and get ready for what happens next. But that's not all. To help with your job search, Chapter 9 will show you how you can get a job lead through 140 simple characters, that is, when you put those characters together on Twitter to answer the ever-important question, "What's happening?"

CHAPTER 9

Twitter Your Way to That New Job

aybe at one time it was easy to dismiss Twitter (Twitter. com) as nothing more than a way to fritter away your time to no good end. That may have been true in 2007. But Twitter has gone mainstream since then, and if you don't make it part of your social media routine, you're making a mistake that could delay the successful end to your job search or cut off a steady stream of new business.

Twitter, shown in Figure 9-1, is the site that asks you to answer one simple question for the rest of the world to consider: *What's happening?* You must answer in 140 characters or less. When Twitter first started, the question posed was: *What are you doing?* That's no longer appropriate. Twitter is now a one-of-a-kind tool for real-time business research (among other things, of course), and it has grown far beyond its roots as a way for people to share status updates about whatever they happen to be doing. One thing that's remained, though, is that Twitter is fun and simple to use. And it has millions of fans worldwide.

Consider that no less than Guy Kawasaki, the former Apple evangelist with an unassailable reputation among techies, told the respected publishing industry blog MediaBistro that while "many people view e-mail and

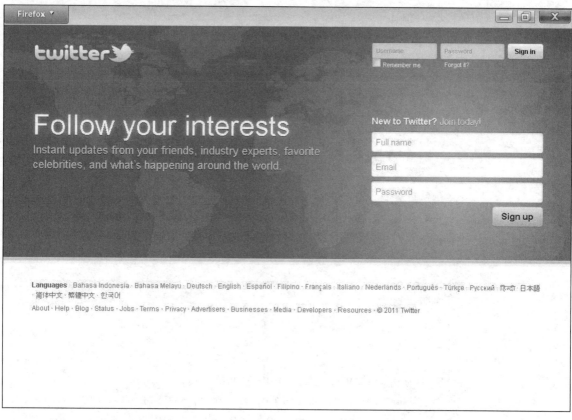

Figure 9-1: Twitter's homepage.

Twitter as kind of an adjunct to their main function, for me, it is my main function, and everything else is adjunct." He continued, "Twitter for me is not something I do when work is done for fun; Twitter is what I do."

So how did we get from a place where Twitter seemed like a frivolous time sink to where it's more vibrant than virtually all the more robust choices we have for social networking today? The story is actually quite fascinating. The *microblogging* site asks no more of you than to tell the world, in a very short phrase, what is happening at the moment. What about that makes a fellow like Guy Kawasaki use it all day long? Beyond the philosophical question, and more important for you as someone exploring new job options, how can you use Twitter to get that next job or freelance gig?

THE LOWDOWN ON TWITTER

Twitter launched in 2006 as a way for people to track what their friends were doing between e-mails, blog posts, and other slower types of communications. No one expected at the time that businesses would grow to use it to communicate in real time with customers and that individuals would use it to find new jobs. Yet that's just what has happened.

Twitter has taken off like a wildfire. Consider these stats from its blog:

- In January 2009, users sent 2 million tweets a day.
- By mid-2011, users were sending 200 million tweets a day.
- More than 25 billion tweets were sent in 2010.
- As of September 2011, Twitter had more than 100 million active users worldwide.

To further illustrate how important Twitter has become worldwide, consider some of the other people already using the site:

- *Leaders*. Twitter says that 35 heads of state worldwide use the site as a tool for communicating with their constituencies. These include Julia Gillard in Australia and Cristina Fernandez de Kirchner in Argentina. U.S.-based tweeters include every cabinet agency, 84 percent of state governors, and every major presidential candidate. Over 40 percent of the top religious leaders worldwide use the site, including the Dalai Lama and the Pope.
- *Athletes*. Many top U.S. athletes actively use Twitter. This includes two-thirds of the NBA, every NFL team, and many baseball, hockey, and basketball players, too. Cricket players from India, football stars from Europe, and many of their fans and commentators are also Twitterers.
- *Humanitarians*. Twitter reports that more than 99 percent of America's top 200 nonprofits use the site. During Hurricane Irene, the Federal Emergency Management Agency (FEMA) maintained a list of accounts to follow for breaking updates and official information.
- *Entertainers*. We don't have to tell you that many famous entertainers use Twitter, such as Lindsay Lohan, Lady Gaga, Martha Stewart, Tom Cruise, Katy Perry, Kevin Spacey, Larry King, Justin Bieber, and Taylor Swift. Twitter reports that as of 2010, 87 percent of *Billboard*'s "Top 100

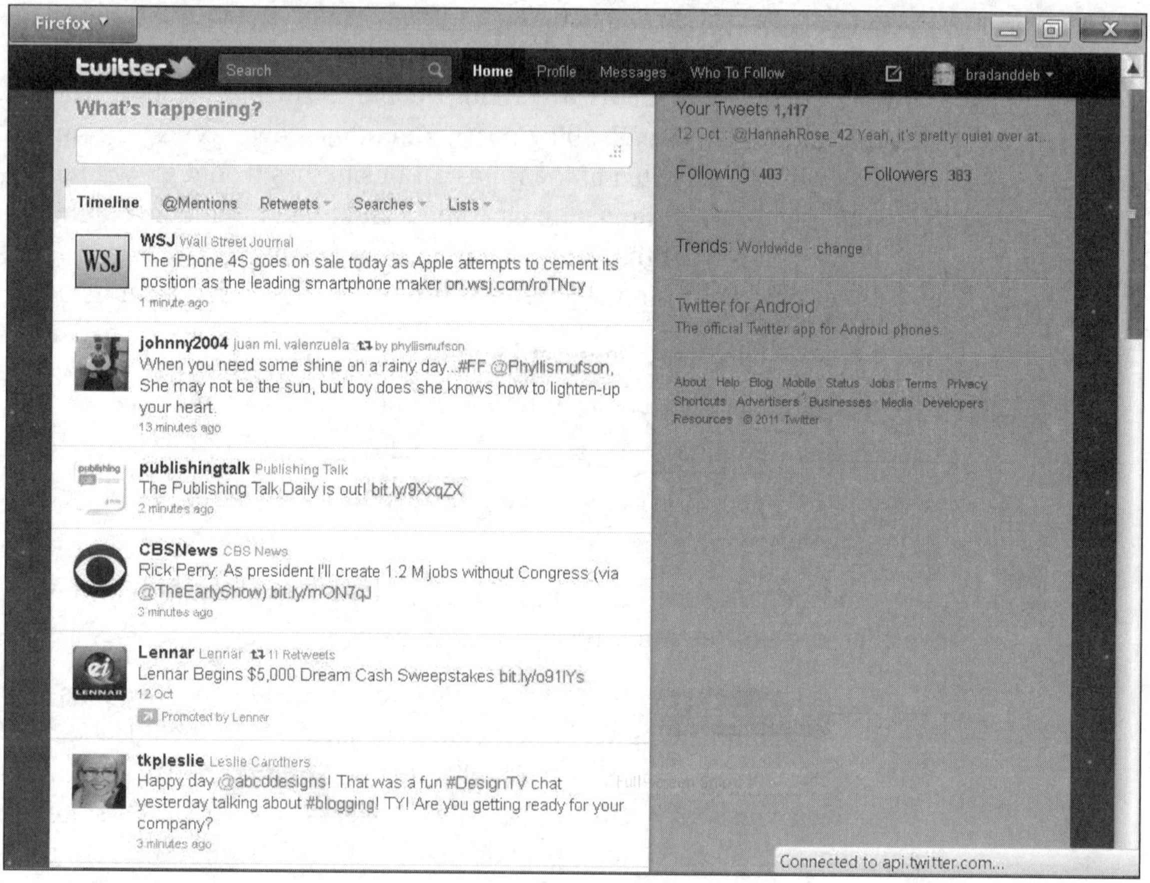

Figure 9-2: The screen where all your tweets will appear on Twitter.

Musicians" actively used the site to connect with fans. Not only that, every one of the top 50 TV shows is represented on the site.

Even with this awesome growth, Twitter is actually faster to use and better organized than it was when it was much smaller, yet it's retained its familiar look and feel. As with any other social networking site, however, you must use Twitter strategically and take advantage of the simple organizational tools it provides to use it effectively. While in the real world people tend to be either leaders or followers, on Twitter, most are both. That is, you can sign up to follow people whose *tweets* (messages) you want to receive, and then others can choose to follow your tweets of wisdom. Log on, and you'll see the latest tweets from your own network, as shown in Figure 9-2. You can choose to observe whenever you'd like. You can participate when the mood strikes or ignore the "tweetering" entirely when the mood passes. The choice is yours, and as in so many things, the more you put into Twitter, the more you get out of it.

Your Twitter Profile

Twitter doesn't ask you to input your life story or even anything nearly as detailed as what you entered for your LinkedIn profile. You just need to input the basics about who you are and why someone might want to take time out of a busy life to follow or connect with you on Twitter, that is, listen to your tweets.

In fact, aside from your username, you have just the following ways to present yourself to the world:

1. A one-line bio that can be no more than 160 characters

2. A "More Info" URL (for example, your website's or blog's address)

3. A picture

4. Your location

Twitter recommends that you include your location (the city will do) because you'll be more likely to turn up in searches that way. In fact, visibility in searches is another reason why you should use your real name (unless, of course, you're better known as Madonna, Lady Gaga, or Pink).

As you can see, a Twitter profile doesn't give you much opportunity to distinguish yourself. You can, however, choose your own background from one of Twitter's templates. From your main page, click "Profile," then edit your profile, and then click "Design." There are also third-party tools available that can help you. Sites that may be helpful here are tweetygotback. com, Threadless, and Themelon. If you are a job seeker, your profile still represents a possible first impression and is as important to your "tweeple" as your résumé. So tweak your profile before you do much tweeting.

And then make those tweets count! To get started, go to https://twitter .com/signup, shown in Figure 9-1. Once you've filled out the form, Twitter immediately asks if you want to follow any of a select group of people (for example, Kanye West), probably just to get you familiar with how to follow someone. Next, you are prompted to "add your contacts securely" by choosing one or more mail services (for example, Gmail) where you have an account. So, as with LinkedIn and Facebook, you'll need to enter your e-mail addresses and passwords for email services that Twitter supports.

Twitter then asks your permission to access your account(s) so that it can fetch your list of contacts. It then loads your address books and shows you which of your contacts are already using the site.

With your contacts imported, just click the "Follow" button under their picture or icon to follow them. Next, Twitter gives you the option of inviting the people who are in your address book but not yet on Twitter to join the social networking site. Twitter will send "invites" to them for you. Tweet! Finally, from that same screen that shows your contacts currently using Twitter, you can click one of the hyperlinks at the top to "View Suggestions" of who to follow or "Browse Interests" and then choose people to follow who are aligned with those interests (we'll have more on finding people to follow later on in this chapter). That's it. From then on, you'll start receiving tweets from the people you are following each time you log on. And soon people will start following your tweets, too, so get ready to tweet yourself!

Those 140 Characters

As you know, you have just 140 characters to work with when you answer the question "What's happening?" and send off those updates. You'll see people send tweets at all times of the day. It's no wonder you will learn that some people are putting their kids to bed, feeding their dogs, and so on. Certainly, tweets range from the mundane to the quite useful. You may be thinking, "Okay, but how do I get to the good stuff?" Fair enough. But stay with us. Soon you'll see how all this twittering can result in inter-actions with contacts at companies that interest you and even queries from employers and news of job opportunities.

We've deleted any identifying information, but other than that, here are some examples of tweets. The true power of Twitter will be clearer as you move down the list:

"Good morning every one! . . . don't let negativity bring you down today . . . stay positive =)"

"Excited to see my kids, tatay and our 3 dogs-Dollar, Sunny and Fufu"

"Thanks to Richard Brody for a lovely New Yorker blog entry. nyr.kr/qiZkWq"

"Google Invests $75 Million in Solar Panel Firm-on.mash.to/nF6ylX"

"Halloween Expected to Scare Up $6.9 Billion in Consumer Spending-adage.com/article/news/h . . ."

"new post: Office Pet Peeves–Are you driving your colleagues up the cubicle wall? bit.ly/nVG9n5 #in"

"Any SEO experts out there? Looking for guest suggestions to join my podcast show next week."

"Technical Analysis Associate - Region 1: Details: Experis Is Looking for a Technical Analysis Asso . . . http://cb.com/r5Wt9p #jobs #hiring"

Now those first couple of tweets, wishing you a friendly good morning and gushing over someone's arrival home from a trip, are time wasters if you're on the site to find work or do related research. But if you're considering a career in green energy, looking for a job in technical analysis, or just need to stay abreast of the current economic climate, there's plenty there to check out. You most likely will click at least a few of the hyperlinks to see what more you can learn. That's a pretty powerful use of 140 characters.

Now, as we said before, people are sending about 200 million tweets per day. Wouldn't it be great if you could just get the tweets that interest you? While it's not possible to weed out *everything* that's extraneous, thanks to Twitter's Lists feature (described later), you can organize the "Twitterverse" to suit your needs.

WHAT ARE *YOU* GOING TO TWEET ABOUT?

As someone who is looking for new job opportunities, you may focus on tweets that showcase articles you have written, very brief first-hand accounts of meetings and conventions you're attending, news you've come across related to your industry, and anything else that would demonstrate to a potential employer that you're bright, connected, ambitious, and hard working. Of course, who you tweet to is even more important than what you tweet about. As you move through this chapter, you'll see, in the section on people who have gotten jobs through Twitter, that they not only happened to say the right thing, but they also said it to the right person. But first, let's take a close look at the structure and vocabulary of Twitter and creating great tweets. Then we'll move on to building the connections with people you follow and those who follow you.

The Ways of Twitter

Just to get started: Here are 140 characters including the spaces. You can easily have your say within these limits. So have fun and make progress by twittering!

Twitter (like all communities) has its own vocabulary. Here are a few terms to get you started:

Direct messages: Messages you send directly to another Twitter user.

Follow: When you decide to receive someone else's tweets.

Follower: When someone is following your tweets.

Timeline: The stream of tweets presented to you each time you log on. These tweets appear in the order in which they were posted.

Tweet: A message, also called an *update*.

Tweetup: A face-to-face meeting of Twitter users.

Tweeple: People, people who use Twitter are the luckiest tweeple. Oh, sorry.

Widgets: Little programs that enable you to perform handy functions. There are Twitter widgets, for example, that enable you to show your newest tweets right on your website.

TWEETING ON TWITTER

As you go about creating your tweets, you can choose to have them be public or private. The setting is absolute, so if you do select to keep your tweets private, only the people within your Twitter network will be able to view and respond to them. For the purpose of job hunting, it seems most beneficial to keep most of your tweets public. How can a vast network of potential opportunities come your way if you've limited yourself to only those within your Twitter network? Plus, since you are exploring Twitter for job-hunting purposes, you are most likely making professional or at least responsible tweets. This is not the time or place to share your wild weekend plans with all the world, so there's no harm in letting others see what you're up to. As a matter of fact, there's a lot of good to it.

You may find a tweet to which you would like to respond. That's easy. Simply mouse over the last line of the tweet, and you'll see three icons pop up. One is a star that will allow you to highlight that particular tweet as a favorite. The next shows two bent arrows almost forming a square. Clicking that allows you to "re-tweet" the tweet, in other words send that same tweet to your own followers. (If you do this, the user name of the original poster and the letters "RT" will appear before your tweet.) The third icon is a left-facing arrow, and from there you can reply to the person who posted the tweet. Clicking there automatically adds the username of the tweeter to your dialogue box. Now it will say, for example, @bob432 before your tweet. You also can just put an @ sign before any username to respond to a tweet directly. As a job seeker, you may want to dialogue with someone, say, a manager, whose tweets have piqued your interest. In that case, you may want to respond directly to that person via a direct message.

The detailed mechanics of using the site are beyond the scope of this book. All the details you'll need are right there on the Twitter help pages, and you'll learn a lot by moving your way through the simple instructions posted on the site. We're going to focus on using Twitter for job hunting and trust that you will very quickly be up to speed on using this simple tool for all your other reasons. And besides, you can read all about it on the web for free.

Tiny URLs for Twitter

After so many years of living online, you've probably noticed that some web addresses are incredibly long. Cutting and pasting makes it easy to put those long URLs into e-mails or blog pieces. That's okay if you have plenty of space, and everyone knows to expect this serving of alphabet soup, but what if your space is limited to a tweet of 140 characters? For example, one retailer's URL for our McGraw-Hill book, *How to Make Money with YouTube,* is 121 characters long. Obviously, we couldn't include this in a tweet and still have anything useful left to say about the book. No worries. Twitter will automatically shorten your link. Copy any link into your Tweet box, finish composing your Tweet, and hit the button to send it. Twitter will automatically shorten the link to 19 characters.

Good Tweets for Job Seekers

It's one thing to tweet about what you're eating, the latest funny thing the dog did, or how your toddler embarrassed you in public yesterday if you're not in the market for a new job. Twitter is a fun place for just "being social." (If you still want to feel free to do this, you can maintain separate Twitter accounts for personal and business use.) But, if you've come to Twitter to have a business communications tool, you'll want each of your tweets to shine as an example of who you are and what you can do. Here are examples of tweets with a purpose. They're good because they provide useful, actionable information and/or cast a positive light on the tweeter.

"See my latest blog post on network security and social networking sites at http/xxx.xxx."

"Have a Fully Integrated Marketing Plan http://short.to/lsy."

"Google+ Traffic jumps 13-fold after opening to the public (Study) http:xxx.xxx."

Don't Let Your Tweets Turn Out Like This

Yes, you eventually may want to use Twitter for fun, and lots of people do. But that point will come only after you've secured your next job and are happily enjoying your new life. By now, you've seen how important it is to behave well on all social networks. They really are your new public persona as much as the clothes you choose to wear or the company you keep. Here are some examples of tweets that really could derail you. So please don't forget for a minute that you are on a public forum that easily could be explored by that hiring manager comparing your credentials with those of your competitor for that single job opening.

"Trying to convince this 2-year-old to sleep!"

"Just ate dinner and am now ready for a nap."

"Any jobs out there in sales or marketing? I'll take anything."

"The Ravens gave it their best but the Steelers are just a better team."

FINDING PEOPLE TO FOLLOW

It's not who you know but who you follow, at least as far as Twitter goes. Start by clicking the "Who to Follow" hyperlink at the top of most Twitter pages. You'll see a search box to let you get right down to finding friends on the site, but you also can let the site help you search by using the tabs that run along the top of the page. Those tabs let you "View Suggestions," "Browse Interests," and "Find Friends." Of course, you will want to follow people from your e-mail address books and other sources who may be in a position to hire you or help you with a job-related question. Perhaps some of the people you'll follow are just intellectually stimulating or competitors you want to track. Increasingly, when you're on a website or blog, you'll see a "Twitter" button you can click on to follow that person or organization. If you are looking for a job in a given field, it definitely pays to follow people in that field who are on Twitter. In Chapter 8 we suggested that you blue sky it and create a list of companies for which you might like to work. If you have that list, you can put it to work again. If not, now is a good time to create it.

Once you have your list of prospective employers, click that "Who to Follow" link at the top of your homepage. Enter one of your company names in the search box on the page that comes up. You may be surprised at what turns up. For example, the pharmaceutical company MedImmune employs a lot of tech writers, and we track it for that reason. We entered "MedImmune" in the search box and retrieved the search results shown in Figure 9-3. As you can see, we found the company's official Twitter feed, recruiters who fill jobs for the company, and some of the people who work there. Now, if you were to do that same search from the search box right on your homepage, you would receive far-ranging tweets that mention the company for some reason. Some of those tweets also may be useful.

After you've pinpointed recruiters or managers and you've done your homework on the company, start a dialog with those managers. Build a relationship. Demonstrate a genuine interest in the company and its products, services, or mission. After you have built a relationship, then you can express an interest in learning even more about the company. And you can do all that through Twitter!

There are also many organizations on Twitter that post jobs related to specific fields. For example, you can find library jobs by following @ala_joblist, @musicjobs delivers music industry jobs, @socialmediajob compiles listings in that field, and @medical_jobs posts, well, medical-related jobs. There are also postings available by region, such as @chicagowebjobs and @sdjobs.

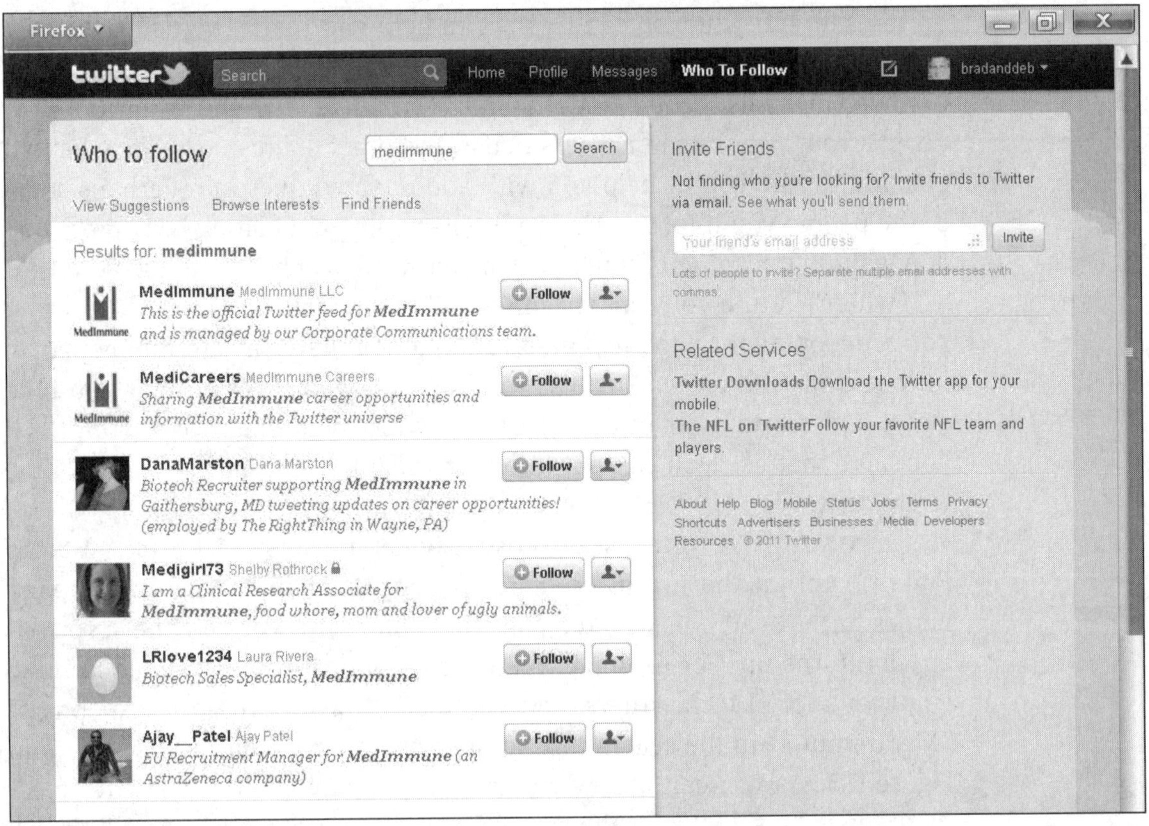

Figure 9-3: Click the "Who to Follow" link on your homepage, and enter a company name to locate key contacts.

Jacob Bettany: Twitter Helped Broaden This Publisher's Reach

Jacob Bettany is the managing director of MoneyScience, Ltd. He is also a publishing consultant. He uses Twitter to both promote his editorial content and highlight external content that he finds relevant to his company's work. "I use Twitter for publishing primarily, as a tool for promoting editorial content I produce and highlighting external content," Jacob explained. "I have five main accounts covering assorted verticals, including accounts for risk management, financial technology, finance education, hedge funds, and a general finance." As we write this, Jacob's combined accounts had approximately 10,000 followers.

Jacob graciously shared with us the story of how Twitter allowed him to locate investors. Here is his story in his own words:

The connection I made on Twitter was with one of the principals of a small venture-capital firm called Thematic Capital Partners. They were using Twitter to promote a new social network for investment professionals called Hedgehogs, which is a test base for a set of proprietary social media tools. Since I'd been keeping a close eye on developments in the social media and finance communities, Hedgehogs stood out as something a bit different, and for several months I observed their progress from a distance. In all honesty, I can't recall who it was that initiated the Twitter conversation, but we moved to a phone call, and it became clear very quickly that our interests and objectives were quite closely aligned. Not only that, but it turned out that my skill set and background in publishing were pretty much exactly what they were missing as a company.

Jacob Bettany used Twitter to expand his publishing business and find venture capital.

Over the course of the next 12 months, we were in fairly regular contact, and when an opportunity came up for Thematic to invest in MoneyScience, we did a deal wherein not only would they give me access to the technology they'd been developing over the previous year, but I would take on a publishing consultancy role across their developing social media portfolio. Following the initial investment in April 2010, things took a while to get going in terms of the MoneyScience development, but I was able to make a general contribution, and then in the early part of 2011, I began working closely with their development team to design and build a content management "front end" for their social platform. In doing so, we significantly enhanced their offering.

That Twitter connection has become, to me, a fairly powerful indication of what social media is capable of. In some ways it felt like pure serendipity that we had made the connection in the first place, but over time, I have come to realize that it was using the tool consistently, raising the profile of my work, and thinking intelligently about my own objectives that made it possible. Indeed, since then, I have repeated the experience time and time again, finding supporters, collaborators, and even customers through the tool.

We asked Jacob to advise others who may want to achieve his type of success through Twitter. "I would say, in the case of Twitter, the key thing is not to expect things to happen too quickly," he replied. "It takes time to build up a reputation, and it helps to have something to support that, a blog or other website. As with many areas of business, patience, persistence, and intelligent opportunism are useful qualities. Identify people or organizations you want to notice you, and find something interesting to say to them, again and again and again."

GETTING PEOPLE TO FOLLOW YOU

Your goal should be not just to follow people of interest but also to get people to follow you, especially if you are a person with something to sell, such as a great work history. Once you have followers, you've become a publisher, and any publisher will tell you that they want as many people (subscribers) to see their messages as possible. Your group of followers will receive your tweets and thus will be the first to know if you've published a savvy new blog entry. Other people can come across you by doing a Find People search, or they may come across your tweets if they're posted on the Public Timeline.

If you're building a following, however, as someone seeking new opportunities should be, invite people to follow you on Twitter by promoting your Twitter address. You can do this in many ways. For example, include it as part of your e-mail signature, within blog articles you write, or on your web page. Include the line, "Follow me on Twitter: http://twitter.com/yourname." Note that you can opt to "protect your updates" and have just the people who you approve be able to follow your tweets. You do this by checking the "Protect My Tweets" box on your Settings page. This means that they will not be part of that Public Timeline we just mentioned.

TWITTER AND JOB HUNTING

There are mixed opinions about whether you should blatantly tweet that you are looking for a new job. Some have done so and gotten work that way. We feel that you *should* alert fellow tweeters that your status has changed. Why not? Nobody, of course, likes to disappoint a job hunter by out-and-out stating that they don't have a job open. But if you tweet that you are open to new challenges in the [fill in the blank] field, that's a lot different. No one has to tell you face to face or over the phone that they don't know of anything. They can just not respond to your tweet. Of course, the ones who may know of an opening may be happy to step forward with a simple tweet in return.

If you just keep up with the culture of social networks, you'll still post lots of tweets that are interesting to the people who follow you. Here's a quick and easy way to prove your industry expertise and your commitment to sharing valuable information and links with people who share your interests and passions. As always, give more than you ask for, and before you know it, your followers will consider you a valuable asset in their own work lives, making it all that much more likely that someone will want to work with you when a job opens up.

Miriam Salpeter: Steps for Starting Out on Twitter

Miriam Salpeter, a career counselor who helps people use web tools to job hunt successfully, is a true Twitter expert. She was generous enough to share her tips for using Twitter. These were originally part of her blog post, "Use Twitter for Your Job Hunt." We highly recommend that you visit her at keppiecareers.com.

- Brand yourself professionally. If you are planning to use Twitter for a job search, set up a designated profile and account. Choose a professional Twitter handle using your name or some combination of your name and profession that sounds good and is easy to remember, for example, JaneSmith or MarketingExpertJane.

- Take time to create a professional profile that will attract your target market. If you don't have a website, link to your LinkedIn profile.

Miriam Salpeter owns KeppieCareers, an executive placement firm.

- Before you follow anyone, start posting some tweets! Don't succumb to the temptation to share your lunch menu! Tweet about an article or an idea, or share a link of professional interest to your targeted followers. Do this for a few days. It may seem strange to be tweeting when no one is following, but you may be surprised to gain an audience before you even try. Once you have a great profile and a set of interesting tweets, start following people in your industry. Aim high! Follow stars—some will follow you back.

- Continue to build your network by using Twitter Search and Twitter's Find People tool. Manually review profiles, and use Twubble to help you find new people to follow. Use directories such as Twellow and TwitDir. Grow your network slowly—you don't want to follow 1,000 people and have only 30 following you. That makes you look spammy, not professional.

- Another tool to use to learn what is going on in your area of expertise is Monitter (hat tip to Steve Cornelius). Steve used it to look up information about a company where he was interviewing. It is also great to see what people are talking about and to find conversations to join on Twitter.

- Give, give, give! Think about what you can do for others. Don't blatantly self-promote. Instead, help promote others. "Re-tweet" (pass along information someone else shared, giving them credit). You will earn followers and friends this way. Those who know (and like) you will become part of your network and will be willing to help you.

Get Organized with Lists!

We've described for you how LinkedIn enables you to organize your contacts and newsfeed and how Facebook lets you do the same through its Lists feature. On Twitter, your organizational challenges can be even greater (depending on the number of people you follow) as tweet after tweet appears on your homepage faster than those chocolates appeared on Lucy's conveyer belt. Not only that, those tweets can come from any one of the people you follow, so mixed in with news from that publisher you've been tracking are updates from your brother about how miserable the weather has been. Talk about distractions!

Now what if you could organize those tweets so that you could view just the ones from your family or just those from clients or companies you're thinking of applying to? You can, through Lists.

Creating Lists

Let's create some lists so that you can see for yourself how simple it can be to organize your Twitter time. Take another look at Figure 9-2, which

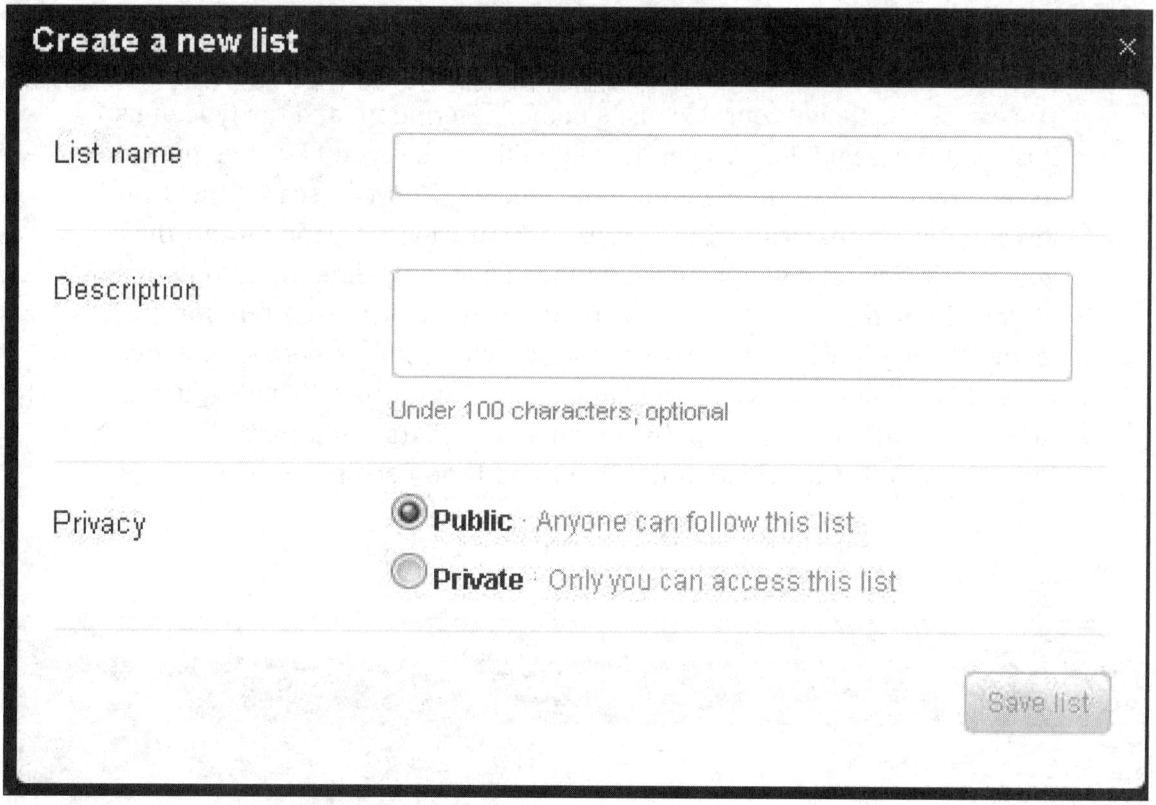

Create a new list   ✕

List name

[   ]

Description

[   ]

Under 100 characters, optional

Privacy   ⦿ **Public** · Anyone can follow this list

                 ○ **Private** · Only you can access this list

                                                    [Save list]

Figure 9-4: From this page you can create lists on Twitter.

happens to be our homepage. Right under the "What's happening?" box, you'll see five hyperlinks. The last one is "Lists." If you were to click on the down arrow by that link, you would see the "Create a list" hyperlink. Click that, and you'll see the box shown in Figure 9-4. Simply create a name for your list (for example, Employers), and write a description if you'd like. The last thing you'll need to do is determine whether you wish for your list to be public, meaning that it will appear on your homepage for anyone to see (including the people comprising it), or private. We find that we keep general lists public, such as those we have for publishers and agents. But lists that are more personal in nature (such as one we have for clients) are private. After you've made your designation, just click the "Save list" button.

Adding People to Your Lists

Once you've created a list, you'll see the screen shown in Figure 9-5. As you can see, it shows your new list's name, description, and the type of list it is (in this case public). Lower down you'll see that you have two options for adding people to the list you have created. You can search the Twitterverse for usernames or businesses, or you can add people from those you are already following by clicking the "Following" link in the right half of your homepage. On the far right side of the description box for each follower, there's a gray box with a picture representing a person. Roll over the down arrows, and you'll see an option "Add to list." Once you click that, a separate box will pop up showing your list(s), and from there you just select the list to which you'd like to add the person (or create a new one right from there).

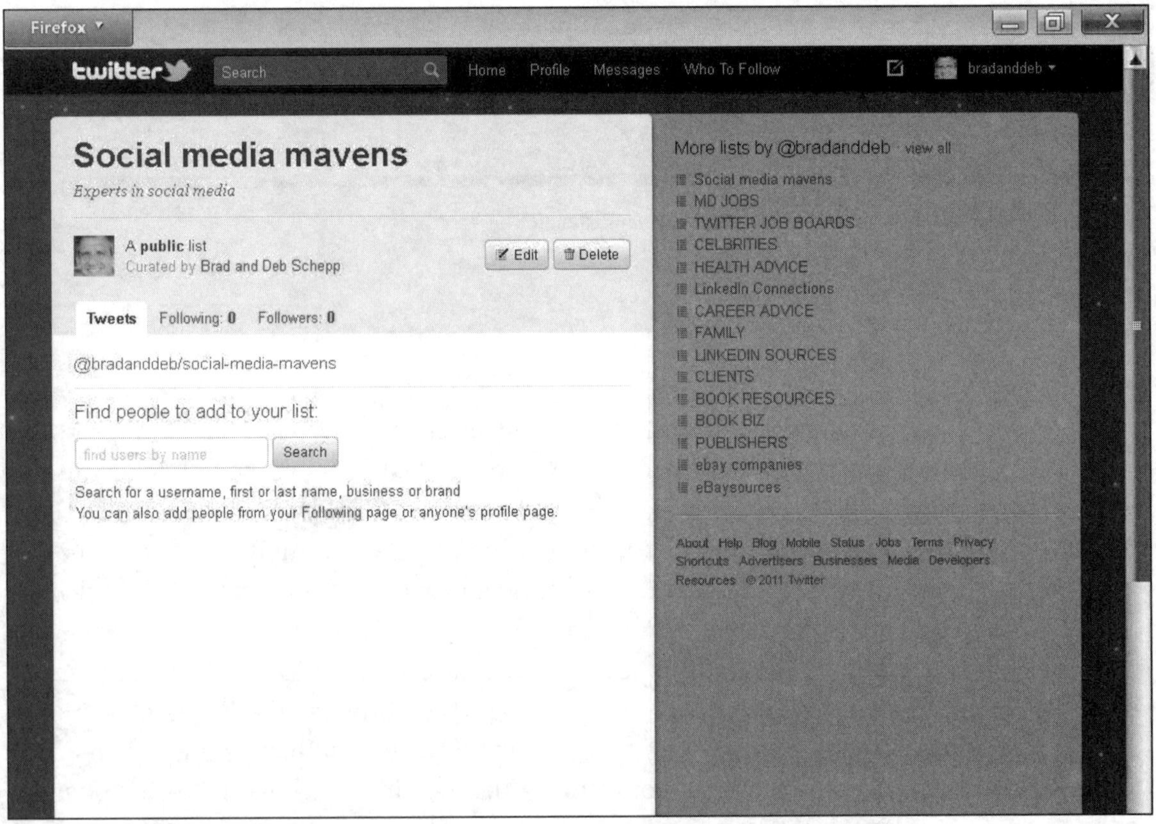

Figure 9-5: This is the screen that appears once you've created a list.

Using Your Lists

Once you've created one or more lists, they will appear when you click the down arrow next to the "Lists" link on your homepage. From there you just click on the list you're interested in at the moment, and you'll be shown just the tweets from the people who comprise that list. Note that you can edit or delete a list at any time.

Subscribing to/Following Other Lists

It's as easy to follow someone else's list as it is to follow a person. Start by going to the profile for a person or entity you truly respect or just want to learn more about. Click the down arrow next to the "Lists" hyperlink above their current tweets. Select one or more lists that you'd like to follow, click the green + box, and a check will appear indicating that you're now following that list. The new list will appear in your own menu of lists under the head "Lists you Follow."

Twitter Tools to Organize and Job Hunt

We don't know if it's the name, the openness of the platform, or the growing number of users, but programmers sure seem to like developing great little programs for use with Twitter. We've listed just a few here:

Listorious at listorious.com. A directory of people on Twitter broken down by category. Using Listorious is a good way to find interesting people to follow. You even can add yourself to the directory.

Twhirl at twhirl.org. This is a desktop-based software program that makes using Twitter easier and staying on top of new tweets even simpler. You can download it right from the site. It runs on both Windows and Mac platforms.

TweetDeck at tweetdeck.com. This organizes and displays your feeds from Twitter, LinkedIn, Facebook, and other sites. You can download it for your desktop computer as well as for your mobile device.

TwitBin at twitbin.com. Can't keep from Twittering even when you're doing other things on the web? TwitBin may be your savior. This little program is designed to work with your Firefox browser. It will let you monitor the latest postings from your Twitter connections and even send messages without leaving your browser screen.

TweetMyJobs at tweetmyjobs.com. This used to be a site for locating job openings on Twitter, but it's now much more. Like LinkedIn, you can use the site to search for job listings by entering keywords and a location. Once you zero in on an ad that looks promising, you click the "Who Do You Know" button to search your social network contacts to see who may be of help.

TwitterJobSearch at twitjobsearch.com. This bills itself as "a job search engine for Twitter." As you may have guessed, it enables you to search through thousands of fresh job postings on the site. It's fast and current, and you also can have results from your favorite searches e-mailed to you.

There are many other tools for use with Twitter. Try a Google search for "Twitter Job Tools" or something similar to see what else you may find useful.

Entrepreneurs and Twitter

In researching an article we wrote for an e-commerce newsletter, we found many examples of entrepreneurs using Twitter to build their brands and drive traffic to their own websites, where they could complete sales. We've already discussed how consultants, for example, have found work through Twitter. Here are some other examples of how entrepreneurs can use Twitter:

- e-Commerce sellers tell their customers about new items they have for sale.
- Promoters such as David Mullings of Realvibez announce new products and clients.
- Anyone with a new website might want to let all his friends and past clients in on special discounts and deals.
- Growing companies that have a lot of people using their products tweet about outages, new services, special promotions, and the like.

Kathy Colaiacova: Virtual Assistant Builds a Thriving Business Through Social Media

When she started her Virtual Assistant business in 2007, Kathy Colaiacovo planned that she would help small-business owners with e-mail management,

Kathy Colaiacova used Twitter to build a thriving business as a virtual assistant.

making flyers, and support for their websites. Then, in June 2008, she discovered Twitter, and "my life changed forever!" she told us.

"I found out I love networking online and did it with lots of gusto. It was such a fabulous way to connect with other people. Within two months, I landed one of my first clients, but one who contacted me directly through Twitter." That same month another client hired Kathy through an online forum she frequented, based on the networking she'd done there.

"I have built my Virtual Assistant business to a six-figure business in three years and now have six virtual assistants working with me as my team of VA associates. I recently branched out more into the social media training part of my business, which I started in 2010."

"My online networking has indeed built my business," Kathy told us. Approximately, 25 percent of her new business comes directly from Twitter and social media. Another 55 percent are people contacting her after online searches for "social media virtual assistant" or other closely related terms. The other 20 percent comes from referrals. "My only real marketing is social media, my e-mail list, and my blogs," Kathy explained. "I do not do any direct mail and only network locally every couple months. The rest is purely via Twitter, Facebook, and LinkedIn. The time I invest is approximately one hour a day on all parts combined (blog included). Then I have a virtual assistant who helps with some parts as well for approximately eight hours a month.

"It's common for me to get an e-mail such as this one from someone contacting me off my website: 'I saw your message on Twitter about being able to assist virtually. I am looking for . . . ,' and she is now a client," Kathy explained. "I say that social media and online networking have built my business, and it is the truth. I only have one current local client. All others are spread out through Canada and mostly the United States, as is my team. This would never have happened if it had not been for the world online that I participate in daily. My business, as it is now, could never have existed five years ago. Social Media, and a big part of that being Twitter, has definitely changed my world," she said.

WE FOUND OUR JOBS THROUGH TWITTER!

When we started writing the first edition of this book in 2009, we admit that we had our doubts about Twitter's effectiveness for job hunters. No more. In fact, we think Twitter is among the social networking sites job hunters must use. Turn over a few stones, and you can find many accounts of people who have found work through Twitter and, as a corollary, who have hired people they've met through Twitter. As Twitter has grown, its usefulness as a tool for locating applicants and announcing new jobs has grown right along with it.

Joshua Bauder: President of Marketing and Advertising

"Twitter is the main site that has helped me get a job," said Joshua Bauder. "It helped me get a job with CityPockets, where I was the marketing and social media intern. That position is what helped lead me to my current position with Happy Toy Machine, where I'm the president of marketing and advertising. The way that it helped me get the job was that it showed that even though I don't have a background in marketing, I was able to connect with specific niche markets and engage in conversation with them. We're currently using social media in our recruiting efforts. We track specific keywords related to our positions, and if someone tweets about them, we engage in conversation with them and work on finding out more about them. After we have tweeted back and forth with them for a while, we then decide whether or not we want to have a formal interview with them. We also use social media to advertise for positions and to track our competitors' hiring efforts."

Joshua Bauder found his job as the president of marketing and advertising with Happy Toy Machine through Twitter.

Brooke Burris: Community Manager

Brooke Burris was an incredibly prolific Twitter user living in Portland. A principal at a marketing and event firm in Seattle started reading and responding to her tweets. When she tweeted that she was moving to Seattle, he reached out to ask if she was interested in a job with his company. She interviewed and soon had a new job. While she loved this job, it was only part time. A friend of Brooke's also was friends with Megan Montplaisir, director of social media for Nology, a Seattle-based social media strategy and content company. Brooke's friend "re-tweeted" a Nology media post about a job as community manager. Brooke got the interview. Megan only learned about the mutual friend after the first interview, but she'd already started following Brooke on Twitter. She saw that Brooke

Brooke Burris actually landed her last two jobs through her Twitter activity.

tweeted a lot about advertising, social media, and the digital industry. Soon Megan offered Brooke the job as community manager, and that's where you'll find Brooke today.

Scarlet Paolicchi: Blogger and Social Marketing Maven

Scarlet Paolicchi is a stay-at-home mom who has built a business blogging and helping companies market their products through social media. Her social marketing business can be found at momswearyourtees.com, and her blog is familyfocusblog.com. She won the prestigious 2011 StartupNation Leading Moms Business Award. "I have found lots of jobs through Twitter," Scarlett said. "As a mom blogger, I work for myself, but only if I keep busy finding clients. Twitter is a great source of finding new clients to represent. I have had so many clients approach me over Twitter and ask me if I would like to do a review. I was actually surprised the first few times because I did not solicit over Twitter at the time. After being approached multiple times by multiple companies on Twitter, I have solicited with success myself. I once found several sponsors for an Earth Day event I wanted to host just by tweeting that I was accepting sponsors for the event.

Amybeth Hale: Talent Attraction Manager

Amybeth Hale found a job within 24 hours of being laid off, and it all happened because of Twitter. "I was working for a PR agency and was laid off in February 2009," she told us. "Ironically, the night before I was laid off I was speaking to the Cincinnati chapter of the Public Relations Society of America on networking during tough economic times with a specific focus on job search. I found myself having to take my own advice the very next day. After being upset for a couple hours, I realized it was a perfect opportunity for me to practice what I'd been preaching for the past six+ years. I started e-mailing and direct messaging select contacts on Twitter, one of whom was working at AT&T. He told me that he just happened to need someone on his team with my skills. I interviewed the next day and was told that the job was mine if I wanted it. I, of course, did due diligence with a couple other interviews I had set up, but ultimately, I took the opportunity—a contract gig—and was working with AT&T for just over a year. I worked as a talent attraction manager (working with the recruiting team). I am not there anymore. I left on my own accord to pursue an editorial position with a recruiting media company, ERE Media, Inc."

Robb Hecht: Consultant

Social media marketing expert Robb Hecht had long used Twitter successfully to network with people "he wanted to know and learn new things about." In the process, however, he struck gold in the form of recruiters seeking him out for paid consulting gigs. "Twitter Search is the culprit for this," Rob explained. "Twitter Search allows you to follow conversations that include keywords that you choose. So, while, for example, I was searching for the latest innovations in the web 2.0 arena relevant to consumer product goods, I ran into recruiters passively who then would contact me, and within say a week, I'd have an offer for consulting work. The key here, the client said, was that I connected my

Twitter account to my LinkedIn profile—which allowed him to passively look at my background and then decide to approach me to see if I'd do any consulting work for their company."

Leslie Carothers: Social Media Campaign Strategist and Virtual Assistant

Leslie Carothers, owner of The Kaleidoscope Partnership based in Minneapolis, specializes in social web conversations for the home industries. Here's Leslie's story in her own words:

> I own a business called The Kaleidoscope Partnership. I have owned it for seven years now and also write online and offline for two major industry publications, *Furniture Today* and *Furniture World*, on how retailers, manufacturers, and suppliers can use social web conversations to connect and engage potential consumers.

> In January, I hired a virtual assistant through Twitter and have been very pleased with the quality and timeliness of her work for me. In addition, I will be signing a contract with a company to conduct a social web media marketing campaign for them. We have never met, and the owner decided to trust me based simply on my "tweets." Interestingly, he lives in Spain, is a very successful businessman, and . . . is 18 years old.

> In addition, I have opened up viable business opportunities for both my clients for whom I am twittering: BiOH Polyols, a division of Cargill that sells a soy-based replacement for foam to the furniture, bedding, and auto industries, and www.yourfurniturelink.com, a website devoted to helping consumers quickly connect with manufacturers directly to order the furniture featured on this site.

Bob Wilson: Director of New Media

Bob Wilson was hired by Moxley Carmichael (www.moxleycarmichael.com), and if not for Twitter, it may never have happened.

"The tweetup was simply a few downtown Knoxville users of Twitter getting together for a few drinks and to meet each other in person," said Bob. "A few pockets of people knew each other, but in many cases the pockets did not cross over. We intentionally kept the size small to facilitate conversation, and that worked well. I had heard of other local events that were larger and did not work as well."

LOOKING AHEAD

No doubt you are now positively atwitter with all the possibilities of using Twitter to advance your career goals, learn new things, share your expertise, and have some fun, too. It's a very good thing that your creative juices are flowing because your next destination is a newcomer to the social networking scene, but it is already garnering a huge amount of recognition and excitement just because its name is Google+. As always, you can expect Google to go in and go big.

CHAPTER 10

Google+—The New Kid on the Block

L inkedIn, Facebook, Twitter—they're all social networking sites that have existed for less than a decade. Yet combined they have more than 1 billion users, and they've helped thousands of people land new jobs or work as independent contractors/ freelancers. In this chapter we'll take a look at the new "kid" on the social network scene—Google + .

As we write this, Google + , which launched on June 28, 2011, has been available for only four months. For all but one week of those four months it was available by invitation only. On September 20, 2011, Google opened Google + to anyone over 18 who had a Google account. Once Google opened the floodgates, its user base grew by more than 1,200 percent in one week!

While it's not clear exactly how many users Google + has as we write this, most sources estimate from 30 to 50 million. This is a mere fraction of Facebook's 800 million, of course, and still considerably below what Twitter and LinkedIn can claim. Yet Google + users are enthralled with the service's possibilities, and with Google and its 1 billion strong user base behind it, there's little doubt that the service has the potential to go from new kid to captain of the football team real fast.

We don't have stories to recount for you of how people have used the site to land work in this chapter. It's too soon for that. Yet we know that were we to revise this book in two years or so, we'd be likely to fill that next edition with scores of such stories.

THE GENESIS OF GOOGLE+

As much as we all admire Google—and it's clear that no other company has come close to it in the online search space—the company has created social media products before only to have them fall short of expectations. The company never truly competed with the big three—Facebook, Twitter, and LinkedIn. We are going to go out on a limb here and say that Google+ is different and that it will succeed where those other Google social networking products did not.

There's no reason to describe in any detail those failed products here. They include Google Buzz and Google Wave. But so far—and again, it's very early as we write this—Google+ looks different. Its users are enamored with it, competitors such as Facebook are enhancing their sites with features similar to Google+'s, and it's more robust than anything Google has offered before. We believe that it will be here for a good long time as a viable player in the social networking world.

Putting Google+'s Growth in Perspective

- LinkedIn, launched in May 2003, reached the 1 million member milestone in December 2004.

- Facebook, launched in February 2004, had 1 million users after 10 months.

- Twitter, launched in July 2006, had 340,000 registered accounts in July 2007.

- Google+, after only 4 months (again, of which it was available publicly only for one week), had an estimated 30 to 50 million users.

We realize that this isn't exactly a fair comparison. The terrain was very different in 2003 and 2004 when LinkedIn and Facebook were getting started. To expect growth rates then that are comparable with those possible in 2011 isn't fair. Yet, undoubtedly, Google + has achieved remarkable growth in a very short time period, and with 1 billion Google users, Google + has a whole lot of room to grow. Plus, let's not forget the simple fact that within our lives in 2011, google is a verb. A lot of folks who may have felt reluctant to venture onto other social networking sites just may take a shot at Google + after having already spent so many years googling.

Why Google+?

For those of us who have already chosen our favorite social media sites, what's the incentive to spend the time and effort necessary to add another one to the mix? Put bluntly, why bother with Google + ? We recently spoke with Jim Prosser, Google's manager of global communication, who characterized the thinking behind Google + like this:

We realize that today people are increasingly connecting with one another on the web. But the ways in which we connect online are limited and don't mimic our real-life relationships. The Google + project is our attempt to make online sharing even better. We aren't trying to replace what's currently available. We just want to introduce a new way to connect online with the people that matter to you.

So Google + offers a "new way to connect online," and we think that by the time you've finished this chapter, you'll agree that Google + as a whole does offer ways to connect with people that its competitors do not—at least not as easily as does Google + .

What exactly does it mean to have Google + come on the scene with the power of Google behind it? For some insights, we spoke with bestselling author and Google + expert Chris Brogan for an article we wrote for the Auctiva website (auctiva.com).

Search is the easiest answer. Google owns the number 1 and number 2 biggest search engines in the world (Google and YouTube), so Google + is indexed by Google, meaning that any public content you share there gives you search ranking potential for this platform. It's the opposite of Facebook, which isn't indexed by Google at all.

So, if it's important to you to reach as wide an audience as possible with your posts, then you could do no better than to use Google + .

With this as background, let's take a look at Google+ for ourselves. If you have not registered yet, just go to Google's homepage and click the "+You" link at the far left of the page. You'll then see the screen shown in Figure 10-1. If you already have a Google account, you can just sign in with that. Otherwise, you'll need to create a Google account first before you can use Google+. This involves entering a current e-mail address and a password, so we won't dwell on that.

Everything you'll need to learn about using the features in Google+ are in the Help area, which you reach by clicking the wheel icon next to your picture or icon on the far right corner of your homepage. Again, we're not

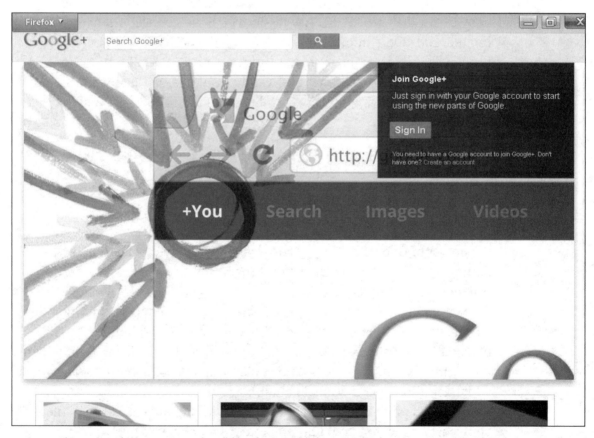

Figure 10-1: The page you see after clicking the "+You" link on Google's homepage (assuming that you're not yet a Google+ member).

going to step you through something so simply found and used; we're just giving you the lay of the land.

Even people who consider themselves experienced social networkers can be a bit baffled initially by Google+. So take a good look around, and give yourself some time to test the waters a bit before diving in. We recommend that you click on the links and view the video embedded in the "Getting Started on Google+" e-mail message you'll receive once you have registered.

When you first look at a Google+ screen, you may think that it looks a lot like Facebook's screen. This is because it does. Your Google+ stream runs right down the center of your screen, much like Facebook's newsfeed. You'll find suggested friends on the right and links to search for more friends, too. It all looks very familiar in a comforting way. Now, let's raise the hood and take a look at each of the site's features.

Circles Make Your Google+ World Go Round

From the beginning, as you first identify people to connect with on the site, you are encouraged to organize them into what Google+ calls Circles. According to Google, the idea behind Circles is to make "online sharing more like your real-life relationships, where you choose who gets to know what." So you can send chatty updates just to your family, thoughts about the latest books you've read to just your book club, and news of your latest accomplishments to one or more of your business circles.

Circles are Google+'s most discussed feature, and we can see why. They make organizing your contacts easy—even fun. With other social networking sites, you're much more likely to have amassed a large number of connections, friends, or people you follow, before setting about organizing them in some way. Google, realizing the value in organization, has you do it from the start.

When you import an e-mail address book, for example, you'll be asked to place each contact into a Circle. Simply drag and drop each contact's photo or icon to one of Google+'s default Circles—Friends, Family, Acquaintances, and Following—or create customized circles of your own (for example, Employers). You may add people to your Circles without them having to reciprocate. In that sense, Google+ is more like Twitter than Facebook. You can "follow" people, whether they have agreed to be friends or not.

What does it mean to add someone to a Circle? Google explains:

- You can share messages, photos, links, and the like with them, and they can do the same with you.

- Google will e-mail them when you've added them to a Circle, and of course, they can return the favor and add you to one of their own. Incidentally, they will never see the name of the Circle to which you've added them.

- They'll appear on your public profile (although this is an option you can change).

If you use Circles to control just who receives which of your postings, there's no need to have separate business and personal accounts on Google +.

Finding People to Add to Your Circles

This step will be familiar to you. Once you've registered, Google + will prompt you to add people you know to your Circles so you can start sharing. Provide the logon information for the e-mail services you use, and Google fetches information for your correspondents so that you can decide which, if any, Circles to add them to. Take your time with this step because organizing your contacts in this way from the start will help you to get the most from Google +.

Next, you can use the "Search" bar to find people who you might like to add to your Circles. Also, when you click the "Continue" button at the bottom of the page, Google will present its current "Picks" for well-known people you might consider adding to your Circles. These include celebrities, well-known tech industry executives, or just people whom Google feels you might find "fun and interesting." We've created a Circle for people like this, labeled "Celebrities." We click on it when we're looking for a diversion from our regular work.

In your quest to find people to add to your Circles, be sure to check out directories such as www.recommendedusers.com (Figure 10-2), which categorizes Google + users by field (artists and designers, bloggers, web celebrities, journalists, and so on). Pick a category, and you'll be shown a list of recommended users to follow on Google +. Another directory we recommend is findpeopleonplus.com. Once you've located new people to add to your Circles (you don't need permission or approval to do this; remember that one of Google +'s ready-made Circles is "Following"), you can check

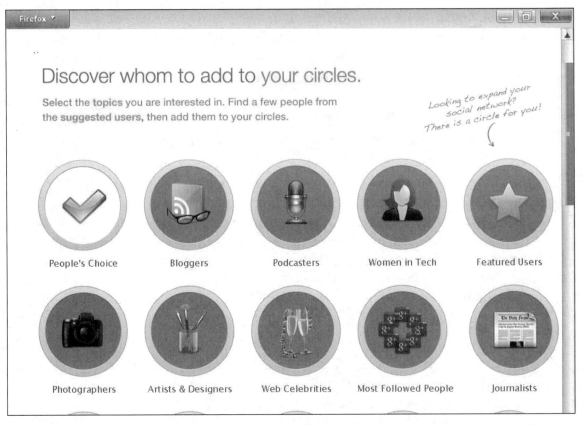

Figure 10-2: Recommendedusers.com is an example of a directory of Google+ members that you can use to find people to add to your own Circles.

to see who some of the people you have added to your Circles have in their own Circles.

You also can share your Circles with others. To do that, go to your Circles tab, and click a Circle to share. To the right you'll see a button that says "Share this Circle." Click that, and follow the prompts. Over time, you'll find people will share Circles with you too as your interests become known. (As we were researching this book, a friend shared a "Job Experts" Circle with us containing more than 100 people.) To find shared Circles, just enter "shared a circle with you" as a search term, and you'll find Circles shared publicly. We did that and found Circles for Women in Tech, Visual Artists & Designers, and Entrepreneurs. Another way to locate Circles is to just try searching for something of interest in the Search box. You can just type something like "librarians circle" in the search box, and see what pops up. Once you've located Circles that interest you, click the link "Create or Add to Circles," and the new Circle is added to your own group.

Other Google+ Features

Circles are great, but they're not the only thing that's unique about Google +. As you might guess, much of the power behind Google has been harnessed to add functionality to Google +. This power is one of the reasons why the outlook for Google + is so promising. Below you'll find a list of features described. In addition, Google + offers other features that will allow you to upload and share photos (Instant Upload), text with a group of people at one time through a group chat (Messenger), and even play games.

Stream

Once you have some people in Circles you'll have your own stream consisting of their posts, images, videos, and links to view and comment on if you choose. You can view posts from whatever stream you'd like or from all of them at once by clicking on the appropriate Circle(s). Figure 10-3 shows you what a Google + stream looks like.

Hangouts

This is a unique Google + feature that lets you "chill with friends that are scrolling through the web just like you!" Google says. It works like this. You and your friends or business contacts agree to a time to meet online, and then through video chat you "hang out" and discuss whatever you'd like. You even can collaborate on Google Docs through Hangouts. (Although if your friends are expecting to "chill," they may not appreciate your suggestion for a group edit of your latest project.)

Search

Coming from Google, you'd expect the search function in Google + to be robust, and it is. Just enter a term in the "Search" box that appears along the top of any Google + screen. By default, you're then presented with results from "Everything" (Figure 10-4), but depending on the hyperlink you choose, you can limit your results to Google + posts, People, or Sparks, which we'll discuss later in this chapter.

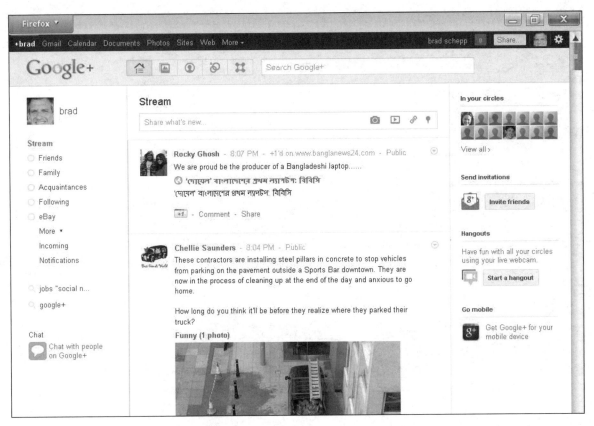

Figure 10-3: An example of a Google+ stream.

+1s

Have you noticed that some web articles now include a " + 1" button that you can click? Similar to Facebook's "Like" button, when you click a " + 1" button, you're recommending that content. You can + 1 web content, as well as any comment someone makes in your stream. Everything that you have + 1'd gets added to your Google+ profile under the " + 1" tab. You have control over who can see these recommendations, making them available to specific Circles or determining whether they are public or private. Be aware, however, Google cautions that + 1'ing something "is a public action." Others potentially could see items you've + 1'd when they visit the same places on the web. Not only that, + 1s may appear "publicly in search, on ads, and across the web," Google says. Others will see your name and even your profile photo as well. Google also may glean insights

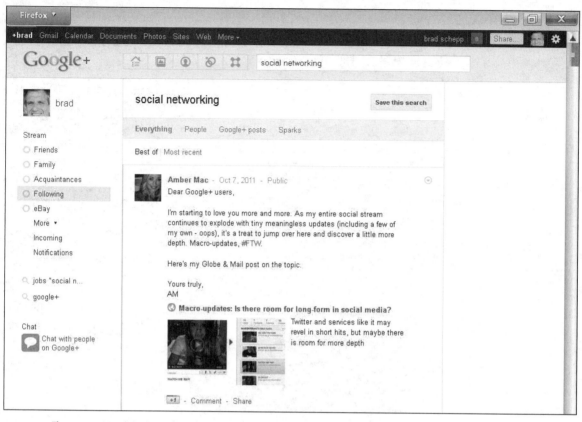

Figure 10-4: By default, your Google+ search results will pull from "Everything."

about you based on what you've designated as a +1 and customize the content and ads it feeds you accordingly, although you can opt out of this feature. So think carefully before you click on that "+1" button.

YOUR GOOGLE+ PROFILE

As with every social networking site, your Google+ profile, which appears under your Google+ "About" tab, is definitely worth spending time creating and keeping updated. It's your public face for the site, and it helps to form your Google+ persona. Therefore, before you post a thing, it affects how you come across to other Google+ users. As we've stressed all along,

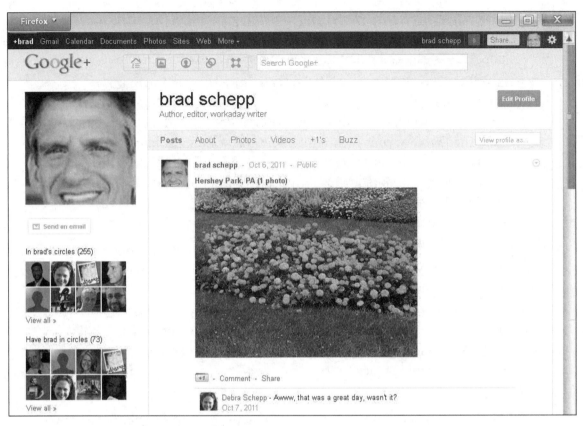

Figure 10-5: A sample Google+ profile.

assuming that you're using a site for business networking, your profile has to have a business-like look and feel to it. For the moment, Google+ isn't LinkedIn, but it's also not as casual as Facebook or Twitter. So wear your business casual clothes, but keep your shoes on, too.

Figure 10-5 shows what a completed Google+ Profile looks like. Much of the information you can include in your profile is self-explanatory. But we did want to touch on some of the ways you have for making your profile sparkle.

From your profile page, click the "Edit Profile" box at the top right corner. As you can see, you have the opportunity to provide information about yourself in the following areas:

- *Introduction.* Here you would put something germane to you as a person so that your visitors know that they've knocked on the right door. This is especially important if you have a common name.

- *Bragging rights.* While Google's examples of what you might put here include "survived high school" and "have three kids," for your purposes, those types of comments will not do. Instead, cogently but unabashedly blow your own horn about the accomplishments of which you're the most proud. If they are work-related, that's all that much better. A good example might be "Boosted sales for my division at Acme Toys by 200 percent in one year." If you're right out of school, just list your top school-related achievements.

- *Occupation.* What do you do for a living? If you're unemployed at the moment, put down what you've done in the past, but consider adding something like "Open to new opportunities."

- *Employment.* You guessed it, here you can list the companies where you've worked, your titles there, and the years you worked for each one. You also have the option of limiting who can see this information, such as only your Circles.

- *Education.* Yes, where you've gone to school.

- *Places lived.* By clicking on the map that appears in this section, you can specify all the places you've lived. If you don't want to get too specific, you can leave your current hometown off the list.

- *Other Profiles.* Here you can include links to your accounts from LinkedIn, Facebook, and similar sites. Through a drop-down box, you can choose to specify who can see this information.

- *Contributor to.* List hyperlinks to pages on the web that feature your work. You might link to your blog, flattering articles about you, articles that quote you, your dissertation, or anything that would impress a potential employer. Don't let this opportunity to shine go to waste!

Other Ways to Make Your Google+ Profile Shine

Just as your LinkedIn profile should live and breathe along with your career, you also can make your Google+ profile an ongoing and ever-changing reflection of the work you do. Add links to articles and other web pages that interest you. Provide content relevant to your industry and stimulating

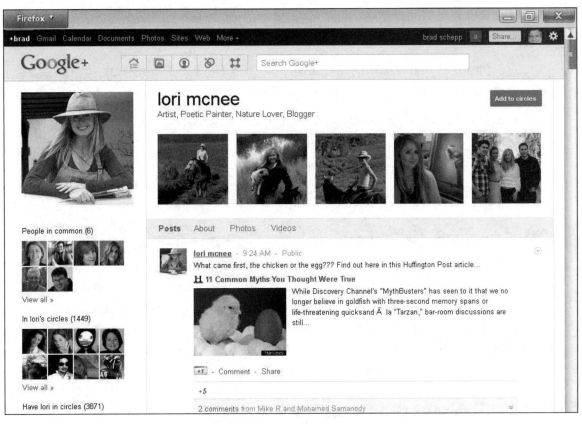

Figure 10-6: Visual artist Lori McNee skillfully showcases her work on her Google+ profile's About page.

to others who share your profession. Again, here's yet another chance to make an impression on employers and potential business partners within your field of interest.

Photos also will help you to stand out on Google+, and the service allows you to share up to five photographs on your profile. This can be a real boon for job seekers. Visual artist Lori McNee makes great use of her profile to showcase her work and presumably attract lots of new work. Her About page is shown in Figure 10-6.

Yet you don't have to be an artist to let pictures speak to your talents and abilities on your Google+ profile. Career expert Donna Svei of avid-careerist.com shared some ideas for photos that would benefit many job hunters:

1. A photo of you accepting an award—you look like a winner.

2. A photo of you doing volunteer work—you look generous.

3. A photo of you crossing the finish line of a 10K race—you look energetic.

4. A photo of you with colleagues—you look like you play well with others.

5. Logos of brand-name former employers.

GOOGLE+ FOR JOB SEEKERS

Again, we don't yet have stories to share with you about people who have used Google+ to land new jobs or freelance assignments. But we know they're coming. "Recruiters are already using Google+ to find candidates," said Sahar Andrade, who operates her own diversity and social media consulting firm. Read further and you'll see why we know that Google+ will become an important tool for job seekers.

It's All About the Organization

As anyone who's been through a job search knows, it's very easy to get disorganized and distracted, especially in a search that involves using the web, and it can span many months. Anything that helps you to stay more organized will save you time, and you know what that equals. It goes back to Google+'s Circles and how they allow you to organize your contacts. "Because of the way G+ is organized, I can create very targeted Circles for my professional connections, such as 'Acquisitions editors, NY' or 'Front-end developers, Bay Area,'" said Debby Afraimi, a senior recruiting consultant. "This enables me to send very targeted job announcements and communications to my network. I don't have to do one hour of prep work in sifting through my contacts to determine who I should send my job announcement to because I've already done that when I created my Circles."

If you're searching for a job, you can create groups of target companies, organizing them within Google+ Circles. Corporate recruiter and career counselor Simon Meth gave this example: "If you're an accountant, you may want to have Circles for Big4 Firms, Second-Tier Firms, Commercial, and Nonprofit. Search for people in each of those types of firms, and add them to your Circles."

You know by now that recruiters can be a big help to you in your job search. Some say that recruiters also will flock to Google+ because (at this time) there's no charge to search through its database to your heart's content. Donna Svei explains: "Google+ has a business model that should prove irresistible to internal and third-party recruiters. It has a huge (already over 26 million) searchable database of some of the most desirable professionals on the planet. Oh, and did I mention that it's free?"

It's not just recruiters who can benefit from Google+. Job seekers, as Donna explains, also can benefit from the advantages Google+ brings to the table. "If you want to be found by recruiters, or prospective clients, or whoever else pays you money to be productive, it's essential to place your profile on the least expensive, most easily searched social network. That's Google+. No contest."

How to Create Effective Posts

After you've created your profile and a few Circles, you're ready to contribute to the public discourse. Almost. First, look around and read a variety of other posts before joining in. Google+ has a techy, serious, academic, but thoughtful air about it as we write this. Poke around a bit, and you may get the feeling that this is a place that doesn't suffer fools gladly. (No, we would never insult you, our reader, by calling you a fool—it's just an expression.) As its user base is growing and becoming more diverse, things are easing up, and people are starting to let their hair down a little. And that makes people more comfortable with using the site.

To create a post, just click on the "Share what's new" box below the Google+ toolbar on your homepage. Then designate which of your Circles you'd like to receive the post. You also have the option of sharing your post with your extended Circles, which are like your second-degree connections on LinkedIn, in that they are the Circles created by those in your own Circles. Finally, you may designate your post as public if you choose.

When you're job hunting, it's important to make your posts effective. You want to stand out among the Google+ community, and your posts will help you to do that. What constitutes an "effective" post? Well, if you're job hunting, it's a post that casts you in a favorable light to prospective employers. Perhaps it's a post where you present an informed opinion on a topic related to your field or a link to a thought-provoking article others interested in your field would appreciate. If you've been featured in a newspaper, a trade journal, a magazine, or a blog article lately, include links to those in a post. Don't make too many of your posts appear self-promotional or you'll turn people off. They may view your posts as a form of spam.

When we interviewed author and Google+ business guru Chris Brogan, he shared with us the example of someone who was ably using the site to gently promote her company's products by getting them to "Feel the Allegiance." Chris explained: "Jennifer Cisney from Kodak shares interesting photo projects that she sees but almost never points out that you should buy Kodak products to do the work. You simply feel the allegiance based on knowing what she shares, and you think more positively about the brand."

Job hunters, of course, are also promoting a product—themselves. If you stay in touch with the people in your Circles and let them get to know you through your posts, links, photos, and other contributions, they may just keep you in mind when they hear of an opportunity that's right for you.

As with other sites, actively sharing is very important on Google+, which gives you the chance to genuinely help people by answering questions and creating postings that highlight your expertise. Once again, it goes back to the 80/20 rule we first mentioned in the context of LinkedIn.

Searching for People Who Will Be Interested in Your Posts

First, search for a company by name. Then click on "People," and you'll see Google+ members who have that company name somewhere in their profiles. (Better pull out that blue sky list of companies again!) At this time, you may find actual employees of that company, or you may find consultants, recruiters, writers, or other support people who build their businesses around that company. Either way, if you're interested in a particular company, you'll find others with the same affinity. You can click through to learn more about each person, perhaps add him to your Circles, and eventually start a dialog that could lead to a job. Click on the "Sparks" hyperlink, and you're shown the "best" results for your topic culled from the web at large.

Searching for Companies

As of this writing, Google+ is only just developing the equivalent of Facebook pages or LinkedIn company profiles. But something along those lines is well underway, according to Google. So keep an eye out for news of Google+ adding pages for companies. Once those are available, your opportunities for researching and reaching out to companies will expand greatly.

Google+ Job-Search Tips

Donna Svei of avidcareerist.com was kind enough to share her tips for job seekers on the best ways they can use Google+:

1. Enter your target companies' names on Google+ in the "Find People" box. See who pops up.

2. Circle people who work for your target companies. Share their posts (great), comment on their posts (great), and +1 their posts (good). Get to know them.

3. Organize job-search clubs using "Hangouts."

4. Ask job-search questions. Post to public by typing "public" in the "Share" box. Post to particular individuals by typing their names in the "Share" box. Some questions turn into multihour, multiparticipant chats. Some don't.

5. Expect that an interviewer will want to talk with you via "Hangouts." Practice using it with your job-search club (see above) beforehand. Get feedback on how you look and on your mannerisms. Get a little better at "performing" online each week.

6. Put together a rockin' profile. Why? Everyone can search Google+ profiles for free.

LOOKING AHEAD

Well, the rest of the story is for you to write. Social networking for job hunting and professional sharing has moved out of its infancy and is now a well-entrenched part of the workaday world. Although it's too soon to say how Google+ will alter the landscape, one thing we know for sure: That landscape is broader, deeper, and wider today than it was just two years ago, and it will be even broader, deeper, and wider two years from now.

We hope that you feel ready to harness the power of social networking for job hunting and professional enrichment. We're confident that you'll find several networking sites that will reward you with new contacts, new business, and new employment prospects. Give yourself some time to learn the lay of the land, and then get in there and make yourself known! You never know where social networking will take you, but we wish you every continued success in your travels.

Index

ABOUT THE AUTHORS

Brad Sch... ...ents and have
been col... ...erests in technology a... ...chnologies and
how th... ...ey've written
20 book... *How to Make
Money* ...

The... ...*ewsweek, The
Chicago*... ...*muter's Handbook,* w... ...and Deb have
both w... ...s also editorial
director...

If y... ...is book or job
hunting... ...t them through
their w...